Blue Devils in Vietnam

Geneseo Central School, Geneseo, New York

Vietnam Veterans
chronicle their lives
Before, During, and After

Compiled and written by
Jim DeCamp
Tony Gurak & Roger Johnson

Edited by
Amie Alden
Livingston County Historian

Front cover: Original concept by Tony Gurak. Collage designed by graphic artist, Rodger Engler, Rochester, NY., with background image of the former Geneseo Central School building now Doty Hall owned by SUNY Geneseo, NY and various images related to the Vietnam War era.

Associated Press photo images in the front cover collage- AP License No: LIC-00254170

926480270306 - Senior U. S. advisor Capt. Robert A. Reitz, center, carries a wounded South Vietnamese Ranger to an ambulance Feb. 6, 1968 after a brief but intense battle with the Viet Cong during the Tet Offensive near the National Sports Stadium in the Cholon section of Saigon. (AP Photo/Dang Van Phuoc)

6710104031 - The address is muddy bunker and the mailman wearing a flak vest is CPL. Jesse D. Hittson of Level-land, Texas reaches out for his mail at the U. S. Marine Con Thien outpost two miles south of the DMZ in South Viet nam on Oct. 4, 1967. (AP Photo/Kim Ki Sam).

Other images used not subject to copyright or known restrictions including: USS Carbonero (SS-337) submarine, USS Oriskany Aircraft Carrier; Iroquois Helicopter (Huey); and image of battle of Xom Bo, June 1967, 1st Infantry Division Archives, (National Archives).

Title page (previous): Top - Vietnam Service ribbon. Photo of Huey exiting after combat assault drop off. 1970.
Courtesy: Roger Johnson.

Back cover: The Blue Devil, Geneseo Central School's mascot. The patch is from Jim DeCamp's High School Varsity jacket.

Editing, book layout, and design by Amie Alden, Livingston County Historian.

For information contact:

Amie Alden, Livingston County Historian
5 Murray Hill Drive
Mt. Morris, New York 14510
Email: historian@co.livingston.ny.us
www.livingston.state.ny.us

Library of Congress Control Number: 2014940698
ISBN 9870991603107

Printed in the United States of America by:
Penny Lane Printing, Inc., Avon, NY 14414

Table of Contents

❀ ❀ ❀ ❀ ❀ ❀ ❀ ❀ ❀ ❀ ❀ ❀

List of map illustrations

Geneseo Central School, 1962, Jen-o-see Yearbook. Livingston County Historian's collection.
Top right:198th Lt. Infantry Brigade military patch. http://www.americal.org

Foreword

❀ ❀ ❀ ❀ ❀ ❀ ❀ ❀

More than forty years ago I proudly served my country during the Vietnam War. The memories of that experience, some extremely painful, remain vivid in my mind after all these years and have made me the person I am today.

Since 2006, the need to share my story with others led to the overwhelming desire to gather the stories of all the Vietnam veterans from the Geneseo–Groveland area who attended Geneseo Central School. This was not an easy task as many vets were hard to locate, others were reluctant to participate, and sadly, many have passed away.

But with patience and persistence, memories that were buried deep in the minds of many surviving local Vietnam veterans for decades began to rise to the surface. Now for the first time their experiences are gathered together and the history of this unpopular and misunderstood war will be preserved.

I wish to express my sincere thanks to my fellow vets and very special friend and biggest supporter, Livingston County Historian, Amie Alden. With the publication of this book, a daunting task turned into a labor of love and my vision has become a reality.

ROGER C. JOHNSON
GCS Class of 1967
U. S. Army 1969-1971
Americal Division
198th Light Infantry Brigade

Some Blue Devil "Senior" Moments

James Adamson   Terrence Alger   James Barber   Bruce Booher   John Carney

Jim DeCamp   Charles Freese   Tony Gurak   Roger Johnson   Charles McLaughlin

Mark O'Neil   Lenny Peri   Francis Rosebrugh   Malcolm Stewart   Carroll Teitsworth

John Thompson   J. Neil Thompson   Wayne Tuttle   Jerry Vickers   Peter Williams

These Blue Devils photos are from different classes between 1961 and 1970 from the "Jen-o-see" yearbooks. Not all Vietnam vets senior photos were available.

Blue Devils in Vietnam

❀ ❀ ❀ ❀ ❀ ❀ ❀ ❀ ❀

The following veterans have shared experiences, stories and photographs for this publication:

James C. Adamson
Terrence F. Alger
James Barber
Rick Bartholomew
Bruce A. Booher
Joseph Kevin Bovill
Roderick D. Bowles
John J. Carney
James K. Clark
James C. Creagan
James DeCamp
Alfred M. Dietrich
Ronald Evans
Charles R. Freese
Tony Gurak
Ronald Hilfiker
Roger C. Johnson
Terry Johnston
Roger Least
Charles McLaughlin
Roger Mustari
Mark O'Neil
Donald Peraino
Lenny Peri
Dennis C. Staley
Malcolm H. Stewart
Carroll Teitsworth
J. Neil Thompson*
John S. Thompson
Wayne Tuttle
Clifton Donald VanDerveer
Jerry H. Vickers
Rodney Wambold
Peter Williams

Unfortunately, J. Neil Thompson passed away on May 5, 2014 before the book was published.

Dedication

❀❀❀❀❀❀❀❀❀

To the three men who gave their lives in service during the Vietnam War.

Francis P. "Butch" Rosebrugh

Robert C. "Bobby" Henderson

Charles D. "Charlie" Wilkie

See the "In Memoriam" section for biographical information on these men.

Dedication

❀ ❀ ❀ ❀ ❀ ❀ ❀ ❀ ❀

"To live in the hearts of others is never to die." - Thomas Campbell, 1825

Dog tags image created by Rodger Engler.

Preface

❀ ❀ ❀ ❀ ❀ ❀ ❀ ❀ ❀ ❀ ❀ ❀ ❀ ❀

The genesis of this book started in 2007. I was taking a course on Vietnam to learn as much as I could about the war that defined my youth through graduation from Geneseo Central School. For my final project I decided to do a study on the impact of the Vietnam War on Livingston County. I knew it would be challenging for a variety of reasons - most of all because after a cursory search, I found little to indicate that any extensive research had been attempted locally on the subject. So I decided to start from scratch and called one of only a handful of Vietnam veterans I knew personally, my old mailman, Roger Johnson. He readily agreed to do an interview and thanked me profusely. I blocked off an hour on my calendar for the appointment and prepared some general questions to ask about his tour of duty and how he was doing today.

Roger was ready to talk the moment we sat down. Over the course of the entire afternoon and several cups of coffee, he described his life before, during, and after Vietnam. I was so mesmerized I barely took notes and just sat and listened. For the first time in my life, a soldier explained, in terms that I could understand, what it was like to be plucked out of small-town Geneseo in western New York, and plopped into a place on the other side of the world surrounded by jungles and rice paddies and live in fear for an entire year. I learned a lot that afternoon about Roger's war experience in Vietnam and how the war continued when he came home. He again thanked me for taking the time to listen and was pleased about my project, offering anything he could do to help. As I prepared to leave he said (and I paraphrase), "You need to write a book so all our stories can be told. We need to find out who these guys are that served in Vietnam from our school and get their stories down before it's too late." I shook the hand of the man I now knew much better and said, "There is no way I can write this story, you and the other GCS vets have to do it. But I will help in any way I can."

Years passed and many projects (including documenting Vietnam veterans) occupied my time. In the fall of 2011, I called Roger and said "It's time to get this book project going," and set aside one year. He immediately organized "the troops" consisting of Tony Gurak, Chuck Freese, Jim DeCamp, Dennis Staley, Cliff VanDerveer, Jerry Vickers, and several others. The core group whittled down to Jim, Tony, Roger and me. They tracked down the Vietnam vets and information to fill in the gaps in Charlie, Butch, and Bobby's stories (the men to whom this book is dedicated) and I facilitated the meetings. In short, it took more than two years with all of us doing whatever needed to be done to accomplish our goal of bringing the bits and pieces of their stories together to share with our community and beyond. It's been a long ride. Along the way we gathered far more information than could be included in this book but all will remain in the expanding Vietnam War section of the County Historian's archives.

Thank you Jim, Tony, and Roger for your hard work and unwavering trust and support. I love you guys like brothers and will miss our lively meetings over lots of coffee and Tim Horton's muffins. This has been a fantastic learning experience, one that I am honored and humbled to have been a part of. There's absolutely no way I would have survived this "mission" without knowing you guys would help with whatever needed to be done. And cheers to all the Blue Devils and area Vietnam veterans who participated in this book project and also to those who were unable. Thank you for your service and I wish all of you the best of everything the "world" has to offer.

Amie (Griffo) Alden
Livingston County Historian
and GCS Class of 1973.
June 15, 2014

BLUE DEVILS IN VIETNAM:

Before, During, and After

❀❀❀❀❀❀❀❀❀❀❀❀❀❀❀❀❀❀❀❀

"I assess all men my age by how they navigated those treacherous draft waters."

by Jim DeCamp

"It don't mean nothing" & "There it is"

a poem by Jim DeCamp

"It don't mean nothing" & "There it is"
were the general issue phrases
of Vietnam.

The former dismissed relevance,
the latter, wonder.
It didn't matter,
it was inevitable anyway.

All purpose, one size fits all
response to any event:
man death,
sock hole,
Lima bean C ration can.

A protective poncho,
impervious.

"I got a Dear John today,
my wife has left me."

"There it is, bro,
it don't mean
nothing."

Previous page: Jim DeCamp (in back row with glasses) with the mortar squad of Co. D, 2nd Bn. 27th Inf. Regt., Cu Chi, Vietnam, Oct. 1970. Above: Jim DeCamp, 11th Armored Cav. Vietnam., 1970. Both photos courtesy of J. DeCamp.

Introduction
❁❁❁❁❁❁❁❁❁❁❁
by Jim DeCamp

"I woke up one morning in Vietnam and I hadn't even been to the State Fair yet." - Roger Johnson

2,709,918* Americans served in the Vietnam War. Approximately 100 were from the towns of Groveland and Geneseo, Livingston County, New York and attended Geneseo Central School. They were the Blue Devils in Vietnam. Some found their way to Southeast Asia via West Point or ROTC, the draft, or recruitment sergeants; others got there at the suggestion of local Justices of the Peace as alternatives to incarceration.

58,272* died. Two were classmates and best friends who grew up in Groveland with their backyards in sight of each other (in fact, if one of them had stepped through the tree line, they could have waved to each other). In between these two farm houses was a future West Pointer who flew helicopters in Vietnam and went on to become an astronaut in the NASA Space Shuttle program. These two friends talked each other into enlisting in the Marine Corps. They were in the same Cub Scout pack, hunted and fished together, and backed each other up in scraps with guys from neighboring towns.

Number of Americans who served in Vietnam: http://www.nationalvietnamveteransfoundation.org/statistics.htm
**The Vietnam Veterans Memorial, The Wall USA http://thewall-usa.com/information.asp*
Photo: Roger's platoon mates. Courtesy of Roger Johnson.

One was home on medical leave, attended the other's funeral in civilian clothes, returned to Vietnam to avenge his buddy's death, and like his buddy, didn't come home alive. Buried, one overlooking Conesus Lake, and the other in Arlington National Cemetery, Francis P. "Butch" Rosebrugh and Robert C. "Bobby" Henderson should be about 67 years old now with grown children and grandchildren. Their service would be a distant memory supplanted by years of work and family. Instead, they are immutable youths who didn't have the chance to grow old. Major Charles Wilkie, Army, was KIA just before Christmas in 1967 and is buried at Temple Hill Cemetery in the village of Geneseo. He died at the age of 33, leaving a wife and two toddlers.

The impact of the loss of Butch, Bobby, and Charlie forever changed the lives of their immediate families, but what was discovered during the process of compiling information for this book was how much their deaths impacted the entire community. This book is about them, along with 32 others who talked to us about their time in 'Nam. It has taken more than two years to compile a comprehensive

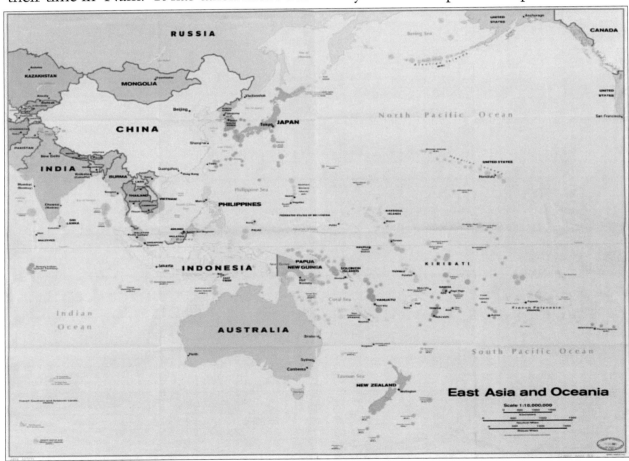

Above: Map of East Asia and Oceania dated 2002 shows Vietnam (long strip of land in green bordering China to the North, the South China Sea to the East and by Laos and Cambodia on the West.) Library of Congress Geography and Map Division Washington, D.C. http://lccn.loc.gov/2002627531

list, then reach out and contact those men from the Geneseo area who served in Vietnam. We have also gathered dozens of photographs, letters home, and moving oral interviews in the process. Quite a few of the guys are still living in the immediate vicinity, but many have already passed away, and despite our best efforts, several were unreachable or preferred not to participate.

From the initial list of about 100 we received surveys back from over 30, almost all GCS Blue Devils. We've also added a few non-GCS men for their long time connections to Geneseo since the war. The survey asked questions under the three categories of the vets' impressions and experiences "Before, During, and After" Vietnam. The "Before" section of the survey is the shortest and least revealing as, basically, nobody had been anywhere before finding himself 9,000 miles away in Vietnam.

Varsity cheerleader Nancy Miceli and a oversize poster with team names of Blue Devils before a sports event. From the GCS "Jen-o-see" yearbook, 1970.

Roger Johnson said it best: "I woke up one morning in Vietnam, and I hadn't even been to the State Fair yet" only 90 miles away in Syracuse. The "During" section revealed a wider variety of experiences in Vietnam along with many similarities as well. And despite the ravages of the unpopular war and decades of battling with the government at home for benefits, many of the vets had positive remarks in the "After" section and sage advice for men and women currently in service.

Before
❀ ❀ ❀ ❀ ❀ ❀ ❀
by Jim DeCamp

"Bowling on Saturday and collecting bottles for nickels and pennies to go to the movies…"
- Rod Bowles

Main Street, Geneseo, NY.
GCS Jen-o-see 1961 yearbook.

A more dramatic juxtaposition of worlds than Geneseo, New York and South Vietnam could not be imagined. The former was a four-season small town of parades, fireworks, lakeside roller skating, high school games followed by sock hops in the same gym, drive-in movies, 4-lane bowling alleys, 100lb girls encased in girdles and petty pants, curfews, and fist fights among town champions. We hitchhiked to the lake, drank illegally on back roads and in speed boats. Wars were old stories not often told from the 1940s and 50s.

Most of us couldn't have found Vietnam on an unmarked world map. A Roper Poll of 18 to 24 year olds in 2006 found that 10% could find Afghanistan, 30% Iran and 37% Iraq. We probably weren't any more accurate in the 1960s. What's remarkable about our experiences prior to military service is how unremarkable they were. This is not an indictment as I'm sure it was repeated all over America, and throughout our pre-war periods. The reason our story is worth telling, and I hope reading, is because of how ordinary it is.

All gave some, as they say, and some gave all. As mentioned in the introduction, for us it was Butch, Bobby, and Charlie. We had our share of Purple Heart, Arcom, Bronze Star, Air Medal, and CIB recipients, and quiet heroes. One could take this small town chronicle and multiply it by all the small towns, and cities too, across America and it would add up to the 3.4 million* men and women (mostly nurses and Red Cross "Donut Dollies") who served in and around that war.

*Number served in the broader Southeast Asia Theater waters). http://www.nationalvietnamveteransfoundation.org/statistics.htm

West Point graduate and astronaut Jim Adamson grew up in the country just a few miles from the village.

"I grew up living in Groveland and attended school in Geneseo from my birth in 1946 until leaving for college in 1964. As a youngster in a small rural community in the 50s we were pretty oriented toward physical outdoor activities…I spent most of my free time hunting, fishing, camping, hiking and making the woods my virtual play-ground. We weren't tempted too much with technology in those days so staying inside didn't hold much appeal for us. Black and white TV was new and sometime during that period we were all amazed that the transistor radio showed up and you could actually carry it around with you! Families were quite nuclear as were the communities. The activities centered on church and community activities were always welcome events. I remember Memorial Day and the 4th of July in Geneseo with particular fondness; the parade, the WWII and Korea Vets handing out poppies, and the National Guard ceremony at the War Memorial in the Village Park. I think I was probably more interested in the Log Cabin than the Memorial. I always thought it would have been great fun had it been located secretly out in the woods instead of in the middle of the park in the "big city" of Geneseo. It was an exciting time and place to be a kid."

Log Cabin, Village Park, Geneseo, NY. Originally built by the Livingston County Historical Society in the 1890s. Photo courtesy of the Livingston County Historian.

Most of us recalled living the Norman Rockwell (or Mayberry) small town American dream. Sports, hunting, farm work, fishing, cars, girls, and rock n' roll were what most remembered. Tony Gurak agreed:

"Hunting, fishing, cars, and a job to support them. Go to school, part serious, part fun. Jump into your car with some friends and ride around town. Life in a small town [was] our whole world. We were happy. That's all we knew."

And Rod Bowles described his life outside of school:

"Basketball, football, haying Hagen's farm, work at Mr. Rost's boatyard and Mr. O'Brien's Appliance Store. Bowling on Saturday and collecting bottles for nickels and pennies to go to the movies, cutting lawns in the spring and driving my Jeepster to the drive-in movies."

Vintage photographs before Vietnam
"Most of us recalled living the Norman Rockwell (or Mayberry) small town American dream." - J. DeCamp

Top left: Jim DeCamp as a toddler wading in Conesus Lake at the family cottage. *Courtesy of Jim DeCamp.*
Top right: Butch Rosebrugh with his dog and lamb. *Courtesy of Brenda Orman.*

Bottom: Groveland Boy Scouts 1956. (L - R) J. Adamson, S. McCauley, T. Magee, D. Aten, C. Adamson, L. Warner, J. Sawdey, D. Sanderson, T. Adamson, F. "Butch" Rosebrugh, W. Rossborogh, unknown, W. Linsner, D. Meyer, R. McCauley. *Photo courtesy of Jim Adamson.*

FIRST ROW: J. Emmons, W. Tuttle, E. LaVigne, E. Rossborough, D. Stolper SECOND ROW: J. Adamson, C. Perry, D. Alger, C. Least, M. Rodamaker, Coach Bondi THIRD ROW: B. Booher, R. Pusateri, L. DeLaVergne, D. Lowery, C. Stevens, M. Orlando, T. Brown FOURTH ROW: J. DeCamp, R. Bryar, D. Hanna, L. Perry, J. Carney, Y. Thomas

Above images from GCS "Jen-o-see" yearbooks. Top: (left) The Palace bowling alley, 1961; (right) Anne Steele, Molly Steele, and Christine Peters, 1962. Bottom image: 1963 Varsity football team with several Blue Devil Vietnam veterans.

Kevin Bovill fondly recalls names, places, and activities of his youth growing up in the village in the 1950s and early 1960s.

"The fifties in Geneseo was a time of innocence and outdoor adventure. Hunting for varmint at the village dump near the Genesee River; hiking the abandoned rail way bed from Court St. to Nations Road with my friend John Staley, Jr. and his brother Steve; biking out the Crossett Road when the surface was still dirt was always exhilarating. Summers spent playing Little League Baseball (Coach Clouser), and Pony League at Kelsey Field (I was not very good) and the ball diamond behind the old high school with Mayor Ryan as coach. Crafts at the log cabin in the park and afternoons being bused to Long Point Park, swimmers and non-swimmers on alternate days.

As we aged, there would be pick-up softball or touch football in the park or on the front lawn of the old high school. Basketball behind

GCS c. 1963. Courtesy Livingston Co. Historian Office.

Bill Cash's home. In the winter there would be sledding down Court Street and skating at the rink in Highland Park. Scouting was very important in those days, both Cub and Boy Scouts. I remember selling apples to raise money so a few scouts could make the trip to a scout ranch in California for the National Jamboree. I could not make the trip as my parents thought I was too young. Some of the scouts on that trip made Eagle.

Growing up I had two paper routes, the Times Union and the Democrat and Chronicle. As I got older I worked for Holden Stickney at the old Minckler Drug Store and during my college years I worked at the Birds Eye plant in Avon. I was somewhat aware of what was happening in Vietnam, but in the early sixties the Bay of Pigs and the Cuban Missile Crisis was paramount. I remember that fateful day, I and a classmate from St. John Fisher College took the bus to old St. Joseph's Church for a prayer service. During this time frame (1959-63), I experienced no strong opinion about Vietnam. My parents did not discuss or have opinions either as the war was in its infancy.

The only extensive travel I made was the summer of 1950 with my mother to visit my maternal grandparents in Ireland for the first and only time. The Korean War broke out while we were there. I felt a great sense of pride in our country and armed forces."

Malcolm Stewart left Geneseo in 1961 before moving on to college, the military, and a career. His remarks about growing up here were brief but appreciative:

Malcolm Stewart was a leader in sports and student activities at GCS. Above: Dance Band, 1960. Jen-o-see yearbook.

"I was involved in a wide variety of school activities, and especially enjoyed football (never defeated) and baseball (often defeated!). Although not fully appreciated at the time, education and small town life in Geneseo were excellent. The extent of my travel before entering the military was limited to New York State, and our senor class trip to Washington, DC and the Civil War battlefields."

Jerry Vickers' interests growing up were typical. Here he writes about his close connections to the area but also the need to get out and explore the world beyond the small town. The deaths of his classmates, Butch Rosebrugh and Bobby Henderson, led Jerry to become very interested in what was happening in Vietnam and eager to join the military and serve his country.

"Interests: My car, '59 Chevy Bel-Air; rock 'n roll music, model airplanes, reading anything and of course: Girls! I liked school but was bored; it posed no real challenge; a job was just that: a job, a way to earn money since I knew that I really wanted to go into the military anyways; until I actually was able to go to the military I feel that I was just 'marking time at home' in Geneseo. Life in 'the small town USA,' Geneseo was alright, considering the fact that at 18-19 years old I had never really been anywhere, so I had nothing to compare it to.

I liked Geneseo. I was 'connected to it' in a way that some people were not. My father, his father and finally his father had all lived here. I've been told by my father, Harold, that our grandfather, at some level, had built the County Court House, the Geneseo Town Hall, and the Log Cabin in the park. Several houses around town were built by my grandfather, John Herbert, Sr. One of the more prominent structures he built was the 'Holiday House' on West Lake Road and the old Girl Scout summer camp.

My home life was good. I suppose you could say that it was 'typical' of what most of the Baby Boomer generation faced: whatever we like, you name it, most of the parents did not. My father and I were famous for being quite opposite of each other. If he said up, I'd say down, etc. So, in part, that's why I was anxious to get out of Geneseo."

Cliff VanDerveer said he worked a lot of part time summer jobs in his teens including carpenter's helper, farm worker, and various jobs at the Amusement Park at Long Point. He moved to Geneseo in 1961 and admits he wasn't a good student and never felt like he belonged, spending most of his free time alone. And Bruce Booher gave another point of view, "As a poor country boy, trouble seemed to find me as did the local cops."

❊❊❊❊❊❊❊❊❊❊❊❊❊❊❊❊❊

High school was often tolerated as a prerequisite to sports. Though we were taught by WWII vets like Core Carmody and my uncle, John Staley, not much mention was made of the Vietnam War. And if it was, the reaction was typically supportive. Consequently, our awareness of what was happening in Vietnam and the politics of the day was limited. Terrence Alger, GCS graduate and West Point Class of 1963, was well informed but even he says:

"I was aware of the Vietnam actions while I was a student at West Point, but the U.S. involvement was only advisors and money. It was a long way off and it did not seem to have any effect on life in the U.S. There seemed to be no strong opinions against our involvement because the world was basically split between the communist and non-communist countries. Fear of the 'domino effect' was very real at the time."

Cadet Terrance Alger, son of Mr. and Mrs. Clifton Alger, will be among the West Point Cadets marching in the Inaugural Parade on Friday in Washington, when President-elect John F. Kennedy will become the President of the United States of America

Photo: (l) Terrance Alger, West Point 1963; (r) Terrance Alger, West Point, 1962. Courtesy of T. Alger.
Left lower: Livingston Co. Leader, 1/19/1961

Eagle Scout James Adamson (seated next to Gov. Nelson Rockefeller) at the "Report to the Governor" ceremonies, Albany, 1963. Adamson reported details of Scouting's participation in the 1964 World's Fair. Photo courtesy of Jim Adamson.

The older we were, the more our awareness increased. Jim Adamson had a larger perspective:

"The Korean War seemed to come and go only as an after-thought of WWII. Being nestled so closely in the shadow of the 'Great War' it didn't seem to gain its own identity. It was however personified for me by my neighbor, Francis Gilbert, who joined the Army and fought in the war. To me, as a preteen, he seemed to just vanish for a time and then re-appeared a hero in uniform to entertain us with his stories and return to normal life. That along with our Boy Scout troop, which had been organized by my mother and several other moms, gave us boys a kind of kinship with our older 'soldier' brothers. It made us feel a part of the larger world. We were all very patriotic..."

Jim Adamson's mention of "patriotism" was correct. Our fathers and uncles had fought triumphantly in WWII, some older brothers fought to a tie in Korea. The American disappointment in that Korean outcome and subsequent disregard for its warriors should have been a harbinger to us about Vietnam. But we, along with everyone else, weren't listening.

Jim DeCamp's narrative continues.

If you're a man (as only males were subject to the draft) from my generation, you were exposed to the draft from ages 18 to 26. You could 'defer' this obligation through various stratagems ranging from permanently for flat feet and other assorted maladies, to temporarily while you were in school. The key, of course, was to keep 'deferring' until you reached the magic age of 26. Some, like former Vice President Dick Cheney, managed this, but it was hard to do. Meanwhile, back at the local Selective Service branch the men (again as only men served) on the Board moved down the list and took the next guy.

Here's the rub: if you managed to elude the draft (and I applaud your success as I tried and only made it to age 24 ½) someone else took your place and you didn't know two vital things about him aside from his name: What happened to him over there? And what did he do to others over there? Your "replacement" could have been a Lt. Calley* clone spreading death and suffering through out his tour or a unlucky guy who stepped on a land mine his last day there.

> ⬦ On Feb. 16 the following men left for military training: James DeCamp and Craig Adamson of Geneseo; Gary W. Forrester of Springwater, Gary O'Donnell of Lakeville James Nettnin and his twin brother, John Nettnin of Livonia; Paul Maloney and Ronald Dickinson of Lima and Larry Briggs of Nunda. The next group is scheduled to leave on March 12.
>
> *Livingston Republican, 3/5/1970*

The draft was a reality looming over everybody and informing all our choices. As Bruce Booher said, "We knew if we didn't go to college we were going to get drafted." And he was right. The draft or selective service existed often in the 20th century, from 1917-20, 1940-47, and lastly 1948-January 27, 1973. From 1-A "available for unrestricted military service" to 5A, "registrant who is over the age of liability" (age 26), there were 29 classifications that allowed for a lot of dodging.

Left:
Congressman Alexander Pirnie reaching into a container of balls with draft numbers (center) as others look on, at the Selective Service Headquarters during the nationwide draft lottery. Dec. 1969.

Photo: Library of Congress Prints and Photographs Division Washington, D.C. 20540 USA. http://hdl.loc.gov/ loc.pnp/ds.01312

---

* 2nd Lt. Wm. L. Calley, Jr., was accused and convicted of murdering hundreds of Vietnamese civilians in the village of My-Lai on March 16, 1968 in what was called the My-Lai Massacre. He was sentenced to life but later pardoned. For more info: http://law2.umkc.edu/ faculty/projects/ftrials/mylai/myl_bcalleyhtml.htm

You could be 1-O, a conscientious objector; 1-S, in high school; 2-S, in college; 2-A, a civilian occupation; 2-C milk farmer; 2-D ministry; or 4-F, "not acceptable for military service." I had four such deferments (one shy of Dick Cheney's 5) and finessed myself to December 1, 1969 and the first National Lottery on television where my newly married wife and I watched them draw June 27 (my birthday), ping pong ball #64.

Scheduled to go in March, 1970, I "volunteered for the draft" and left on February 16 at the age of 24 years and 8 months old. The highest lottery number called for induction in Livingston County was 195 and later statistical analysis determined that the 366 balls weren't randomly mixed and birth dates later in the calendar year were disproportionally low.

Roger Mustari, GCS class of '69 has the "distinction" of being "the last young man to leave Geneseo from Local Board No. 72 before the no-draft law went into effect." That law came in on December 30, 1972 and Roger left on the 27th. Fortunately for him, he didn't have to go to Vietnam.

Mustari, Last Draftee

Roger Mustari, son of Mr. and Mrs. Guy Mustari, 14 Temple Hill Acres, Geneseo, left for the Armed Services Dec. 27. He was the last young man to leave Geneseo from local draft board No. 72 before the no-draft law went into effect.

Avon Herald, 1/31/1973.

We were as ignorant, generally, of politics as we were of the geography. Jim Creagan (who came to SUNY Geneseo in 1964 and still lives in town) pointed out, "Aware of the politics? I had no clue and still am not sure. My decision to enlist was pretty much my own call, wanting to get in on the action, I guess." If our parents weighed in at all it was with a maternal note of caution and some paternal patriotism. Mark "Bucky" O'Neil explained,

> "My father was a hawk and couldn't understand why we were not 'in it to win it', with all the comparisons to WWII. My parents were afraid of communism and came from the 'we need to stop it wherever it is' school [of thought]."

There was a definite sense of duty for many like Wayne Tuttle who came from a family of WWI and WWII veterans and said,

> "I knew the military was in my future while still in high school. I went to SUNY Cobleskill but knew it wasn't for me. I left there to work at SUNY Geneseo until the military grabbed me. I looked into the Air Force and once I was drafted by the Army I joined the Air Force thinking it might keep me out of Vietnam."

To some, the military seemed like a good idea at the time. Avon's Jim Clark, who taught art at GCS for many years reasoned, "It was just another adventure, something to do, friends were joining and at the time I was not interested in college or being a homeless bum."

Thoughout the Vietnam era editorials in the local newspapers
questioning the politics of the war became more frequent
as the war became more controversial.

Morals and War

By Don Sanders, Jr.

The United States is becoming a victim of its own moralistic propaganda. In The First and Second World Wars this nation fought from the basis of a moral commitment, the defense of democracy against the threat of tyranny. Yet nothing was done until this moral commitment was forced upon us by act of direct violence, such as the attack on Pearl Harbor. Then The United States went to war because the American people believed that they were right. It was as easy as telling black from white.

In Viet Nam there is no such easy distinction. It is a country rocked by civil war, in which various foreign powers have intervened, but none in such a heavy handed manner as has The United States. This is a war in which many people believe that the United States is the aggressor. Americans, who seriously think about the war in Viet Nam, have trouble justifying our position from a moral point of view. No one has sunk the Maine or bombed Pearl Harbor. Instead it has been The United States that has rapidly pushed escalation.

Today, we as a nation face a grave peril. Some say bomb Hanoi and Red China, others call for a complete and unilateral withdrawal, and still others advocate no concessions until an honorable peace has been reached. How to settle the war in Viet Nam? This is the dilemna that faces not just President Johnson, but every one of us. We must ask ourselves if we are prepared to participate in an Asian war, not only physically, but mentally. This is a war that could last for fifteen years. This is a war that could become nuclear.

It appears that if the war continues at the present pace, The United States will become involved in a situation where the advantage will be with the enemy. This naturally increases the odds that nuclear weapons will be used, since intelligent men will rationalize that a few carefully placed atomic bombs would settle the whole affair in our favor.

Once the die is cast there is no turning back. Therefore we must not let our need to fight take complete possession of ourselves and dominate our doubts. So Americans, lets not be so complacent and smug. Are we prepared to accept the moral responsibility of starting an all out Asian war? Are we mentally prepared to fight this war once it has begun? Now is the time to search out these answers in a free and open dialogue, leaving all partisan political interests aside.

By now President Johnson will have delivered his State of The Union Address, and these questions might have been answered for us. However, it seems as if more soul searching should be done before we decide the destiny of the world.

LETTER HOME
by
Ray C. Sherman

Dear Folks:

On another page of this issue (and without United Press's consent) we have reproduced pictures appearing on the front page of the Wednesday, Dec. 2, 1970, Democrat & Chronicle which is the graphic answer to the "bleeding hearts" for the Kent rioters and other rioters every where.

The first picture shows at least four anti-war demonstrators "ganging up" on a single policeman whose is armed only with a Billy Club. The second shows the policeman being beaten by at least three of the demonstrators. The last picture shows the policeman (law and order) abandoning the scene and leaving it to the forces of "violence."

In this case the policeman is walking away but we do not know how badly he was hurt nor how far he was able to "walk."

If the situation had been reversed the scream would have been "police brutality."

The question is do we want our police, our National Guardsmen, etc., to be forces to maintain "law and order" or do we want them merely to be something to be on hand so rioters can "vent their spleen" on "symbols of the establishment?"

Let's bleed a little for the outnumbered policemen.

• • •

Above Left: Livingston Co. Leader, 1/19/1966
Above Right: Livingston Republican, 12/3/1970

Jim DeCamp's narrative continues.

For others, going into the military was personal. Chuck Freese, who was befriended by Butch Rosebrugh, a kindly GCS upperclassman on the volleyball team who lost his life in Vietnam, put it simply, "I felt that I could settle a score with the bad guys." And no doubt, the Country Joe & the Fish smash hit song expressed the sentiment of several with the lyrics, **"What are we fighting for? I don't give a damn, next stop is Vietnam."** *

Back then you might ask a girl what her astrological sign was but she was more likely to ask about your draft status. Al Dietrich explained:
> "Opinions on the campus and elsewhere were extremely polarized. It seemed that whoever I was with, a group or at a party that there were many heated discussions about the war with some supporting it and others vehemently against the war."

This awareness grew exponentially every year during the 1960s and when I was drafted on February 16, 1970, America was all too aware (and tired) of this war. My advanced infantry training, as a 11-C mortar man at Ft. Ord, CA coincided with the Kent State shootings. I heard the news on the practice range from a tiny transistor radio. The National Guard guys from Oklahoma who were training with us draftees let out a cheer. Shocked, I asked what was cheerful about the deaths. They replied, "fuck those college kids, we hate 'em." I asked why they were staying home given their bellicose demeanors, and I, a recent convert to pacifism, was on my way to 'Nam. They replied, "Don't you know what NG stands for?" To my answer of "National Guard?" they answered, "No, <u>N</u>ot <u>G</u>oing."

Roger Johnson and his future wife Linda, just before he was sent to Vietnam.
Courtesy Roger Johnson.

Refers to "I-Feel-Like-I'm-Fixin'-to-Die Rag" by rock group Country Joe and the Fish, released in 1967. The title track remains one of the most popular Vietnam protest songs from the 1960s.

Main Street Geneseo, N.Y.

c. 1968-1971

Photos courtesy of Livingston County Historian

Top: East side of Main Street, north of Center St. Middle: The Bear Fountain in center of Main Street, facing Center Street. Lower: West side of Main Street at corner of Bank Street.

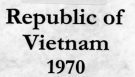

Republic of Vietnam 1970
Photos courtesy of Ron Hilfiker

Top: Funeral with ARVN truck for hearse. Middle: Three-wheeled Lambretta bus near Camp Eagle. Bottom: Pagoda at Phu Bai.

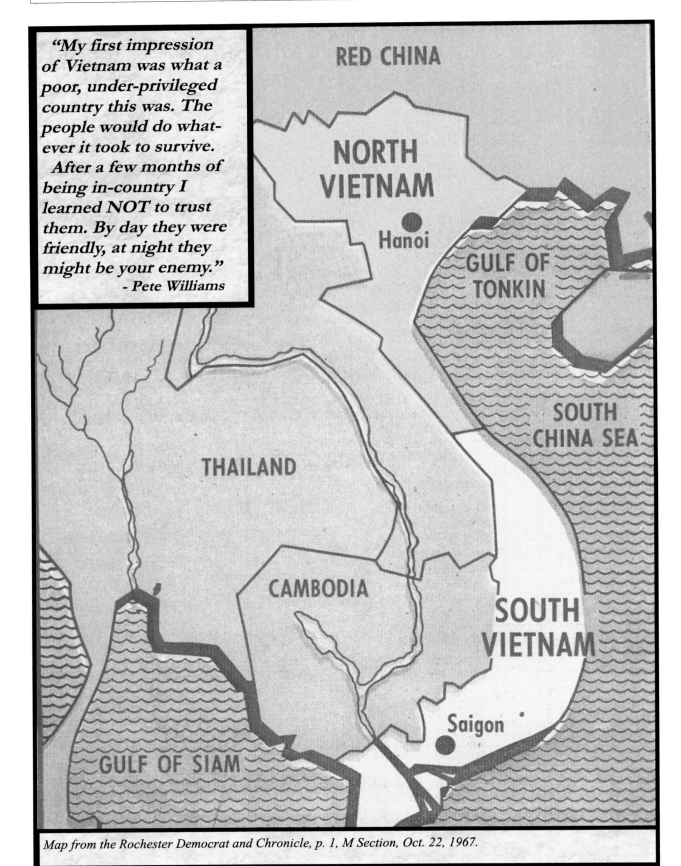

"My first impression of Vietnam was what a poor, under-privileged country this was. The people would do whatever it took to survive.

After a few months of being in-country I learned NOT to trust them. By day they were friendly, at night they might be your enemy."
— Pete Williams

Map from the Rochester Democrat and Chronicle, p. 1, M Section, Oct. 22, 1967.

During
❀ ❀ ❀ ❀ ❀ ❀ ❀
by Jim DeCamp

"I finessed myself to a 143 on the IQ section by peeking ahead and taking a little extra time...They assigned me to the infantry."
- Jim DeCamp

Joe Heiler, 11th AC, hootch mate of Jim DeCamp. Vietnam 1970. Courtesy of Jim DeCamp.

BASIC TRAINING

We started our "during" section the same way the armed services did: Basic Training consisting of a six- to twelve-week introduction, indoctrination into military life. Whether at Great Lakes Recruit Training Command, Illinois; Lackland Air Force Base, San Antonio, Texas; various army forts; or US Marine Corps training depot at Paris Island, South Carolina, or San Diego, California, the drill was similar: Off the bus, yelled at, stripped of civilian clothes and hair, uniformed and marched to spartan barracks. Up early, formation and morning run, mess hall and a series of mind- numbing classes and body-numbing physical training. The army instructors were a varied and fascinating lot.

Jim DeCamp's narrative continues.

My first favorite was the guy who administered the aptitude test in basic. He was on a raised platform in a huge room filled with long tables. He was mic-ed up and imperious. I was taking this test very seriously as I was still dumb enough to think the army cared. I finessed myself to a 143 on the IQ section by peeking ahead and taking a little extra time…They assigned me to the infantry. But this instructor was good. If anybody lagged behind in any aspect of the administration: not passing or picking up stuff quickly, distributing pencils, etc. - he had a one word sentence: "Latrine!" The miscreant was banished to stand up in the bathroom for the duration and come back later to be retested. He had that latrine jammed full of shoulder to shoulder guys by the end of the next day.

My next favorites were the guys in front of the outdoor bleachers imparting some arcane Army bullshit to us. To keep us focused, they told us to stay seated when they said, "On your feet!" and to stand when they said, "Take your seat!" You can imagine what this did to the collection of minor felons and dropouts I was training with. The consequence of being intuitive was a forced duck walk around the perimeter of the bleaches with the rifle in your lap. One poor recruit I trained with failed to salute the car of a one-star General driving by, he missed the little one star flag on the fender, and spent the night walking down a hallway, saluting the General's picture, about facing, all the way back, then repeat, and he trained all the next day.

Our West Pointers had different versions of the experience. Jim Adamson described the insular world within the military academy:

"After spending a year at Clarkson College I finally was selected to attend West Point. My awareness of Vietnam and the meaning of the war had just taken a quantum jump to being front and center in my life. Basic training consisted of four years of intense physical mental and emotional immersion in military life with an academic twist.

We were surrounded by professors, tactical officers, mentors and trainers who were either just returned, or just going to Vietnam. While the outside world was wrestling with the growing antiwar movement and protests, we were insulated. In our world we honed our bodies to enjoy the punishment of war and our minds to seal out the agony emotion of the tragedy. We all knew that we were going but we were neither afraid nor happy about it. It was simply our job…we were young, hard as nails, invincible, and horribly ignorant.

The four years at the Academy once again transformed my attitude. My first encounters with the casualties of war were my fellow scouts and neighbors from back home in Groveland. Butch Rosebrugh was KIA in 1966, and Bobby Henderson was KIA in 1968. And then many more. There were countless friends, professors, and tach officers with whom I had learned and trained. I discovered that one could actually die in this business.

(J. Adamson cont.) The war seemed closer than ever. Gradually, my dream of adventure and space travel receded to the back burner and preparing myself for war came to the fore. The feelings were sobering and strengthened my resolve to train harder than ever so I could survive. I gradually became a soldier first. Space would have to wait. While these thoughts were sobering, they were not necessarily frightening. The fear, if that's what it was, was more about not screwing up. We were after all supposed to be leaders of men in this war. The thought of not making the right decisions and causing my own death or the death of others needlessly was my only fear. My prayer became just one: "Please God, don't let me screw up!"

"The war seemed closer than ever. Gradually, my dream of adventure and space travel receded to the back burner and preparing myself for war came to the fore...
My prayer became just one,
Please God, don't let me screw up!"
- J. Adamson

Top: Jim Adamson at West Point graduation 1969. Below: West Point 1968. Courtesy of Jim Adamson.

Terry Alger went through basic a half-dozen years before Jim: "My basic training consisted of the West Point instructor, Officer Basic School, Airborne School and Ranger School... My biggest concern was to complete the training and get to my first duty assignment." ROTC offered an easier introduction as Carroll Teitsworth, a Cornell Navy ROTC grad described, "ROTC probably involved less rigorous basic training than any other avenue into the military. One week of intro to Marine life that included one day of recon training. A few push-ups was about as tough as it got. Later SERE (survival, escape, resistance and evasion) training was more rigorous. But still it was only a few days in length."

> Roger McCauley and Carroll Titsworth, Jr. attended the graduation exercises at Cornell University at Ithaca. Afterwards Mr. Carroll Titsworth left for Norfolk, Va. to take a North Atlantic cruise in connection with his ROTC course, which he has been taking at Cornell University. He expects to be gone for about 8 weeks.

Livingston Republican, 6/25/1964, p.7

Al Dietrich, another ROTC naval officer offered more details:

"As a midshipman in Navy ROTC we had four years of courses during college and drilled one afternoon per week. We had Marine drill instructors and Navy officers with several years of sea duty behind them as our course instructors.

The Marines were tough and, at first, scared the hell out of me... They and the instructors in class would talk about Vietnam and at sea. I felt/knew that my life had suddenly changed in a much more fundamental way than just leaving home for college.

Sometimes when we marched, there would be a group of students next to the drill field protesting against us. They went out of their way to make it very personal with various insults.

Al standing watch on the ship. Courtesy of Al Dietrich.

As a midshipman, our basic training with sea duty on the ship was during the summer break. I was assigned to a destroyer out of Newport, Rhode Island and spent the summer out in the Atlantic chasing Russian submarines. It was during the height of the Cold War and all business, definitely not a pleasure cruise. That summer aged or matured me very quickly."

Jim Clark's wake up to the Navy took place in January 1967 at Great Lakes Naval training base.

"I had a good friend pick me up at my home and take me to a train (never was on a train) in Rochester. From there I traveled to Buffalo to be inducted into the Navy. It was just a lot of waiting and confusion (the confusion and waiting lasted four more years) until we boarded the plane for Chicago. In Buffalo the Red Cross gave us a box of toiletries and other survival gear that was taken away when we got to our final destination… arriving very early in the morning. We were given bunks and no sooner had we got to sleep we were woken up and made ready to face the day. This is when I realized I had made a huge mistake… From learning how to brush your teeth, getting a haircut (no hair), getting your clothes and stenciling everything you own, shots and other BS…I learned early in my naval career if you had a very low IQ (borderline challenged) no dexterity, no skills/talents whatsoever and you really didn't like people, you became a Navy barber…

Camp was easy because I was made permanent service week recruit because I knew how to type. Extra liberty, no classes, no marching, no taking apart weapons no nothing (just typing). I did have to prove I could swim. This was great until the light bulb came on and I realized I knew nothing about the United States Navy. This is hard to believe but I was even given answers to many of the Naval tests we were required to take, escape

USS Oriskany (CV-34). http://www.history.navy.mil/photos/images/h97000/h97408.jpg. Image not subject to copyright or any known restrictions.

and survival or what to do and say if you are captured. This came back to haunt me not that I was ever captured but when pulling guard duty aboard my ship. A Marine officer asked me what the seventh general order of a sentry was and I told him I had no idea. This did not set well with him but I could care less, but he cared. There was a Marine unit aboard the ship I was on (USS Oriskany, CVA 34) and to this day I do believe they did not understand the true Naval warrior. I was also not able to march with my unit at graduation because I was never taught how to march, but I did graduate. Did this part of my career (basic training) scare me, no - I just wanted to get it over with and move onto the next adventure."

Right: Dennis Staley and Navy buddy. Courtesy of D. Staley

Dennis Staley seemed to have a stress-free time during his time at the Great Lakes Naval training base in 1961:

"I joined the Navy with my best friend, Richard Maybee. Basically what I expected, no up or down emotions, no culture shock, was not scared."

❀ ❀ ❀ ❀ ❀ ❀ ❀ ❀ ❀ ❀ ❀ ❀ ❀ ❀

Our Air Force guys were shocked not by the cold Great Lakes but the heat and humidity of San Antonio's Lackland Air Force Base. For Jerry Vickers it was a long awaited baptism:

"Finally I thought I was on my way. I was quite excited and ready to rock 'n roll. The only real shock to me was the weather: Texas in June for six weeks. I had no time or room to be scared."

◆ Jerry Vickers, who is now in the Air Force, is stationed at Lackland AF Base in San Antonio, Texas.

Livingston Republican, 7/11/1968.

Bucky O'Neil enlisted on the buddy system but that didn't last long,

"Basic training was a very big adjustment and culture shock. I went in on the buddy system with my friend from high school, Donny Parker. We were supposed to be there for 30 days, but because we were there through Thanksgiving, Christmas and New Year's, it seems like forever. The training was easy and I was 'dorm chief' and that gave me some ways to make it more fun. I remember being screamed at as we got off the bus at about 2 AM by a little guy who threatened to break my arm. I looked at Donny and said 'what did we do?' I was not scared, but did miss home and was a bit lonely. I remember getting our orders to go to our next stop. I went to Fayetteville, North Carolina and Donny went to Mercedes, California. I think they wanted us to be as far *(continued from previous page)* apart as possible! I was assigned to the 39th tactical airlift squadron at Pope Air Force Base and shortly after arriving we went on our first TDY assignment to Vietnam. So much for my plan."

> Mark O'Neil left from Mt. Morris Wednesday bound for Lackland Air Force Base near San Antonio, Texas. He will undergo six weeks of basic training. He is the son of Mr. and Mrs. Mark O'Neil of Geneseo.

> Donald Parker left Wednesday for six weeks basic training at Lackland Air Force Base at San Antonio, Tex. He is the son of Mr. and Mrs. Grant Parker.

"I went in on the buddy system with my friend from high school, Donny Parker...So much for my plan." - *Mark "Bucky" O'Neil*

Photo: Varsity football team, Jen-o-see yearbook, 1970. Both clippings from the Livingston Republican 11/18/1971.

Kevin Bovill also experienced the intense Texas summer heat at Lackland:

"I graduated from St. John Fisher College and entered the US Air Force officer training school Lackland Air Force Base, 9 August, 1963. It was the difference between night and day. We left the bus on the run: Up at 0500 hours [5:00 AM] lights out at 2400 [midnight], fast-paced, lots of stress, both physical and mental. Enormous amount of training compacted into 90 days."

J. Kevin Bovill, USAF. 1963. Courtesy of J.K.Bovill.

John Thompson felt the psychological effects more than the physiological: "Basic training wasn't physically difficult but it was emotionally challenging." For some like Rod Bowles, it was their first leadership experience. He was "proud, to be a squad leader, then barrack leader" and recalled one poor soul who used the long urinal, which was forbidden. Rod said, "After he cleaned it, he slept in it."

Wayne Tuttle said he "adjusted quickly, became a squad leader in basic, in Tech school. Also at Amarillo Air Force Base I was our class leader and graduated top of my class." And John Carney felt a little dislocated in Texas, "My first airplane ride was to basic and I was homesick and missed my wife. We had been married 14 months by then. Lackland Air Force Base is a large, lonely and desolate place."

"The experience was larger than life."
- J. K. Bovill

After leaving Lackland AFB, J. Kevin Bovill, standing (dot on chest) was eventually assigned to a unit of the 552nd Air Early Warning and Control Wing as Senior Weapons Director. During 1967-68, the unit's area of operation was over Laos bordering N. Vietnam and the Gulf of Tonkin. The Air Force generally had two bombing missions per day for 3 weeks, then 10 days of maintenance and relaxation. In Vietnam, J. Kevin Bovill flew a total of 87 combat support missions and received numerous awards for his service. He remained with the Air National Guard until 1991 retiring as a Lt. Col. Photo courtesy of J. Kevin Bovill.

✿ ✿ ✿ ✿ ✿ ✿ ✿ ✿ ✿ ✿ ✿ ✿ ✿

"Fear of the unknown was how it was going to be for the next four years." - Tony Gurak

Of all our Air Force guys, perhaps Tony Gurak summed the transition from small town life to military life best:

"Basic Training was not just culture shock, it was total shock. One day I was drinking beer and eating pizza with friends and a couple days later I was being yelled at and controlled every second. I had never felt so alone. Soon I made new friends and got used to the routine, there was hope, not as scary. Then we received orders for our next assignments and all the new friends scattered in different directions. Then the whole process started over again. Fear of the unknown was how it was going to be for the next four years."

Most of our vets were Army guys so Basic was 8 weeks, mostly at Ft. Dix, New Jersey, with a few less fortunate sent to the dreaded Ft. Polk, Lousiana. Their impressions were varied but all had 'basic' similarities.

Roger Least said he had no problem:
"Having ROTC and military school - no big deal. "

Jim Barber got a "snow" day or two:
"I started my Basic Training at Ft. Dix, NJ on December 15, 1965. In January we had a blizzard that shut down Fort Dix and most of the Northeast for several days, and, needless to say, training was halted until things got back to normal. As far as culture shock…some. Scared? No."

Chuck McLaughlin saw some positives, as well as some confusion:
"Important to work together, one person in charge, I was not certain that I understood the ranking status, whom to salute."

Neil Thompson was a squad leader:
"No, I wasn't scared; I just wanted to get through it and they kept shipping us around the country. First to Ft. Dix, then to Ft. Bragg where I had my first encounter with Green Berets, Rangers and Army Drill Sergeants as instructors. The Green Berets and Rangers had just come back from a tour of duty and their experiences were very graphic. You didn't want to goof off when they gave their lectures."

Terry Johnston was determined to get through Basic also:
"On Jan. 10, 1966 I was on my way to Ft. Dix, New Jersey for Basic Training. I knew I could do this because of football practice in school. It was not easy but I got through it, but in my mind I knew where I was going."

Malcolm Stewart, our only "Gyrene" summed up his Paris Island, South Carolina Boot Camp, in simple terms:
"Culture shock and scared would be understatements."

But Don Peraino asked the question that all of us pondered:
"My basic thought was what the Hell am I doing here?"

Jim DeCamp's narrative continues.

For me basic training was OK. I was 24 and ½ and out of shape but it was less grueling than most of my sports experiences. I was made "Trainee Field First" due to my age and education but mostly because I am 6'3" and the Captain was about 5'6". I had my own room and took morning attendance before the D.I.s showed up from their off-post homes. They tried to keep me there to help push troops but my 11C MOS (Mortor Crewman) sent me off to Advanced Infantry Training at Ft. Ord, California and I knew my future was growing ominous. I carried all the paper work for my plane load of guys flying to Ord. By then I had decided not to play along with their bull shit and didn't want any more pretend leadership roles that wouldn't keep me out of Vietnam.

I was shaken awake that first foggy, cold April morning by a "Shake 'n Bake" E-6. Shake 'n Bakes were guys who did a few more weeks after AIT and were made instant NCOs. They were pretty universally derided as inexperienced assholes, hence the culinary nickname. This guy asked me if I was the "BBMFIC." *"The what?"* I sleepily replied and he translated, the "big bad mother fucker in charge." I told him I was just the sorry asshole with the paper work. I did accept a squad leader post to keep my no KP streak intact. But I was through cooperating.

Jim DeCamp (right) cleaning his M-16. Courtesy of Jim DeCamp.

Ron Hilfiker, a long time resident of Geneseo, vents his frustration during basic training in a letter to his parents.

Sun Night
Oct. 27, 1968

Dear All,

I do not know if I told you but I am in the same platoon with Ted Flood. He is our platoon leader. The guys in my platoon range in age from 17 to 26 and take in four college grads and four ex cons. The ex-cons are from Reading Pa and were thrown in jail for non support of their wives and children. They are real bone heads and I will be lucky to get out of here without nailing one of them.

Last night we had to do K.P. duty. We work from 6 to 6 but it was 13 hours because of the time change. Working at a normal pace we would have been done in two hours, but we had to fake working for the full thirteen. The sergeant in charge would not even give us soap to wash the walls and floors down. I'll

I got in on a touch football game with some bone heads. It was like playing with eight year old kids. My ankle held up very well. I was afraid that it would be messed up for the running to come in the next few weeks.

I met a fellow that I saw in the Phelps hotel before I left. He is from Newark and there might be a possibility of getting a ride home with him if we stay together until Christmas. He used to work for a trucking firm, so we might be able to get a ride with the truckers.

Tomorrow we take some tests for job placement. It better get better or it going to be two years of wasted time.

Ron.

Roger Johnson explains how he quickly learned to adjust to the unknown:

"For a kid that had never been any farther away from home than Rochester, going to Buffalo, where I was sworn into the US Army, I truly had no idea of what to expect. I was about to become an entirely new person in (8) weeks. Uncle Sam would see to that. Fort Dix was a massive place and with no doubt it seemed like everyone there was telling us how we were no good, useless and hopeless. Getting quarter assignments, uniforms, shots, hair cuts and all was tiring because everyone with one stripe or more on his sleeve was in charge. Yes, it was difficult but as time went by I got used to it. After basic I was sent to a place I had never heard of, Fort Lewis, WA, at that time I knew I was going to the jungles of Vietnam. Everything from that moment on took on a much more serious and complicated feeling. I was training to become an infantry soldier."

Many of us did feel some of the stereotypical conditioning that most associate with Drill Sergeants. Cliff VanDerveer who went through Basic at Ft. Polk said,

"I trained with men from all parts of the U.S.A. The physical and classroom training was more 'drudgery' than challenging.
The D.I.s did their best to take away our individualism, only see Green."

Left: Sign at Fort Polk, Louisiana, also known as "Tiger Land". Photo: Livingston County Historian's Collection.

Roger Mustari's memories of the "psychological beating" are still vivid after all these years:

"We were shouted at from the time we were awake until lights out. At first this was frightening and intimidating. As Basic Training progressed it became very clear to me that this was all fluff. The sergeants and staff doing the noise were no more important than us, the new recruits. In time these people were called 'lifers.' These were the people who could not make it in the civilian world or who had been given the options of jail or the military... As soon as we got off the bus in Ft. Dix, New Jersey we were semi-marched to a location and everyone had his head shaved. This was during the long hair era and for some a traumatic event. I still clearly remember my first night at Dix in a cold, drafty, old wood barracks listening to fellow draftees crying in the dark...There was no leadership or accountability."

Jim DeCamp's narrative continues

The culture that shocked us wasn't so much the military's as it was the "flotsam and jetsam" washed up from the rest of the country with us. The Army was a local alternative sentence offering in the late 1960s and a parade of low level felons and misdemeanors found themselves doing 0 to 2 (years) in the Army. It was a multi-ethnic, multi-regional free for all and also a fast track to citizenship.

Far from the isolated Genesee Valley, we met Chicanos, southern and urban Blacks, Hispanics and "good old boys" and I trained with a sharp guy from the Virgin Islands with a diamond inlay in his front gold tooth. I also remember a bunch of North Carolinians shipped to Dix from an overcrowded Ft. Bragg. They were from a region where fluoride was considered a communist plot and they had brown, stubby teeth to show for it. Uncle Sam got them up at 4 AM, pulled those "stubs" and sent them out to be trained.

Jim Creagan was at Ft. Polk and made note of the melting pot of America that was bubbling in the military in those days.

"It was interesting to see differences in geography, weather, and culture. I had never met a con man or a prostitute before. Fear was mostly directed towards the cadre who could mete out punishment for a variety of discrepancies, real or imagined. It was quite amazing meeting men my age but with a very different background. Most were Blacks from Chicago."

Lenny Peri enjoyed meeting a lot of friends,

"Ah, Basic training!! I wasn't scared and it wasn't a 'culture shock', but it was a different way of life. A daily regimen of the same routine, mixed with a constant barrage of verbal harassment. All designed to insure that all 200 'slick-sleeves' knew they were all on the same level - the bottom. Once an individual understood that concept, the rest was easy to take. I met a lot of G.I.s in Basic and made a lot of friends there, but 8 weeks was about as long as that friendship lasted."

All those new "friends" jolted some as Pete Williams said:

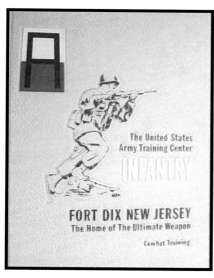

"Basic Training at Ft. Dix was tough. However, when I was finished I was in great shape! It was kind of a culture shock living in a building with 30-40 men. I was scared at first of the Drill Instructors. They were brutal on new recruits. They did prepare you for the days ahead in the Army though."

Left: U.S. Army Training Center, Fort Dix yearbook. Private collection.

Rodney Wambold worked hard to keep his cool:

"Basic training, physically, was not bad. At the time I was in decent shape. I did, however, have a bit of difficulty with people shouting in my face and saying demeaning things to me for what I thought was no good reason. At times it nearly got me in hot water, because, as people who know me would tell you I am not the calmest person. I also had never been away from home and missing my family and future wife."

Chuck Freese had a hilarious close encounter with one of his Drill Sergeants:

"Scared, confused, tired, hungry were my biggest emotions at the time. One morning while running in formation, dark out, cold, and I had to clear my lungs I spat out a large hunk of phlegm. I hit our Drill Sarge who was running up the outside of our unit, hit him on the side of his face. He happened also to be our hand-to-hand combat instructor. I was yanked out of line and taken to HQ, really thought I would not make it there, Sarge was so mad he could not talk. Our First Sergeant was an older man, WWII, Korea, and very strict. I explained what happened: I could not breathe, so I spat. He looked real mad at first, then smiled and said he had the same thing happen when he was in Basic. He calmed our Sarge down, he laughed also. I said I was sorry. I was picked a few times for demo during hand to hand, guess Sarge was trying to even the score."

WELCOME TO

SAND HILL

HOME OF THE

192D INFANTRY BRIGADE

AND THE

198TH INFANTRY BRIGADE

FORT BENNING
Maneuver Center of Excellence

Rather than Sand Hill, Bruce Booher described the Ranger post at Fort Benning, Georgia as "Sand Hell" and expressed what most of us felt to one degree or another:

"I went in as a draftee. They beat you down mentally and physically til they thought you were a soldier. You had to pretend or they would drill more Army into you.

I was taken from a small town in Geneseo to a place of misery. I did not volunteer for this and wondered why I was there. Yes, I was scared."

Above: Ft. Benning brochure. http://www.benning.army.mil/infantry/198th/Content/PDF/SandHill%20Brochure.pdf

A winter soldier's chronicle:

❀❀❀❀❀❀❀❀❀❀❀❀❀

One day in Advanced Infantry Training at Fort Ord, CA.
I found myself half-assedly loping through the bayonet course,
missing most of the target and neglecting to yell,
"Kill!" with every thrust.

I was called over by a Sergeant First Class
and informed I had a "bad attitude."
I replied, "I don't know Sarge,
I'm 25 with a wife and a Master's degree
and I'm out here stabbing these fucking dummies."

He pondered this and said,
"Carry on, troop" and waved me on.
Thus the seeds of the all-volunteer force were strewn.

- Jim DeCamp

Above: Postcard of Fort Ord, Monteray CA.. http://www.calhum.org/news/blog/new-multimedia-exhibit-brings-history-to-life

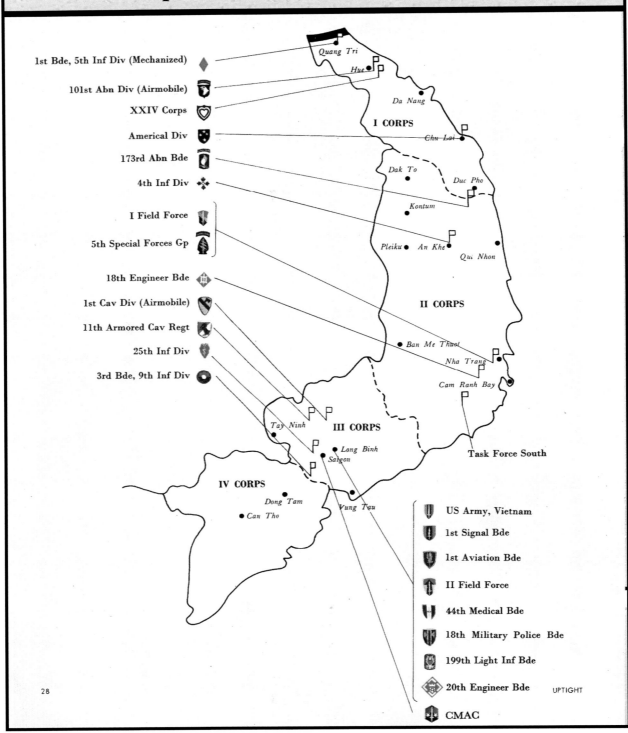

Above map was issued by the US Army to soldiers stationed in Vietnam. Courtesy of Roger Johnson.

"FNGs" & FIRST IMPRESSIONS "IN-COUNTRY"

These small town boys and a few men were flown 9000 miles away on very somber chartered flights. Guys read and slept and there was an oppressive air of fear and uncertainty on the planes. We were set down in 100 degree heat or the afternoon monsoon at Ton Son Nhut or Cam Ranh Bay, the blasts of engines in the air, the smell of diesel fuel and incinerated feces greeted us. Hurried into buses with chicken wire over the windows "to keep the grenades from being tossed in" as the driver explained. We rode the narrow roads amid convoys of olive drab "deuce and a halfs" to various posts throughout the south and started ticking off our calendars - one day down - 364 to go.

On March 8, 1965, thirty-five hundred U.S. Marines came ashore near Da Nang. They were the first non-advisor troops in Vietnam. They traveled on a troopship, knew and trained with each other. Company leaders knew the strength and liabilities of their troops. Grunts were familiar with their leaders and either trusted them…or knew not to. Attrition, KIAs and the wounded quickly necessitated replacements and they arrived in Military Airlift Command commercial 707s. They came mostly alone, knowing few or none of their fellow travelers. Maybe a friend or two from Advanced Training but usually a plane load of scared, lonely troops soon to be plugged into up-and-running units as the dreaded FNGs.

Above: Mortar firing. Courtesy of Ron Hilfiker.

Jim DeCamp's narrative continues.

I had been mildly attentive during advanced infantry training but I was all ears during newbie training in Vietnam. We were in a small three- or four-row bleacher set one day when the sergeant popped the handle of a grenade and handed it to the first guy in the row and told him to pass it along. Assuming it was a dud we casually did so and handed it to the instructor at the end. He threw it into a nearby hole where it promptly exploded. Now, it may have been a percussion grenade and not fragmented and there was a guy in the bleachers ready to catch a drop, but I always admired that attention-getting device in my subsequent years as a teacher myself.

FNGs were worthy of dread. "The Fuckin' New Guy" was a distinct liability until enough experience made him less dangerous or just inept. Walking through triple canopy jungle and 'wait a minute vines' that reached out and ensnared us one day I had the latest "Newbie" stumbling behind me. On a rest stop I asked him what setting he had his M-16 set to. There were three choices: safety, single shot, or full automatic known as "rock 'n roll" which emptied the 20-round clip in 1.8 seconds. When he replied, "rock 'n roll," I suggested he walk in front of me so I "can keep an eye out for you."

This isolation, disassociation and constant turn over would have profound effects on morale, discipline and mission effectiveness. It enforced the idea that each of us was essentially a cog in the war machine and on his own. *Esprit de corps* was hard to muster when there really was no corps. You were either the FNG or the "short-timer" with an endless stretch of 300+ days in between. Once you got the hang of your job you were too short to pass it on or too scared to keep doing it. Coming and going at a steady pace made long term relations difficult.

Many of our first impressions of Vietnam mirrored those of the fictitious disk jockey, "Roosevelt Lee Roosevelt," played by actor Robin Williams in the 1987 movie

> ## Thus my tour of duty began
> When I arrived in Cu Chi with the 2/27 "Wolf Hounds" Regiment in July of '70 they were still in Cambodia mopping up from the May offensive. SFC Luna was the first Wolf Hound I met, in the outdoor, solar, gravity fed showers. He was a nut brown, wizened up, small, Hawaiian native. His first words to me were, "Take a look at my ass, troop. What do you see?"
> What I saw was one cheek and the other replaced by scar tissue that went from his leg to his back. "You seem to be missing a cheek, Sarge" I replied. "You're right, and it's your job to make sure I don't lose the other one." Thus my tour of duty began.   *- Jim DeCamp*

Good Morning, Vietnam. Roosevelt's responses to the question about the weather:

"It's hot, damn hot, hot as my shorts. I could cook things in it, crotch-pot cooking. Fool, I told you it's hot, were you born on the sun? It's damn hot. It's so damn hot I saw a little guy in an orange robe burst into flames. It's that hot. Tonight it's going to be hot and wet, which is nice if you're with a lady, but it ain't no good if you're in the jungle."

The movie's character was right about the country's meteorology. Vietnam is located from 9 to 23 degrees north of the equator. Over the course of the year south of the DMZ the temperature varies from 71 to 94. The warm season is from March 15 to May 15, then the monsoons come in until September. The length of the day does not vary substantially over a year, staying within 45 minutes of 12 hours throughout the year.

Chuck Freese described the heat's brutal intensity:

"Wow, it's hot there and the streets were really hectic with scooters, bikes, cars, people walking in the street. We were on a bus with chicken wire in the open windows. We were told to watch for someone hanging anything on the wire, if they did, unhook it and let it fall as it would be a bomb device...I thought then and there, this is going to be serious and very bad."

Cliff VanDevere added humidity and stink to the mix:

"Arrived at Cam Rahn Bay (Feb, '69) Temp. 90. Had left Ft Lewis, Washington, rainy, 30s! The heat, humidity and stink struck me. The base was incredibly busy."

Ron Hilfiker, a Phelps Central School graduate and long time Geneseo resident, went to Vietnam as a college educated 11B (Infantry) and his first impressions were,

"Dangerous, stay alert, stay alive, hurry up and wait, don't let your guard down, very cautious at first, experienced, then overly cautious as a short timer."

Left: Ron Hilfiker at hilltop chopper LZ. Courtesy of Ron Hilfiker.

Malcolm Stewart put it all together:

"My impressions of time in Vietnam were heat and humidity, periodic torrential rain, constant fatigue, immense responsibility, and thankfulness for survival."

Jim Clark experienced Vietnam on the USS Oriskany, an Attack Aircraft Carrier:

"I arrived by helicopter from another vessel after a very long flight from California and a two-week stay in the Philippines (Olangapo City). Olangapo was a dream come true, women and bars and here we are in the middle of paradise and only 19 years old. I later found out it was the home port of the Oriskany (Yes!). Needless to say my attitude changed…I was doing something, and I was involved - right or wrong, I was doing my part and proud to be a part of it. (It was a totally different feeling than the stateside Navy BS.) My primary job was Naval Tactical Data Systems (NTDS) and surface radar and I was assigned to CIC-Combat Information Center (got lucky). It was a great place to work especially when you were in port as all of these operating systems were shut down. When at sea it gave you a total picture of what was happening around you. On Line (combat operating area) you would work 8 hours on at your primary job and 8 hours off. Your 8 hours off were most of the time not yours. You usually pulled a working party which included moving bombs on the hanger deck to standing in a very long line moving boxes of stores from the hanger deck to their respective storage area below for many hours. I believe the longest we were at sea was 48 days. We provided air support for our troops and bombed North Vietnam. Then we would go to a port for two weeks to be resupplied and rest and relaxation. The ports were a wild time…"

Al Dietrich served aboard a repair ship and also made regular excursions into Saigon:

"In Vietnam I served on the USS Tutuila ARG-4, a repair ship for the river boats on the west coast. We were anchored off Phu Quoc Island which is just off the northwestern coast of Vietnam and just off Cambodia. It was a beautiful tropical island with fishing villages, beaches, lagoons and jungle. During WWII the island had a Japanese prison camp for Americans and British. When I was there it was a prison for North Vietnamese soldiers and Viet Cong. I believe about 20,000. I was really quite safe being on a ship anchored off the island as there was no combat in our area.

As a ship's supply officer I had to go to Saigon periodically and that was always more than interesting. Travel was usually on a small plane carrying mail with many stops in various towns and villages along the way. I was usually in Saigon for several days. The totally different culture along with the war was difficult to comprehend. I appreciated quickly the phrase 'back in the world' as this was just so different

(continued next page)

(A. Dietrich continued from previous page) almost exactly halfway around the world and so totally different even without a war. Most disconcerting were all of the children (mostly orphans I believe) in the streets trying to sell you every-thing from watches and cameras to drugs and girls. They were every-where and you couldn't walk any-where without them quite forcefully approaching you.

Child with handmade replica of a M-16 rifle trying to sell to US soldiers. Photo courtesy of Ron Hilfiker.

You could see what a beautiful city it had been before the war but now it was sad and surreal.

Our ship was a busy operation and the days were long with regular day job and standing watch on a rotating basis at night. I certainly can't complain though. I was quite safe, had a room to share with another junior officer and good Navy food. We really did eat well. For the river boat crews that we supported, life was a very different story. They would leave for days or weeks on operations that definitely put them in harm's way and at times the boats would be shot up and towed back for repairs, but some of the crew did not return with them.

Life was so busy that the year went by relatively quickly and you just put home and your previous life in the back of your mind."

Left: Hoisting a Navy Swift boat up for repairs. Courtesy of Al Dietrich.

Dennis Staley's view was from under the water,

"Hawaii was my first duty station, U.S.S. Carbonero SS-337 was my first submarine, it was a WII Diesel Boat test depth 400 feet. My culture shock was here with all the inter-racial marriages. I adapted quickly because it was the norm here, everyone was very nice. My perspective didn't change, we had a job to do on patrol, and we did it. We had one patrol in the Gulf of Tonkin and one long patrol, 64 days, South China Sea off the island of Hoinan."

Left: Dennis Staley on top side watch aboard the USS Carbonero, 1964. Courtesy of Dennis Staley.

Nearby Thailand wasn't much different. John Carney was at Korat Royal Thai AFB in Thailand in Oct, 1972, describing it as,

"Hot, humid, stinky, insect and snake-infested 'paradise'. Our third day there we got hit with sappers trying to get to our planes... People in Thailand are very poor, they gave their money to the rulers of the country. I couldn't believe how they lived. It was incredible, such a culture shock."

We were surrounded by a sing-song tongue that was nothing like high school French or Spanish. "Señora Sacco" (our foreign language teacher, Barbara Bagg at GCS) was not going to help us here. For Lenny Peri,

"Vietnam is what I'd call my first culture shock. It had a distinct odor to it and it was the first time in my life I realized that not everyone could speak English."

Right: Lenny Peri worked as an Army radio operator. Photo courtesy of Lenny Peri.

Language was even a challenge for West Point's Terry Alger who had studied Vietnamese:

"The biggest problem that I had was the language. Although I attended the Army Foreign Language School and studied Vietnamese, it was still difficult to communicate with the people.

My first assignment was as an Asst. Battalion Advisor to a Vietnamese Infantry Battalion in the Delta area of South Vietnam. It is sometimes difficult to understand the manner in which the Vietnamese handled the war, but one had to understand first that it had become a way of life for many of the soldiers and their biggest concern was to stay alive to the end. For the American advisors it was a one- year tour of duty and we to make a big impact on the war in a short time. Sometimes the two objectives would clash. Looking back it is easy to understand the Vietnamese attitude."

Vi Thanh Market, 1965. Courtesy of Terry Alger.

The Vietnamese people made a quick impression, both positive and negative. The children were especially notable. Rodney Wambold said,

"In our motor pool we had a 14-year-old boy who worked for us and I got to meet his family. It was an experience to see the way they lived, but they were very gracious.

I would like to know what happened to that young man. These people were poor, but extremely proud."

Right: Mt. Morris Enterprise, 01/06/1971.

Sgt. Wambold In Vietnam

Sgt. Rodney Wambold is serving as a Motor Sergeant for the U.S. Army in Can Tho, Vietnam.

He is the son of Mr. and Mrs. George Wambold of Nunda. His wife, Leslie, and son, Darryl live at 518 West Lake Rd., Geneseo at the home of her parents, Mr. and Mrs. Everett Lewis.

Sgt. Wambold entered the Army in Oct. 1968, received training at Ft. Dix, N.J., Aberdeen Proving Grounds, Md. and Fort Knox, Ken.

Pete Williams describes the darker side of the war-torn country:

➥ Peter Williams, son of Mr. and Mrs. Bill Williams, is now a Post Engineer in Vietnam. His address is Sp/4 Peter M. Williams, US 51778266, 589th EBC- Co. "D," APO, San Francisco, Calif. 96377.

Livingston Republican, 04/03/1969.

"My first impression of Vietnam was what a poor, under-privileged country this was. The people would do whatever it took to survive. After a few months of being in-country I learned NOT to trust them. You learned that by day they were friendly, at night they might be your enemy. I watched people die. I experienced losing friends. I learned that war was terrible and terrible things happen in war."

ARMY PRIVATE FIRST CLASS Donald D. Peraino (right), 22, son of Mr. and Mrs. Nunzio Peraino, 5 Highland Road, Geneseo, hands a gift to a Vietnamese boy as other children look on. The gifts were sent by the student council of the Geneseo High School where Pvt. Peraino graduated in 1964. Pvt. Peraino, assigned as a mail clerk with the 199th Light Infantry Brigade's Headquarters Company, entered the Army in April 1967 and completed basic training at Ft. Benning, Ga. He was stationed at Ft. Polk, La., before arriving overseas in October 1967. He holds the Combat Infantryman Badge. The private attended the State University at Geneseo. Before entering the Army, he was employed by the Star Super Market in Geneseo. (U.S. ARMY PHOTO)

This gave way quickly to questions of why we were in Vietnam in the first place. Roger Least saw "a beautiful country and people, realized the politics and it became a cluster fuck." Chuck McLaughlin said he "didn't understand the Vietnamese culture and why we were fighting them."

Donny Peraino's first impression "very soon after I got there was that these people didn't want us there."

Right: Livingston County Leader, 05/01/1968.

Carroll Teitsworth's view was from a P3 Orion aircraft,:

"The country is spectacularly beautiful. Among our crew we talked about how if we could do away with the war and build hotels on the beaches we could get rich. The closest we came to that was swimming and playing volley ball in the sand. When I returned home I was in a cast - due to a turned ankle in a volley ball game.

The plane I was flying was the P3 Orion (Navy's version of the Lockheed Electra). It was not a carrier plane. But one time as we were finishing our patrol around the coast, we ended up in the Tonkin Gulf.

Navy Lt. Carroll G. Teitsworth has his "Wings" pinned on by his wife. Navy Lt. Teitsworth, son of Mr. and Mrs. Carroll A. Teitsworth of Barber Hill Rd., Groveland, has been awarded aviator's "Wings of Gold" upon completion of flight training at the U.S. Naval Air Station at Corpus Christi, Tx. Livingston Republican, 11/21/1968.

(C. Teitsworth continued from previous page.)

The carrier on station had just finished recovering its fighters, and its CCA (Carrier Controlled Approach) radar was still up. We asked for and received clearance for an approach. Of course we didn't land - our right wing tip and #4 engine would have taken out the island. But it was cool - sailors on deck were taking pictures of us as our crew was all in the cockpit taking photos of them.

I had done 'Carquals" (Carrier Qualifying) during training as all Naval Aviators did at that time, but most of our crew members had never been that close to a carrier before."

Future astronaut Jim Adamson flew helicopters in Vietnam:

"Of course all the training I received never prepared me for what I actually found when I arrived in Cam Rahn Bay, Vietnam in late 1971. Hours and hours of boring flights over the Pacific were sandwiched in between horrendously hurried equipment issue, unit assignments, transportation orders, medical checks, and a barrage of instructions. The whole thing was quite surreal and very helpful. Had I had more time I might have been scared. Instead, arriving 'in-country' was all a kind of dissociative blur.

In the end I was assigned to C Troop 16th Air Cavalry. The Air Cavalry was pretty new to the Army, having been formed in 1965. The Air Cavalry was designed to increase troop mobility and extend the reach and flexibility of the ground commander. C/16 had originally been assigned to the 1st Infantry Division as D Troop, 1st Squadron, 4th Cavalry Regiment and was later detached after the 1st Inf. returned home in 1970 and moved to the Mekong Delta. That's where I found it, or it found me.

Over the course of the war the mission had morphed from being the 'eyes and ears' of the Division to performing a kind of all-in-one 'Find-Fix-and-Destroy' mission for South Vietnamese ground commanders in the Delta. We were a 'Have Gun, Will Travel' outfit.

(continued next page)

(J. Adamson continued) There was good news and bad news about being in the Cav. The good news was we came home every night and therefore got to sleep in a relatively secure bed. The bad news was that we were in a fire fight every single day. Our mission was stopping enemy supplies coming down the Ho Chi Minh trail. It was our job to start the fight and we did, every day. We definitely paid the price in aircraft and blood. During the year I fought with the Cav. we lost more than a complete complement of aircraft and flight crews to combat. It was almost before the end of my tour before I saw a single pilot go home walking upright."

Jim Adamson in Vietnam, 1971 with C/16 Air Cav. Troop. Courtesy of J. Adamson.

Jim Creagan was also a chopper pilot, serving three extended tours:

"Vietnam is quite a lush geographical area. I had nothing in my life to compare it to. I was impressed by the magnitude of the military presence, probably because I had never prepared for it. I'm not even sure I could have found RVN on a globe. I enjoyed meeting and knowing many of the citizens there. They seemed like a friendly, humble and often thankful sort of folk. I imagined we were on the side of right and naturally would be victorious. Oh well.

I was a helicopter pilot in RVN during 1967, '68 and '69 and received numerous commendations from the Army. I also enjoyed touring Hong Kong, Tokyo and Europe while on leave. I was shot down twice, crashed in the Gulf of Thailand on a separate occasion. Although getting a bullet hole through my flight helmet, I was never wounded."

> *"In June 1966 I landed in Vietnam at Saigon & when I got off my plane I looked over to see body bags being loaded on another plane headed to the U.S.*
>
> *This was my wake up call and I figured this will be the way I will get home: in a body bag."*
>
> *- Terry Johnston*

Terry Johnston, Vietnam 1967. Courtesy of T. Johnston.

Terry Johnston's welcome to Vietnam was a rude one:

"In June 1966 I landed in Vietnam at Saigon & when I got off my plane I looked over to see body bags being loaded on another plane headed to the U.S. This was my wake up call and I figured this will be the way I will get home: in a body bag.

Scared was now a reality and I changed my perspective of the war. That same day I was sent to Cam Rhan Bay to the 1st Aviation Battalion and was assigned to the 48th Assault Helicopter Co. in Tuy Hoa. That night, my first day in-country at Cam Rahn Bay, we got mortared by the North Vietnamese but survived the hit. Next stop was Home Base Phan Rang the very next day then on to Tuy Hoa where I got my first education of war.

We set down in a UH-1B helicopter in Tuy Hoa where I was assigned with the 48th. As I got out of my chopper and it left to take off, another chopper was sling loading a shot-up rotor blade and the air current caught it and shot it up into the helicopter blades and it plunged to the ground.

On that flight (64-13772) on August 1, 1966 we lost 5 men and as this all unfolded, I realized it was going to be a hard road for a year, to get back to the United States alive. The afternoon of this crash was not a pretty sight."

Roger Johnson had a similar welcome, this time from the local fauna,:

"I arrived at Cam Rhan Bay in Vietnam on Oct. 1, 1969 and when the airplane's doors opened I was greeted by a terribly oppressive heat, and to seeing a huge military complex, with so much activity going on it was difficult to take it all in. We were placed in a huge, simple metal building where we were housed until our placement orders came in. My first evening after "chow" I was laying on my bunk when something hit my chest, just as in the next bunk someone yelled 'Did you see the size of that fucking rat?' It had run across my chest on its way to who knows where. Now awake, I watched the rats run across the beams of our building and they were huge, what kinda place is this? In a few short days I was assigned to the 198th Light Infantry Brigade of the American Division in I Corps in Chu Lai, my home for the next year."

Jim DeCamp's narrative continues.

I almost joined Roger at the 23rd American Division but a little chicanery and some great serendipity sent me to the much calmer 25th, Tropic Lightning Division. Heat, noise, smell as we disembarked from a very quiet, sober trip over. The bus had chicken wire over the windows and the driver gleefully told us it 'kept the grenades out.' I spent over a week at the massive camp where we lined up every morning behind a telephone pole with our destination on it. Mine was Chu Lai and the 23rd American Division.

I saw no reason to hurry and by lingering at the end of the line I avoided the trip long enough to run into a guy from Mt. Morris, only a few miles from Geneseo, one day playing pool volleyball. He recognized me from high school football, told me he had hated my guts then but was going to see if he could help me out over there.

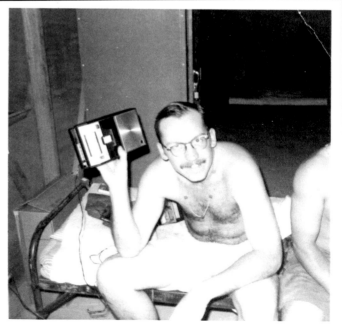

He was a base electrician and the clerks owed him a favor. He got my orders changed to Cu Chi and the 25th. They went home in November and I lucked out with a clerk's job in the 11th Armored Cav.

Right: Jim DeCamp, Vietnam 1970. Courtesy of J. DeCamp.

BRUCE A BOOHER, 21, Army Specialist Four, son of Mr. and Mrs. Walter Booher, 3878 North Road, Geneseo, is taking part in "operation Yellowstone" in Vietnam with the 25th Infantry Division. The operation began Dec. 8 in an area of heavy jungle 60 miles northwest of Saigon known as War Zone C. Search and destroy missions are being conducted in the area with support from helicopters, artillery, armor and mechanized units. U.S. and Vietnamese infantrymen involved in the operation are attempting to cut off and destroy enemy units using the area as a supply route from the north and a storage point for weapons, ammunition and food. Spec. Booher is a combat engineer with Company D of the division's 65th Engineer Battalion. --

Above: Livingston County Leader 1/31/1968.

Bruce Booher's first impressions were the most salient:

"What the hell am I doing here? I said this on the plane over, Cam Rahn Bay and wherever I was over there every day. Scared is not the right word.

You don't sleep, every day you don't think you're going to make it - then you just say, fuck it, do it and get it over with."

"Winning the hearts and minds..."

❋ ❋ ❋ ❋ ❋ ❋ ❋ ❋ ❋ ❋ ❋ ❋

Phan Thi Kim Phuc was a little girl
burned up by US Army-delivered napalm,
a product from the "living improved daily"
Dow Chemical Company.

She was in Trang Bang,
a town that we flew in and out of.
We would ride our deuce and a halfs
out of Cu Chi to a helicopter field there.
Little kids would run along side our trucks
and we would toss candy and C-Rats to them.

Once in a while a Private joker
would toss a smoke grenade instead
and kids like Phan, or Phan herself,
would be enveloped in the yellow or red smoke.

Winning the hearts and minds
one napalm bomb and smoke grenade at a time.

- Jim DeCamp

SHIFTING POINTS OF VIEW

Evidence of widespread chemical defoliation. Courtesy of Ron Hilfiker.

Our guys were asked how their perspectives changed during their tours and about some of their experiences. Here, again, the eras of service mattered. The early (pre-1969) arrivals were ripe for disillusionment as they all believed we would do this right and ultimately prevail, leave triumphantly or on our terms. Peace with honor, kind of, though that phrase was corrupted by Nixon's cynicism.

These early warriors thought we were fighting the "Red Menace" and defending the dominoes from falling all over South East Asia. We would be welcomed in the country and welcomed home by America, WWII style. Somehow, we as a nation forgot how our older brethren had been greeted home from Korea. And they fought to a tie.

By my time in 1970-71, it was time to 'turn out the lights' and we echoed Ensign John Kerry's question to the Senate Foreign Relations Committee: "How do you ask somebody to be the last man to die for a mistake?"*

*Refers to John F. Kerry, currently US Sec. of State (appt. 2013), highly decorated Vietnam veteran and subsequent anti-war protester. He asked this question while testifying before the Senate Foreign Relations Committee in 1971. http://www.state.gov/r/pa/ei/biog/203657.htm.

> *"The day in and day out exposure to combat started tugging at my mind.*
>
> *Several very intense fire fights, loss of close friends, and the constant exposure to the bloodshed made me weary."*

Right: Vietnam 1971. Courtesy of Jim Adamson.

Jim Adamson explains how his perspective shifted in separate stages:

"I went through three distinct psychological phases during my tour with the Cav. When I first went into combat I expected the enemy to be everywhere and to shoot accurately and fully expected to be shot at any moment. I soon found out that they were somewhat predictable and my training had been quite good and I was able to survive if I paid attention and did my job well.

The second phase was definitely the best and lasted most of my tour. I felt very confident and even a little cocky. I was a gunslinger and damned good at it. I didn't think too much about death and I tried not to think about the odds. I simply focused on the mission and doing the best I could. I reasoned that my training had been the best and if I could only stay focused, I would be fine. Eventually however that phase gave way to doubt about my survival. The day in and day out exposure to combat started tugging at my mind. Several very intense fire fights, loss of close friends, and the constant exposure to the bloodshed made me weary. I couldn't stop the feeling that one of these days I would find the bullet with my name on it. I started getting apprehensive before the day's mission to the point of vomiting. Would today be the day?

Thoughts about the morality and reason for the war began to creep into my thoughts. That began the third and most dangerous phase which lasted until I came home. The thought that my luck was running out and I wouldn't make it home started to affect my behavior in combat. That's a very bad thing. Being over-cautious is definitely the enemy of success in that game and I knew it. For the rest of my tour I fought every day to recapture the boldness that had saved my life. Fortunately for me I was able to do it well enough to get home alive."

Jim Clark felt conflicted between his military and civilian self:

"I did feel a strong part of this anti-war social movement but as long as I stayed in the Navy, Vietnam (7th Fleet) is where I wanted to be. But when my time was up I wanted to get the hell out. It is like being pulled into two different directions. I wanted our government to stop killing our troops and finish the war by killing their troops. We did have the capability. An unpopular war that we should never have got involved in, but since we did we should have the common sense to use every means available to win it, and win it fast. Get out and never have a doubt who was the victor. Then we can return to peace/love."

Rod Bowles' mindset went from naïve to realistic:

"I arrived to help others and soon learned that everyone was helping himself. Focus was work though I still did not know what we were trying to win. Glad that I volunteered, sorry to learn that I was idealistic, young, and easily fooled."

Roger Johnson's perspective definitely broadened with experience:

"These young men became my teachers, mentors and, most of all, brothers. They told me what they expected of me and what I needed to learn so that one day we might all go home…I learned so much about those super special guys I was serving with, and their being killed and how that pain has never completely healed…those ghosts will always be with me. It was a year of terror, fear, agony, and hope with some good times with some of the best guys on this planet."

Half a dozen or so of us were married at the time so communication with and support from our wives was especially critical and poignant. I got great support from

home, as most of us did. My wife, Doreen, wrote every day, my Mom often, my Dad twice, and I received care packages from my four sisters. I enjoyed my status as a combat GI and wrote U. S. Senator Jacob Javits when I thought I was being mistreated. I also wrote the head of Selective Service when he said publicly that he didn't know of any college graduates who were enlisted men in the infantry. I introduced him to one - me.

Jim DeCamp sent this photo to the ladies at the local draft board office to show how bad he looked like after 18 days in the field with no shower. It was meant to be cynical but they found it endearing, assuming he was enjoying being a soldier in 'Nam and posted it on the bulletin board for all to see. Courtesy of Jim DeCamp.

As I mentioned earlier, I had gone over to Vietnam right after the Kent State shootings so was very aware of politics at home. *Stars and Stripes* was actually a pretty good newspaper. I had a ten-day leave right in the middle of my tour and was able to fly home (arriving at the airport in Rochester in my short sleeves). It was strange to be back in Geneseo in January of 1971 and know I was only halfway through my tour.

Mail call was a special time for all of us. It would get choppered in with a hot lunch (and two cold beers apiece) while we were in the field. Mail seemed to bunch up coming over, so a few days of a dry spell would be followed by a downpour of half a dozen letters or more. I have all my letters home to Doreen still and as I re-read them I realize I left a lot of the danger and fear out. I didn't always date the weekday so continuity is hard to establish. I'm always impressed at how wildly in love I am with Doreen in those letters. She was my sounding board and I also bucked myself up by assuring her that I was being careful and that I would be coming home so we could resume our life together.

Terry Alger said that support from family and friends was always very positive, "I was married and my wife lived in Piffard with her mother. The Livingston County and Geneseo, in particular, residents were very supportive. I never had the coming home experiences that many of my friends from the large cities complained about."

Rodney Wambold's new wife sent letters and pictures of his son daily. Carroll Teitsworth, also a new dad, said his wife and new baby spent the deployment time with their families back home.

John Carney had two young sons at home and said, "My wife supported me. But not a lot of family support, didn't seem to care.

Gets Second Bronze Star

Army Caption Terry Alger, 25, receives a second Bronze Star Medal for outstanding meritorious service in combat operations against hostile forces in the Republic of Vietnam, August 1965-1966. Livingston Republican, 11/24/1966.

My uncle Jim was wounded in WWII and the exception." Rod Bowles' father had also been a POW in WWII and "understood."

Terry Johnston said how vital contact from back home was,

"My family & friends are what kept me going and my wife at home was all I thought of. My Mom would send packages of cookies, they were in pieces & crushed but it was a taste of home."

Tony Gurak said he was glad to get letters and "crumbly cookies" from home.

"Kept me connected just to read about my family's every day life. Letters from my girlfriend always assured me that not every college student was a protester. I always appreciated her support."

Bucky O'Neil appreciated the much maligned and often re-gifted fruit cake:

"One of my favorite presents each year was a fruit cake from Mike Kelly, my girlfriend's mom. Even though Nancy and I were over shortly after I went in the Air Force, the fruit cake came reliably every year I was in."

Jim Creagan said he got cookies and "the omnipresent cheese and cracker packages with that horrible summer sausage in there."

Al Dietrich relied on recordings to communicate:

"We all had small reel-to-reel tape decks and would send tapes to each other almost every week. I rarely wrote nor did they as being able to get tapes was really great. You could hear the voices and say much more than you could in a letter."

Wayne Tuttle made audio tapes but "background noise" made it difficult:

"I felt I had full support from family and friends while in Vietnam. My relatives sent 'care packages' as did Ruth Magee in Groveland. Ruth's banana bread and cookies were great. I made an audio tape soon after I arrived. Our base at Na Trang was being mortared and the Air Force was bombing and strafing the perimeters. It sounded so scary that I never sent it home. My only real scare was one night we went through a rocket attack. The rockets were landing all around, when one hit behind our barracks. I figured the next would be right on top of me. It hit the front of the barracks, with shrapnel sounding like pebbles pounding the metal exterior."

Top: Wayne Tuttle (right) and Rene Sylvester, also from Geneseo, in Nha Trang. Right: Wayne with one of the 23 planes he rebuilt while serving with the 21st Tactical Support Squadron. Courtesy of Wayne Tuttle.

Many mothers were occupied in wider care package distribution. Malcolm Stewart said, "Family support was outstanding during my Vietnam service. My mother, Eleanor Stewart, was involved with a local Vietnam support group which kept me and my Marines well-supplied with baked goods and other items." That group was called "Operation Morale," and the local branch was started by Jim Clark's mother, Kathryn Clark of Avon. To the soldiers she was affectionately known as "Mama Kay."

Below: Rochester Democrat and Chronicle, May 14, 1972.

Combat GIs Salute 'Mama Kay'

By PAUL PINCKNEY

Town Traveler

"Mama Kay."

That is how thousands of GIs in combat zones address a charming, energetic Western New York woman who long ago declared war on apathy.

Even in her own Livingston County community, Mrs. Relly S. Clark is known as Kay, an affectionate appellation for her first name, Kathryn.

This mother of two sons and a daughter, a grandmother of four, is, in a sense, a saleswoman, a cheerleader, fervent in her commitment to "remember the men over there" on the lonely warfronts.

Gift, birthday card and letter programs, requiring endless hours of preparation, packing and writing, make up the project called Genesee Valley G.I. Morale, a two-year-old successful offshoot of disbanded Operation Morale.

As unpretentious as your next-door neighbor, the Rochester native, a 37-year Avon resident and author of children's books, has never slackened her drive. Her inexhaustible faith, bolstered by the contributions of "many, many

volunteers," continues to lift the esprit de corps of servicemen.

"I have packed thousands of gift boxes for boys from all over the United States, not necessarily Livingston and Monroe counties," said Mrs. Clark at her home, 152 Clinton St., where even a severe case of laryngitis did not deter her efforts to aid the fighting men.

"All we need is each man's name and address — and funds, of course." There is a great need for packages in all combat areas," she emphasized, noting that the gradual troop withdrawal policy of the government has affected the program somewhat by reducing the sense of urgency about the need to boost morale.

"Frankly, in our area the group, so faithful in the five years that I have been involved in this work, has weakened a little bit. We still need volunteers and financial support, for we are determined to

carry out the program, to let the servicemen know we care."

As evidenced by grateful GIs — "Thank you for letting us know someone really cares" — the shipments, cards and letters are well received.

Contributors have received visits from men after they're discharged and, as a group, the Livingston-Greece organization accepted a plaque from a special advisory team in Vietnam for "outstanding performance."

Oriental dolls, green berets, Viet Cong flags and other "souvenirs" also have been sent to area residents in "thank-you" messages.

It's a monumental task for the large army of volunteers. Mrs. Clark pointed out, paying tribute to "all those wonderful people who are cooperating," especially the officers of GVGIM, which she heads as president.

Mrs. Richard F. Hughes of

D&C Photo by G. Paul Burnett
Mrs. Relly S. Clark (Mama Kay) packing GI gift packages.

Greece is vice president; Mrs. Laurence Hinkley of Greece, secretary; Kendall Seybolt of Avon, treasurer, and William

J. (Bill) Bruckel, an Avon lawyer and former University of Rochester athlete, legal adviser.

"They work so hard without ever any mention," said the

Please turn to 3B

From 1B

charismatic leader, modestly shrugging off her duties with, "We don't work as individuals; this is a group effort. Take Joan — Mrs. Hughes — for example, she has been very active for many years."

Mrs. Hughes, 3 Florence Ave., Greece, is another superb organizer.

"We feel it is necessary to keep this program going as long as our servicemen are in Vietnam," iterated last year's "Monroe County Mother of the Year."

"It's not that we believe in war, or even support it. In fact, many of us don't. But as long as our servicemen are over there, we want them to know we're thinking of them."

In her family, besides her husband, are "two of my own children, two foster children and one adopted child."

"Only last month," said the

buoyant and diligent suburbanite, "our organization sent 22,000 pounds of foodstuffs and clothing to the men in combat areas — Thailand, Okinawa, and most of it, of course, to Vietnam.

"We had a great deal of difficulty raising funds. As a matter of fact, our goal never would have been reached had it not been for an anonymous contributor.

"The morale in Vietnam is low — just terrible. Just look at the letters we receive. They tell the story. We should be sending gift packages in a few weeks again because of the situation, but we just don't know how it can be done without getting donations."

Although names of contributors are never disclosed, it is important, Mrs. Hughes declared, to shower praise on the "junior high school students at Britton School in Greece."

Without their help, she said, the most recent project would

not have been completed. "They did all the packaging — 800 five-pound gift boxes — and letter-writing. They should be commended."

Said Mrs. Clark: "We are completely funded through public donations. The law requires us to have our officers registered with the Internal Revenue Service so that donations can be deductible."

Among the goodies sent in each mailing overseas are tuna fish, sardines, smoked markerel, hard-tak, beef stick, cheese spreads, snack packs of pudding, raisins, meat spreads, fruit juice, fruit cocktail, olives, pickles, potato sticks, tin-wrapped rye bread, packaged gum, peanuts, canned nuts, dehydrated soups, gravy mix ("the GIs mix this with C-ration"), small packages of candy ("the kind that doesn't get sticky in humidity"), cookies . . .

And that's not all: white (sweat-type) socks ("they wear these as liners"), self-

seal envelopes, ballpoint pens, paperback books . . .

There are always flaws in the operations, acknowledged Mrs. Clark, who has No. 1 rooter in her husband, Relly, a sales engineer, chairman of the Livingston County Planning Board and of the Policy and Goals Committee of the Finger Lakes Regional (eight-county) Board.

Two sons, James K. of Avon and R. William of South Livonia, and a daughter, Mrs. Robert T. (Kathryn) Valleau of Summit, N.J., complete the family.

James, a student at Geneseo State College, served two Vietnam tours of duty with the Navy.

Somehow, though, Mama Kay always manages to hurdle the obstacles, group spokesmen assured newcomers.

"Use any superlative," one suggested. "Kay will qualify."

Editor note: In 2008, Jim Clark donated the entire "Operation Morale" collection (bulk 1968-1970) organized by his mother to the Livingston County Historian's Office. The collection includes the organization's activity records plus thousands of documents including surveys, letters, and photographs from Vietnam soldiers (local vets and vets from almost every state in the U.S.) as well as nurses and nuns who received packages.

Remember our Men in Vietnam through **operation morale** LIVINGSTON COUNTY

Remember our Men in Vietnam through **operation morale** LIVINGSTON COUNTY

1 July

Dear "Mama" Kay Clark —
Your packages and mail are very much appreciated by all marines, particularly by those serving with field units.
Thank you, and keep them coming!

Malcolm H. Stewart
Lt, USMC

Dear Momma Kay,

First off, I would like to express my thanks to you and all of Operation Morale. I want to thank you for the packages which I have received since I've been here, and they and letters have really help my morale it's great to know people at home care and think of us while we are here and would take time to participate in operation morale. I'll be leaving Viet Nam about about the 20th of August and I hope all others that have to come here can also experience and know the joy of Operation Morale. I don't really know how to express my thanks, but to all back home, it's wonderful to know that your hearts are with us alot of fellows can get very lonely while over here, and I have been myself, but Operation Morale has really helped this year go by for me. Once again thank you Momma Kay and Operation Morale. You are wonderful people, and I'm proud to be part of the Livingston County people

Sincerely,
Sp/4 ___ J Pici

Operation Morale
LIVINGSTON COUNTY GROUP

QUESTIONNAIRE (It Helps Us)

PLEASE FILL IN THE FOLLOWING:
RANK, NAME & SERIAL NUMBER: _PFC. PETER WILLIAMS   US51778266_
ADDRESS AND ZIP CODE: ___577 ENGINEER BN (Const)___
___APO 9636 SF. Calif___
___Tay Hoa, Viet Nam___

BIRTHDAY: MONTH __12__ DAY __9__ YEAR __48__
WHEN ARE YOU RETURNING TO THE U.S.? MONTH __SEPT__ YEAR __'69__
MARRIED?: YES _____ NO __X__
IF YOU CARE TO, IT WOULD BE NICE TO HAVE YOUR HOME ADDRESS.
___26 ELM ST___
___GENESEO NEW YORK 14454___

PLEASE TELL US IN WHAT CONDITION THE BOX ARRIVED: GOOD __X__ FAIR _____ POOR _____
ARE THE ARTICLES USEFUL? YES __X__ NO _____ COMMENTS, QUESTIONS, REQUESTS (Don't Be Shy)
___ALL articles are very very full. Thank___
___you very much for the trouble you went through___
HAVE YOU EVER RECEIVED OPERATION MORALE - LETTERS? _NO_ BIRTHDAY GREETINGS? _NO_
HOLIDAY CARDS? _NO_ DO YOU WANT MAIL? _YES_ FROM WHOM? _18-20 yr old girls_
IF YOU ARE NOT REQUIRED TO KEEP A TIGHT SHIP, IT WOULD BE NICE TO KNOW WHERE YOU ARE
STATIONED IN VIETNAM. _I'm stationed in Tuy Hoa in Engineer Mech._
IF YOU ARE BEING RETURNED TO COMBAT AFTER HOSPITALIZATION, PLEASE LET US KNOW YOUR
NEW ADDRESS. NOTE OUR NAME & ADDRESS ON ENVELOPE.
IF YOU RECEIVED THIS BOX IN A HOSPITAL, AND YOU WILL BE RETURNED TO THE STATES, PLEASE
KEEP IN TOUCH. (TEAR OFF AND KEEP FOR REFERENCE.)   MRS. RELLY S. CLARK,
___G-___   Chairman Livingston County Chapter
                                                      152 CLINTON STREET
                                                      AVON, NEW YORK 14414
HURRY THIS ALONG, AND THANKS SO MUCH FOR YOUR TROUBLE.
ENVELOPE ENCLOSED.

Your Mamma Kay

Top: Soldiers in Vietnam unloading boxes from Livingston County Operation Morale. Letters on this page, photo, and logo all from the Operation Morale collection donated to the Livingston County Historian's Office.

Dear Mom and Dad
"You were probably beginning to think I was dead for not writing in such a long time." - Rick Bartholomew

Most soldiers said their letters home didn't reveal much about dangerous situations in Vietnam. Rick Bartholomew's letter is an exception.

[Handwritten letter, dated May 18, 68, beginning "Dear Mom + Dad,"]

Rick Bartholomew, who dropped out of Geneseo Central School at the age of 16 and enlisted in the Marines, is the author of two books. Both books are graphic, no-holds-barred accounts of his experiences both during and after the war.

Dig In (2002) is comprised of his letters home and *Vietnam Battlefield for the Soul* (2004) chronicles his 'war' with PTSD. Rick is currently working on another book. Right: Cover of *Dig In* by Rick Bartholomew.

LETTER TO EDITOR

*"Soon I can leave this nightmare and come back to the wonderful world
I live in and live like a normal person again..."*

Words of passion, frustration, and determination by Army Pfc. Ronald G. Evans

Jan. 24, 1968

Dear Sir:

I'm a soldier who is in VIETNAM. I would like to know if you would put an article in the Geneseo and Mt. Morris town paper, for me. I live in Geneseo on the Lima Road, or I did until I was married. I will pay any charge. So will you please send me the bill and I will send you the right amount. This is what I would like you to put in the paper. For Example, maybe you can word it a little bit different.

"Army Pfc. Ronald G. Evans spends honeymoon in Vietnam after being married Dec. 23 to Linda M. Gullo of Mt. Morris. His short leave made him return to Vietnam where he is stationed at Chu-Lai, to the "A" Btry., 3rd Bn., 18th Artilliary, 175 mm. self-propelled Howitzer cannon which is being hit by mortars just about ever night. We have one famous saying here. (In God we trust). There is temperature here of 100 or higher. I sure wish I was home shoveling snow. You people can't believe how it is over here until you really see it yourself. I plan on being home Jan. 20, 1969. You don't realize how you miss your wife, until you are gone for a year."

(continued above)

If you would put something like that in the paper I will sure appreciate it. Whatever it costs, send me the bill. And is it true that I can get the paper free, as long as I'm in Vietnam? If so, would you send me the paper, please. I would like to read how you reworded it. I always read your paper back home. It gets pretty lonely over here. Thank you very much for listening to this letter. What ever the cost is, I'll pay for it, just as soon as I get your reply. Again I thank you for your trouble.

Your fighting men
from Vietnam
Ronald G. Evans

(Ed. note: There's no charge. Sanders Publications have already put you on the list. Write us anytime and may God bless you all.)

_____

*Left and above: Avon Herald, 2/7/1968.
Right: Avon Herald, 3/20/1968
(both Sanders Publications)*

March 7, 1968

Dear Editor:

I am with "A" Battery, 3rd Battalion, 18th Artillery, known as the Ghost Battery, Chu-Lai,

Vietnam, which was on the 175 mm Howitzer self propelled section.

I have been transferred to the 8" Howitzer Self Propelled. The need for this 8" gun is tremendous at the DMZ line, where our section is heading for shortly.

The 8" gun is a lot of gun, but she does the job! and does it well. We fire H.L missions every night which averages 200 to 275 rounds per night. That sounds easy.

But try carrying a 215 lb. pro-joe (shell) from the pro-joe bomber, to the gun, 275 times a night. You soon get tired out! Sleep is something, we very seldom get, 2 hours of sleep a night, is what we call a good night's sleep.

Charlie has been hitting us with rockets and mortars. My best buddy was hit by flying pieces of metal by a rocket the night before last. It landed 4 foot from our bunker. Soon I can leave this nightmare and come back to the wonderful world I live in and live like a normal person again, which will be Jan. 25, 1969.

LETTER FROM VIETNAM

Caution non-Vietnam Veterans: Before reading this sarcastic, but honest and humorous letter; take a deep breath. By the end you will have a slightly better understanding of the life of a combat soldier re-adjusting to the 'world.'

"This is to inform you that a certain de-Americanized, demoralized, dehydrated, mud bound, water soaked, and slightly crazy individual…is ready once more to take his place as a human being."

The following was a letter sent to Robert Booth's parents, Mr. and Mrs. George Booth, before he was sent home from Viet Nam. It was composed by a couple sergeants in Robert's battalion.

This is to inform you that on the 22 day of April, 1967, a certain de-Americanized demoralized, dehydrated, mud bound, water soaked, and slightly crazy individual known as SP/4 Robert L. Booth is ready once more to take his place as a human begin with freedom and justice for all, engaged in life, liberty and the somewhat delayed pursuit of happiness, is leaving our little village known as Sewer City, securely nested among the jungles and rice paddies of Qu-nhon, which is located in the south central part of a semi-tropical country in the Far East, known as the Republic of Vietnam.

In making your joyous preparations to welcome him back into respectable society, you must make allowances for the crude environment in which he has suffered for the past twelve months. In a word, he may be somewhat Asiatic (Ha) suffering from stages of Viet-Congitis, or too much Ba Maui Ba Biere. Here is a few words of advice:

Get your women off the streets, hide the corn liquor, lock the cow in the barn, and put a lock on the refrigerator.

This man has survived the worst the Far East has to offer, -- mud, rain, heat, lonesomeness and monsoons, not to mention a liberal sprinkling of typhoons.

He is your son and is still yours. He may look a little strange and act somewhat the same, but this is to be expected after twelve tiresome months in water soaked, tea sipping, mud plastered Viet-

Continued next 2 pages.
Avon Herald, 9/13/1967.

Letter from Vietnam continued

"Any of the following sights should be avoided since they can produce shock: People dancing, television, and 'round-eyed' people...By no means ask or mention if it rains in Vietnam..."

nam.

Show no alarm if he prefers to pad around in throng-sandals, and a towel wrapped around him, slyly offers to sell cigaretts to the postman, and insists that everyone sit squat legged and eat their soup with chop-sticks and picks at his food suspiciously, as if you were trying to poison him. After this pay no attention when he stirs soy sauce in his potatoes, or mixes raw snails in his rice in hopes to make it taste better.

Don't be surprised if he answers all questions with "I hate this place" or "number one' or "sorry about that". Do not say anything to him if he stands around muttering Vietnamese phrases such as "Di di, Toi Met, Toi, SinLoi, or Hi Chi Biere". Do not argue with him when he asks for sulphur to put in his bath, or if he is continuously flushing the toilet. Just go along with him and he will get over it, eventually.

Be tolerant when he tries to buy everything at less than half the asking price, accuses the grocer of being a thief, and refuses to enter any establishment that doesn't have steel mesh over the doors and windows.

Any of the following sights should be avoided since they can produce an advance state of shock: People dancing, Television and "round-eyed" people. In a relatively short time his profanity will decrease enough to permit him to associate with mixed groups and soon he will be speaking English as well as he ever did. He may also complain of sleeping in a room and refuse to go to bed without a mosquito net.

For the first months (until he is housebroken) be especially watchful when he is in the company of women, particularly young and beautiful specimens. The few American girls he may have seen since arriving overseas are either thirteen years old or married to personnel who outrank him, therefore, his first reaction upon meeting an attractive "round eye" may be to stare. Wives and sweethearts are advised to take advantage of this momentary shock and move the young lady out of his reach.

Neglect to say anthing about powdered eggs, dehydrated potatoes, fried rice, fresh milk, ice cream and above all do not mention or even hint on the words "you want to change money or PhucEt (which means ambush).

By no means ask or mention does it rain in Vietnam, are

Letter from Vietnam continued

"Any souvenirs he may bring home (such as M-14's, Shotguns, Carbines, Pungi Stakes, Crossbows, or Saigon Barmaids) should be confiscated..."

the women good looking or did the mail always get there? for he may get very violent.

He is strictly forbidden to watch "Combat, F Troop, or 12 O'Clock High" on television for fear of causing him to go into a permanent state of shock. Any souveniers he may bring home (such as, M-14's, Shotguns, Carbines, Pungi Stakes, Crossbows, or Saigon BarMaids) should be confiscated for a period of not less than ninety days.

If he offers you 200 P's to go Chop Chop, humor him and go along but do not ask him such questions as "You buy me one drink?", "You want picture cards?", "You have American Cigarettes," "You go to PX buy me lipstick and hair spray?"

When he crosses the street, take care of him for he has become impartial, indifferent and completely oblivious to car horns, pedicycles, water Buffalo and horse drawn carts and above all never, no never let him get into a blue and white taxi cab.

Remember that beneath this rough and water soaked exterior there exists a heart, sweet and pure, though a little wet. Treasure this for it is the only thing of value he has left. Treat him with kindness, tolerance, and an occasional Fifth of Good Whiskey and you will be able to rehabilitize this hollow shell of the man you once knew.

If any problems arise that you can't handle please call the Vietnamese Police in Qui-nhon. It won't do any good but they like to use the telephone and it makes them feel good and important.

Send no more letters to A PO San Francisco 96316, because this sorry looking, good for nothing bloody eyed, mud soaked, damp drunkard is leaving the tropics in nine days.
  /S/Ho Chi Minh
  Viet Cong
  Commanding

Editor note: We don't know the whereabouts of Robert Booth but hope his parents took heed of this advice and that he adjusted well upon his return home!

RELAXATION AND RECREATION

Troops arriving for a USO show. Photo courtesy of Ron Hilfiker.

Jim DeCamp's narrative continues.

The military culture was a hard-drinking one. Pabst or Black Label was $2.40 a case at the post PX in Vietnam. My unit got a 'cold one' choppered into the field with our hot lunch. On most returns from the field we had a 'stand down' party with grilled steaks and pickup truck beds filled with ice and beer - to be used later in the night as the baptismal font for the Newbies - I chose the nearby drainage ditch for my immersion as it seemed less chilly.

Every unit on the vast bases had its own enlisted and officers' club with the obligatory Philippine band playing the Iron Butterfly hit, *"In A Gadda Da Vida"* and our anthem, The Animals' *"We Gotta Get Out of This Place."* Those literal 'floor shows' forever ruined a great song for me, Credence Clearwater Revival's *Suzie Q.*

I stumbled upon a show one night, paid my $5 at the hangar door, inside a circle of smoked-wreathed GIs, a little Asian girl bumped and grinded to this tune. Nearby a mattress for the horizontal part of her act, I guess, as I left before she got there (it can be a very long song in some versions). That scene seemed to encapsulate our whole impact on that country: we were corrupting its youth…and ourselves in the bargain.

Philippine bands playing American music.

Left: Courtesy Ron Hilfiker

Center: Courtesy of Roger Johnson.

Far left: Jim DeCamp on R&R in Hawaii with his wife.

Left center: Roger Johnson and platoon mate having fun.

Below: Ron Hilfiker at Eagle Beach Recreation.

WELCOME
EAGLE BEACH
101ST AIRBORNE DIVISION
(AIRMOBILE)
RECREATION CENTER

Being "Short"

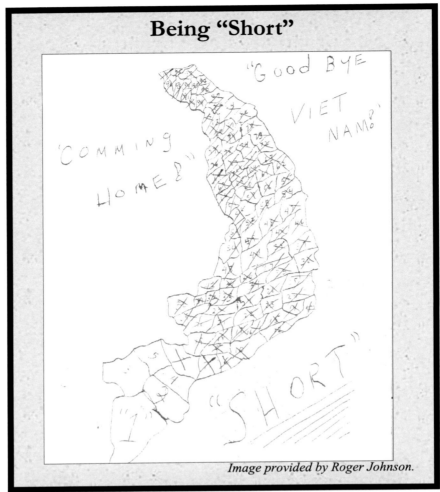

Image provided by Roger Johnson.

The last part of a tour was known as being "short." For some the countdown started upon arrival with a "short-timer's stick" notched once a day, but didn't begin in earnest until 100 days or less and didn't get dramatic until less than 10 days was achieved. You were a "single digit midget" with a descending number of days until DEROS (Date Estimated Rotation Over Seas) or a "wake up" or "bag drag."

Being "short" led to a whole litany of "I'm so short" lines. Many of the punch-lines were currency based: "I'm so short I have to stand on a nickel to piss on a dime" or, "I need a ladder to get on a dime" or, "I can sit on the edge of a dime and swing my legs." Other varieties were: "I have to look up to look down," "I trip over rugs," "I left yesterday," and "I can do chin-ups on curbstones." And my two favorites: "I'm so short I can't even have a long conversation," and "I'm so short I have to look up to a lieutenant." You get the picture.

Being "short" afforded some privileges. Combat grunts were often taken off line and brought to the rear. Not enough though, as it was estimated that over 1,400 died on their last day in-country. A short-timer with the 2/27th was placed in the middle of our column as we hiked through the boonies. He stepped on the booby trap that 10 guys in front of him had stepped over and was instantly killed.

Reactions to Politics & Protests

What was going on politically back home received surprisingly bland answers to our survey except for Jane Fonda, of course. Cliff VanDerveer said, "The lack of support hurt! What I read and heard about some things made me angry. 'Hanoi Jane' still makes me puke." John Carney was a little angrier: "Politics in the States was getting our men killed. If Jane Fonda was on fire, I would not piss on her to put her out." Terry Alger said, "Jane Fonda actively supported the

Anti-Vietnam war protesters demonstration in front of the White House. Jan.1968. Library of Congress Prints and Photographs Division Washington, D.C. http://hdl.loc.gov/loc.pnp/pp.print

enemy. In WWII her actions would have been considered treason." You would expect that the deluded *Barbarella* posing atop an NVA anti-aircraft gun would annoy all the vets but a surprising number were unaware of or untouched by politics.

Malcolm Stewart said, "We were too focused on our missions and survival to be concerned about politics at home." Kevin Bovill said, "I cannot remember how I felt about politics going on in the states." Jim Barber "didn't pay much attention to what was going on back home" and Ron Hilfiker didn't know much about politics at home either and blamed the lack of information on the overseas versions of *Time* and *Newsweek*. Bruce Booher was brief and to the point, "Politics - what the Hell are they doing and what the Hell am I doing here?"

However, the protesters at home troubled many. Though the "anti-warriors" and the soldiers both wanted an end to the war and a safe return, there was little common ground. Jim Creagan and I were college guys before we were soldiers and were more aware of politics back home and sympathetic to protesters. Jim Creagan said, "Some folks wanted to go home and 'beat up a Hippie,' I wanted to become one." Roger Least noticed that the anti-war protestors liked our fashion sense, "the anti-war groups were awful to us, but they liked wearing fatigues. Go figure!" Jerry Vickers said he paid little heed to the anti-war stuff. "To me, those people were useless draft dodgers looking for their 15 minutes of fame."

And Rod Bowles felt the lack of support even before he left the U.S.:

> "Before going [to Vietnam] I went to a formal Valentine's Dance at my wife's college in my dress blues only to leave quickly, unwanted and rejected. Both my wife and I felt unwelcome. I was still proud to serve my country."

Dennis Staley expressed annoyance with the process of ending the war:

> "I would get upset with the Paris Peace Talks because they could not see eye to eye; in the meantime our men were getting killed."

Terry Alger blamed media:

> "I was very angry with the politics in the U.S. The mass media outlets were doing their best to hurt the morale of the troops and convince the public not to support the American effort…I firmly believe that the actions of the newspapers and anti-war activists helped to strengthen the North Vietnamese to stay in the war."

Tony Gurak watched the same channels:

> "We could see from the TV news that the war was being taken over by the politicians."

Chuck Freese was also angered by the anti-war movement:

> "The protests at home made me mad. I feel they didn't have the whole story of what was happening. The communists really made life miserable for the peasants: stole their crops, stole the boys to fight, shot anyone who didn't help them. Many mass killings by the communists and no pictures about that. The media would not report it. I saw that first hand."

And Terry Johnston did not mince words in his distaste for the actions of the politicians and summed up the situation of the war that dragged on too long:

> "The politics were a farce and that was more hurtful than the war itself. The people running our country back then and now are 'idiots' and will always be in my mind. This war should have never happened and we should learn to stay in our own country & never mind everybody else's problems."

Lenny Peri playing the guitar in Vietnam. Courtesy of Lenny Peri.

> ## "Some folks wanted to go home and 'beat up a Hippie,' I wanted to become one." - Jim Creagan

Barber Conable Evaluates Opinions

Dear Friends:

WORD FROM HOME --One in my position never knows how seriously to take individual comments and opinions expressed on a returned questionnaire form, but when you multiply the opinion by ten thousand and find a pattern, a Representative is likely to be soberly respectful of the pattern. The questionnaires I sent to postal patrons in the 37th District started coming back on March 25th, and by the end of the first week more than 5,000 had been received. It will take several weeks to analyze them thoroughly, although the outlines of some of the patterns are already discernible.

To begin with, it is surprising to me how many people are willing to accept a federal tax increase if it is coupled with a spending cutback. Most people think the War on Poverty program is having little or moderate success. High priority for federal spending is given to law enforcement, to job training and to water pollution control. With respect to Viet Nam, a majority still seem to favor decisive military action to end the war, but an even larger number think Congress should have the chance to pass on overseas commitment of troops before the President acts in an undeclared

Barber B. Conable

war.

The most interesting reading early in the analysis of a general mailing questionnaire of this sort is the response to the question, "What do you consider the nation's number one need today?" Most people answer this very generally with phrases like: "End the War" or "integrity in government" or "Unity." There are always few answers like this: "Inteleck," "Birth control -- QUICK!!!," "A new congressman," but most answers reveal a widespread and deep-seated concern about the broad issues with which the country is wrestling. As usual, the processing of these questionnaires is shattering the routine of my office staff, but it is well worth any difficulty it causes in terms of the citizen advice and perspective which are such necessary ingredients of representative government.

Above: Soldiers catching up on news reports from Vietnam. Courtesy of Ron Hilfiker.
Left: Editorial from the Avon Herald, 4/10/1968. US Congressman Barber Conable (1922-2003) represented the Livingston County area from 1964-1984.

> ## "The protests at home made me mad. I feel they didn't have the whole story of what was happening." - Chuck Freese

College Group Plans War Protest Oct.15

By BOB BICKEL
Livingston County News Service

GENESEO — Strong support is expected on the Geneseo State College campus for the Oct. 15 "Vietnam Moratorium" being organized nationally by the dissenters to the U.S. policy on the Vietnam war.

The chief organizational force behind the local effort is a new group, "Veterans Against the Vietnam War (VAVN), formed about three weeks ago. It is directed by a board of 12 members, most of them veterans, and assisted by a volunteer corps of about 55 students.

Students John Bruno and Gerald McCarthy are the leaders of the group.

Its immediate goal is to have classes canceled and the college closed on Oct. 15.

Bruno said yesterday this aim is important to the group because it would add a measure of seriousnessness and purposefulness to the moratorium demonstration. "We'd like people to take some time to think about what we're doing over there," Bruno said.

The VAVN is moving toward the campus closing through three channels. It would prefer to have the closing ordered by the college ad-

ministration, and to this end is circulating a petition asking for the action. The goal is 2,000 signatures. About 1,500 have been obtained so far, Bruno said.

If the petitioning fails, the VAVN would like to see instructors dismiss their classes for the day. Verbal agreement to do so already has been obtained from the majority of the faculty, according to Bruno.

If this fails, VAVN will ask students to stay away from class.

The business men are being asked personally to close on Oct. 15, and letters are being

addressed to Geneseo Mayor Vincent Ryan and Robert Hart, chairman of the Livingston County Board of Supervisors, reading in part, "National Vietnam Moratorium is an effort to maximize public pressure to end the war by encouraging a broad cross-section of Americans to become involved against violence.

"We would like to make this a joint effort of the community and the students. This can be accomplished by closing your offices between 1 and 3 p.m. on Oct. 15."

Faculty, clergy, townspeople, and VAVN will be repre-

sented among the signers.

They have little expectation that the request will be granted.

As preparations for the moratorium, the VAVN has held a fund-raising dance at Letchworth Dining Hall, attended by more than 500, and for the past week has been showing a film and lecturing in three different residence halls each night.

The main pre-moratorium event will be a rally tomorrow at 7 p.m. in Wadsworth Auditorium. Several professors and veterans will speak on the economic, sociological, and moral implications of the war.

Rochester Democrat & Chronicle. 10/4/1969.

War Stories

Photo of "Lucifer" - A Company 155m artillery at LZ Sally. Courtesy of Ron Hilfiker.

"The US military tactical defeat of NVA and VC forces during Tet and the war was strategically 'irrelevant' to the war's outcome (USA Col. Summers and NVA Col. Tu, Hanoi, 1975), despite the professionalism and tremendous sacrifices of America's warfighters, who had paid too much for too little." - M. Stewart, GCS '61

❈❈❈❈❈❈❈❈❈❈❈❈❈❈❈❈❈❈❈

by
Bruce Booher, Jim DeCamp
Malcolm Stewart, Tony Gurak,
Jim Creagan,
C. Donald VanDerveer,
Ron Hilfiker, Chuck Freese,
& Roger Johnson

We asked the guys to share some experiences while in Vietnam and some wrote poignant short stories while others wrote lengthy memoirs. These are scattered throughout the book. Here are a few more passionate and insightful stories several of the vets submitted, often sharing painful details of events they have never shared with anyone before.

A Story of Death & Survival
by Bruce Booher

"During my time in 'Nam I saw a lot of killing, blown-up bodies. Comrades would turn to drugs (which you could get from the villagers or black market) to get through one more day there. I didn't choose drugs, just drinking and whores. I was a mine-sweeper. We cleared up to a bridge - while on the bridge, the ends blew up.

After the dust settled I found a comrade's hip; in the pocket was his wallet with his family's (wife and kids) picture. An 8 or 9-year-old child had the demolition controls that blew up the bridge. The guys behind us shot him. My first mission and I look over to the left and see someone got a bullet right between the eyes. *And you ask if I was scared.*

During our mine-swipe we loggered the tracks (so we couldn't get attacked). One track hit a mine next to me. I was sent to the hospital blind for 10 days then sent back to base camp and then back to the field.

Every day you just try to stay alive. You never think you're going to go home. My mother sent me a Christmas package which I got on New Year's Eve. It contained cookies, rotten pepperoni, and a bottle of Black Velvet. The next day we got run over by the Viet Cong. Whatever side was winning the ARVNS (South Vietnam soldiers who fought with us) would go on. You never knew who was who - we shot our barber in an ambush one night. You couldn't trust anyone.

Four or five of us made a pact we weren't going to kill ourselves. We were going to try to die of old age. Events in Vietnam made me hate the army and government even more. I am a survivor of prostate cancer; so I am on my way. God Bless America."

"Things I carried"

❋ ❋ ❋ ❋ ❋ ❋ ❋
T.P., razor,
tooth brush and paste,
pen, stationery, paperback book,
C-rats (fruit cocktail only),
rollup floor mat, olive drab miracle fabric blanket,
bug juice, quart size water bladder/pillow,
short handled shovel,
bandolier of 10-20 round clips with tracer bullets alternated,
fragmentation and smoke grenades,
1 claymore mine (front toward enemy), wire and clicker,
M-79 grenade launcher, M-16 rifle,
either the plate, tube or legs of the 81 mm mortar,
1 white phosphorous round, 1 High Explosive round,

and the neglect or derision of most of America.

- Jim DeCamp

Photo: Soldiers going out on a mission. Courtesy of Ron Hilfiker.

"Sweet little shit burner"

Photo: Woman who cleaned out the bathrooms at Jim's base was a Colonel for the Viet Cong. Courtesy J. DeCamp.

One of my favorite Vietnam privies was an elegant, elevated 4-holer maintained by the woman in this photograph. She may have been 40 but hard work and betel nut had wizened her up. I used to sell her my weekly-allotted carton of *Kools* at par value so she could make some money on the black market. Strangely enough, competing with *Park Lanes*, filtered marijuana cigarettes in cellophane packs, the mentholated smokes were very popular.

She would pull out the sawed-off 50-gallon drums filled with waste and set them on fire to dispose of it. A solution that seemed questionable even back then. One day a GI went to put the seat down on the empty outhouse and noticed a thin wire trailing off. Investigating, he found it wired to some pilfered claymore mines and the sweet little "shit burner" was revealed to be a Colonel in the local VC.

"Everybody wore black PJs"

This tale is clearly apocryphal as I didn't see it but I trust the guys I heard it from and it is consistent with the attitude I did observe. Now, that is inadmissible hearsay evidence, which is good, as it's surely a war crime.

We were surrounded by indigenous personnel who were indistinguishable. Everybody wore black PJs and the Viet Cong were everywhere. The Wolf Hounds of the 2/27th would take two trussed up suspects up in a helicopter, throw one out and have the other questioned by the attached ARVN officer.

- Jim DeCamp

Malcolm H. Stewart's Story

❀ ❀ ❀ ❀ ❀ ❀ ❀ ❀ ❀ ❀ ❀ ❀ ❀ ❀ ❀ ❀ ❀ ❀ ❀ ❀

I was wounded January 27, 1968 along Route 9, north of Camp Carroll, south of the DMZ, I Corps, in north-central South Vietnam while serving as an enlisted commissioned 2nd Lt. Platoon Commander of 65 battle-hardened Marines. Route 9 was the main supply road for 3rd Marine Division combat bases from Dong Ha in the East to Khe Sanh in the west, including isolated interior bases at Cam Lo, Camp Carroll (new 4th Marine Regiment Headquarters and a major artillery base), the Rockpile and Ca Lu.

In preparation for the 1968 TET Offensive, in late 1967 and early 1968, the North Vietnam Military Command began positioning forces, supporting artillery, rockets, recoilless rifles, rpgs, mortars, land mines, machine guns, and small arms, south of the DMZ. In late January, the NVA simultaneously attacked Marine bases east at the Cua Viet Port Facility (supply port) and west at Khe Sanh, subsequently at the center, and set up ambush sites along Route 9 to isolate Camp Carroll for an NVA attack by interdicting supply convoys traveling west to it and to the other interior bases.

On January 24th, there was an initial NVA ambush of an artillery supply convoy en route to Camp Carroll and subsequently against the reaction force deployed from Camp Carroll, which resulted in 52 Marine casualties. Three companies of the 3rd Battalion (including my platoon), 4th Marine Regiment, 3rd Marine Division were deployed by helicopter to the Route 9 ambush area and ordered to clear the ambush site, set up separate defensive perimeters on higher ground, and re-open Route 9 for supply convoys.

During the night of January 26th, a regimental size NVA force, fully uniformed and equipped, from the elite 320th NVA Division (veteran of the 1954 Dien Bien Phu campaign which ended the first Indo-China War) attacked the Marine company positioned on what became known as "Mike's Hill," and also moved back into the valley along Route 9, using tunnels, stream beds and gullies to re-occupy

2nd LIEUT. MALCOM STEWART son of Mr. and Mrs. George R. Stewart of 55 Center St., Geneseo, was wounded in action while leading his marine platoon in the DMZ zone, Vietnam. He telephoned his parents a week ago Sunday night from the Hospital in Cameron Bay. While the connection was not to good, his mother said he seemed to be in good spirits. Malcom said it was a clean wound, and he expected to be sent to Hawaii for a month and then he would probably return to active duty.

Livingston County Leader, 2/7/1968.

and establish additional well-camouflaged ambush sites against an anticipated reaction force for Mike's Hill, in foxholes in the dense vegetation, hedgerows and brush.

On the morning of January 27th, our company was ordered to attack the NVA forces along Route 9, eastward from our defensive position at the west end of the valley and link up with the two Marine companies located 1,000 meters to our east at Mike's Hill and the nearby NVA-destroyed bridge. Our eastward attack through the valley bisected by the road was across open ground interspersed with dense vegetation, hedgerows, brush, gullies, and dry stream beds, in a two platoon one-line formation perpendicular to the road, with my platoon attacking from the south side of the road, another platoon attacking from the north side of the road, the company command group in the center, on and near the road, and a reserve platoon in the rear. While the Battalion had ordered pre-attack artillery fire north of our attack direction to protect our left flank, no pre-attack artillery anti-personnel fire or air support east and ahead of our attack against the well dug-in and camouflaged NVA was provided.

Consequently, the NVA raked our company, especially the most visible Marines in the open areas, with recoilless rifles, a .50 caliber machine gun north of the road, light machine guns, mortar, and AK-47 fire as we began our attack, killing our Company Commander and stalling the attack. I was ordered by the Battalion Commander to assume company command and continue the attack.

When my Radio Operator and/or I saw NVA firing from a hedgerow foxhole adjacent and perpendicular to the road on its south side ahead of us, with covering fire, I ran southeast to the hedgerow, cut north, ran parallel along the hedgerow, and dropped a grenade into the foxhole. As we again attempted to advance eastward, I was immediately shot in the upper right thigh and disabled by an NVA AK-47 round fired from an NVA position north of the road. I reported my injury and condition to the Battalion Commander who then committed our company reserve platoon to reinforce our already engaged platoons.

Subsequently supported by Huey gunships and a platoon deployed from the company at the bridge near Mike's Hill, the NVA forces were overrun and dispersed in the early afternoon. Artillery fire and B-52 bombers were directed against suspected NVA retreat and reinforcement avenues along and north of the Cam Lo River. On January 29th, engineers constructed a by-pass bridge near Mike's Hill and Route 9 was re-opened for supply convoys. The anticipated NVA attack against Camp Carroll had been pre-empted.

Our 83 Battalion casualties (21 KIA and 62 WIA) were evacuated by helicopter from the battle scene as soon as the area was secured. NVA losses (including 40 KIA by my platoon) were estimated at Battalion size. Our Platoon Sergeant, Robert Espinola, and a Platoon Squad Leader, John Blair, were awarded Silver Stars for their combat leadership and aggressive action.

After surgeries in Vietnam and Hawaii, I returned to Vietnam March 27, 1968 and served as an Air Operations Officer coordinating helicopter missions for the 3rd Marine Division forces by Army and Marine helicopter units until Dec. 12, 1968,

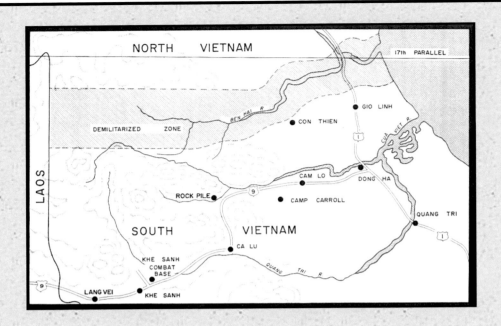

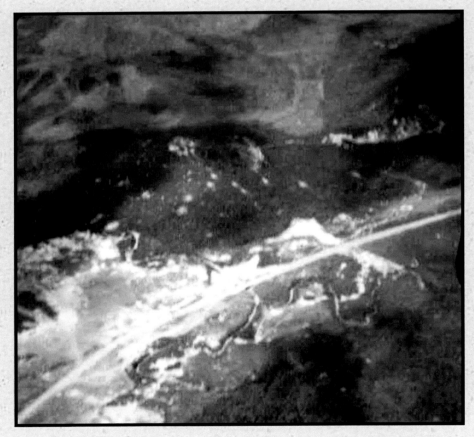

Top: Map showing DMZ, Vietnam. Map in public domain. No known restrictions. (PD-USGOV; PD-USGOV-MILITARY-MARINES.) Lower: Aerial view provided by Malcolm H. Stewart. Shown in picture is Hwy 9 which runs from Dong Ha to the east, to Khe Shan Village in the west. http://thundering-third.org/4members/RGHarriman/RGHarriman.html.

when my tour ,which began December 5, 1967, ended.

A personal comment: The Tet Offensive (January – February 1968) at the beginning of what has been called "The Defining Year – 1968," while a military disaster for North Vietnam, became an irreversible media, political and diplomatic victory for it was a result of the "Cronkite Effect," the increasing anti-war agitation, and the inability of the overly confident Johnson Administration ("...light at the end of the tunnel.." statements in late 1967) and the strategically ill-prepared Westmoreland Command to reverse the consequences of their failed political and military planning and leadership. The rapidly eroding and already weak US public trust and support for the protracted war of attrition resulted in the eventual withdrawal of US forces, defunding of South Vietnamese support by Congress in 1973, and the successful NVA invasion of South Vietnam in April 1975.

The US military defeat of the NVA and Viet Cong forces during Tet and during the war, had been "irrelevant" in the blunt one-word response by NVA Col. Tu to US Army Col. Harry Summers in 1975; despite the professionalism and tremendous sacrifices of America's warfighters who had paid too much for too little.

Above: India Company platoon leaders, 3rd Battalion, 4th Marines, 3rd Marine Division, taken in December 1967 south of the DMZ. Left to right: Spaulding White, Malcolm Stewart, and another unidentified 2nd lieutenant. Courtesy of Spaulding White.

Tony Gurak's Story

❋❋❋❋❋❋❋❋❋❋❋❋

B-52s Over Vietnam

Airman Anthony C. Gurak, son of Mrs. Gladys M. Gurak, who resides on Booher Hill Road, Geneseo, has been selected for technical training at Chanute AFB, Ill., as a U.S. Air Force aircraft maintenance specialist.

The airman recently completed basic military training at Lackland AFB, Tex. His new school is part of the Air Training Command which conducts hundreds of specialized courses to provide technically-trained personnel for the nation's aerospace force.

Airman Gurak is a 1965 graduate of Geneseo Central High School.

Livingston Republican, 11/11/1965.

The B-52 was created during the Cold War as a long range nuclear weapons delivery aircraft. If the Soviets had actually initiated a nuclear war by launching a missile at the U.S., within minutes the U.S. would have launched countless missiles and hundreds of B-52s (there were a total of 744 built) towards the U.S.S.R. It would have been enough to assure mutual destruction. Neither side would have won. However, both sides stayed in constant readiness. We were in a stalemate situation for decades until the fall of communism in Russia. That readiness was the mission of the Strategic Air Command (SAC). My job as a ground crew member and later as crew chief was to keep our aircraft operationally ready.

The flight crews constantly flew training missions to hone their skills for the ultimate mission that we all hoped would never happen. Every training mission included a simulated bomb run that was scored electronically. Every crew member's duty performance on each mission was scored and the entire crew was rated.

Above: B-52D Stratofortress dropping 500-lb bombs. (Historical U.S. Air Force photo in public domain.) http://en.wikipedia.org/wiki/Boeing_B-52_Stratofortress#mediaviewer/File:B-52D_dropping_bombs.jpg

The maintenance crew's performance was also constantly under the microscope as well. All launching and recovery of aircraft was observed. All refueling, towing, inspections, repairs, management of specialist maintenance, and turn around time was evaluated. Rightly so, as lives were at stake.

My base, Clinton–Sherman AFB, Oklahoma, like every SAC and TAC (fighter aircraft) base had several aircraft on alert, nuclear loaded, fueled, and ready to launch on a moment's notice. These aircraft would have been the first to respond to an attack. The rest of the aircraft would have been quickly uploaded with weapons (bombs) and launched. The alert pad was separate from all other aircraft on the flight line. It had its own living quarters and chow hall for flight and ground crews. This was the only time officers and enlisted men were allowed, by military regulations, to mingle. We lived, ate, and watched TV and movies together. Needless to say, we became quite familiar with each other, at least on the pad. When you know the men who will be flying your aircraft, you feel an extra responsibility for their safety.

When your assigned aircraft was on alert you would spend a week on the pad, a week off, and back on the pad again until your aircraft was replaced by another. Every month there were seven practice alerts. The klaxon, an electronic alarm, could sound at any time, day or night. The klaxon had such a distinctive sound that once heard, you could never forget it. When the klaxon, also referred to as the horn, sounded, all hell would break loose. Everyone scrambled for the trucks and aircraft. When the flight crews boarded the aircraft they would crank engines and wait for further orders. Five times a month that was all that happened. However, twice a month all aircraft taxied out to the runway and waited. Eventually, they would taxi down the runway for the turn around to the pad.

You never knew if it was just a drill or if it was for real, but was always treated as if it were for real. It would make you real jumpy after a while. To this day, a loud telephone ring will make me jump. The sound isn't even close, but it doesn't matter. At least I don't try to take off running somewhere, anywhere, like I used to. I'm getting better.

The long hours on the flight line working on the aircraft in brutally cold or incredibly hot weather, the readiness inspections, all the time spent on alert, were all pretty serious business.

Tony Gurak (far left) and fellow crew chiefs receiving Golden Bomber Crew Award, 1968. Courtesy of Tony Gurak.

That was how we were called upon to serve our country. That was how I thought I would spend my enlistment in the Air Force. Then along came Vietnam, and everything changed. The B-52s with their long range and tremendous bomb load capability became the war bird of choice for Vietnam. In the early days of the war, aircraft and crews were randomly selected from different bases to go TDY (temporary duty) to Guam. Almost every model of 52 was used. Since the 52s were not designed to carry conventional iron bombs, their bomb bays had to be modified to carry them, then converted back to carry nuclear weapons when they rotated back from TDY. This was a time-consuming process.

In 1965 Operation Arc-Light was initiated. Arc-Light was the intense, heavy bombing of targets in South Vietnam by B-52s. The Air Force wisely chose the "D" model bomber to carry out these missions. The "D" model was the most numerous of the 52s with 170 built. Their bomb bays were modified only once, external bomb racks were installed under the wings, and were given the familiar black and camo paint scheme. Most "D" models spent the rest of their service life in Vietnam service.

After Arc-Light began, bases in Okinawa and Thailand were added to Guam to increase the number of bombers and bomb runs. Many more flight and ground crews were needed to carry out the increased missions. The Air Force began sending entire bomb wings for six month TDYs. Every SAC base eventually took a turn. In late March, 1968 my base joined the rotation. We began to un-cock our alert aircraft (down load weapons). We started to receive black "D" models, and to send our "E" models to other bases. We never saw them again. We received orders for Okinawa, and by early April we were ready to deploy.

On Easter Sunday 1968, I boarded one of our KC 135 tankers and departed for Okinawa. We flew non-stop to Hickam AFB, Hawaii. We were allowed to go into the terminal to stretch our legs while our tanker was being refueled. It was dark out, so we couldn't see anything of Hawaii. I wandered over to a window and was able to see one lone palm tree. First trip to Hawaii and all I saw was one palm tree.

View out the window over the Pacific on Tony's flight from Okinawa en route to Vietnam. 1968. Courtesy of Tony Gurak.

Until now all we had done was to prepare for a war we hoped would never happen. Now we were going to join a very real war.

A U.S. Air Force Boeing B-52F-65-BW *Stratofortress* (s/n 57-0139) at Andersen Air Force Base, Guam, during the Vietnam War. http://www.nationalmuseum.af.mil/shared/media/photodb/photos/061128-F-1234S-006.jpg (Photo in public domain.)

In October, 1966, I was on alert when I called home and my mother told me that my good friend and classmate, Butch Rosebrugh, had been killed in Vietnam. I'll never forget that terrible, numbing feeling that came over me. I did not want it to be true. 19-year-olds just aren't supposed to die. We had just graduated from high school a little over a year before. Butch and I did a little partying before he left for Marine boot camp. I'll always remember the good times we had. Butch was very proud to be joining the Marines.

In January, 1968, I received the news that another friend and classmate, Bobby Henderson, had also been killed in Vietnam. Butch and Bobby were best friends and neighbors. Bobby had convinced Butch to join the Marines. I'll always feel their loss. We'll never know what their lives could have been. I wanted revenge for my friends, but I was stuck in Oklahoma and couldn't do anything about it. Finally, I was in Okinawa and could do something about it. I made them a promise that I would do whatever it took to make sure my plane made every mission. I wanted to make sure that all those bombs did something good. When we arrived in Okinawa there was no period of adjustment, we hit the deck running. As soon as we reported to the flight line we replaced a ground crew member who was rotating back to his base. Until all of our own guys arrived we had mixed crews. Every organization does things a little bit differently. Sometimes it was difficult doing things someone else's way, but we got by. When everyone finally arrived and we took over flight line operations things smoothed out, and we fell into our routines.

I had already been on flying status for over a year and flew regularly before arriving in Okinawa. It wasn't very long before I was able to fly my first bombing mission. I'll never forget my first sight of Vietnam. We entered from the south, over the Mekong Delta, and headed north towards our target. All I could see was brown, muddy water and thick green jungle. It looked so forbidding and hostile all I could think was that no American should ever die in a crap hole like that. I renewed my promise to do everything I could to get my plane in the air for every mission, for revenge and to help keep any other Americans from dying there. I know it sounds hokey and melodramatic, but that's the way I felt, then and now. I wish I could have done more. We all wanted to do more.

The role we played in the war was very different from that of the Marines and Army fighting on the ground. We were based far away from Vietnam, away from danger. We went back to a clean bed, in a safe barracks every night. We had good, hot food to eat. We could go to town for entertainment. The soldiers and marines did not have those luxuries. We weren't being shot at, or ambushed, did not face booby traps, jungle rot, or any of the other horrors of war that they faced every day.

Our planes were only occasionally targeted by artillery or light rockets. My plane was targeted twice, but I felt that we were safe. We were aware of the effect the 52s had on the V.C. and N.V.A., they were very afraid of them. We knew how important our missions were to the guys on the ground. We felt a great responsibility to them. We worked long, hard hours to get our planes in the air. That's what we could do to help them. By the end of May or early June our squadron brass decided that we needed more maintenance crews to handle the increased work load. Existing crews were thinned out to create new crews under the direction of new crew chiefs.

I was one of those chosen to become a crew chief. I quickly became responsible for a multi-million dollar aircraft, the lives of a six-man flight crew, the performance and safety of a six-man ground crew, and the mountain of paper work that the 8th Air Force so dearly loved. Shortly after, I became authorized to sign off red X symbols in the aircraft forms.

The aircraft forms were a permanent record of everything about that aircraft and stayed with the plane. A red X in the maintenance section of the forms was the second most critical symbol, signifying the readiness of that aircraft. An open red X usually meant that the aircraft did not fly. My initials and signature meant that I guaranteed that the maintenance had been done properly, the problem was eliminated, and the aircraft was operationally ready to fly. The consequences for signing off on something not done correctly would have been life changing for sure.

Previously, only those with a lot more stripes than I had been on red X orders. I was a twenty-year-old E-4. Three years out of high school.

Every day we would check the flight schedule posted in our barracks. If the tail number of your aircraft was listed, it was to fly a mission that day. We flew two eight-hour missions of six aircraft each day. Six planes may not sound like a lot until you consider that each plane carried 74 bombs. That's 444 bombs, twice a day, just from Okinawa. Guam flew two twelve-hour missions each day, and U-Tapao, Thailand flew several four-hour missions also. The bombers flew in two groups of three, in an arrowhead pattern. They could concentrate on one target or spread out to carpet bomb a large area. If you were an enemy soldier on the ground and suddenly your whole world began to explode, what direction could you run? You couldn't! Captured North Vietnamese soldiers confessed that they were absolutely terrified of the 52s.

Many years later, in Operation Desert Storm, just the distant sound of B-52 strikes caused entire units of Iraqi combatants to surrender. Just the mere picture of B-52s dropped from Psy Ops aircraft (bullshit bombers) also caused combatants to surrender in droves. Such was the world-wide recognition and reputation of the 52s earned in Vietnam. I am very proud of that!

Our days fell into a routine. Either I or my assistant crew chief, Sandman, would arrive four hours before launch time to begin the pre-flight inspection of our plane. Sandman wasn't his real name, but his first name was so bad that Sandman was much better. He was a very innocent, shy, naïve kid from Kansas. We all know about Kansas. We kind of made it our mission to "alter" his innocence before we left Okinawa. We succeeded. Kansas would never be the same for him.

When the flight crew arrived, I would go over the forms, and accompany the pilot on his walk-around inspection of the plane. After all the crew completed their pre-flight check lists, we would wait for engine start time. That's when things became exciting. Engine start and aircraft launch was my favorite part of the day. After the engines were started, and all systems were on line, the aircraft taxied out in the order of their take off. We would drive the truck to a spot with a clear view of the runway, close enough to the planes to be able to assist the flight crew if there was a problem, and wait for takeoff. I will never forget the sight and sound of those big guys roaring down the runway and lifting off! To me that was the most satisfying part of my job. I knew that we had done our jobs right, and that those planes were on their way to do something very important.

Several hours later we would return to the flight line to begin preparations to recover our aircraft. After the planes were parked in their spots, refueled, water injection tanks filled, engine and hydraulic systems serviced, a basic post-flight inspection was conducted. The entire aircraft was inspected for damage, or basically anything that required repair. Everything had to be repaired and signed off before the aircraft was buttoned up for the day. If repairs took all day or night, so be it. I would stay with it until everything was completed.

I've really simplified what we did. There was a lot more to the job than I've described. The last thing I want to do is bore readers to death with too many details. It just took a lot of work by a dedicated, unselfish crew to keep the planes flying. Sometimes when the planes came back we would have some surprises waiting for us: "hangers" (bombs that did not release properly and hung up in the racks). Sometimes we knew that they were there, sometimes we didn't. If the bomb bay doors had not been opened by the flight crew we could open them manually. There was a cable in the rear landing gear well that required a sharp downward pull to release the door locks. That's where the surprise would come in. The bomb loading crews assured me that the hangers were safe. The bomb had to fall a certain distance before it could detonate. Sure thing. I noticed that those guys were never around when I popped open the doors.

We were in Okinawa for the typhoon season. Hurricanes are called typhoons in the Western Pacific. Why, I don't know. Whenever a typhoon was due to hit Okinawa, we would fly our planes out. I would have to load up all my gear, tools, and all the equipment I would need to be self-sufficient wherever we were sent. We would always fly a bombing mission first then proceed to our temporary base. I went to Guam once and Thailand twice. I always flew at least once a month, but always welcomed the chance to fly on more missions, and to see new places. It's always interesting to see how other people live. It sure makes you appreciate what we have here at home a lot more.

Top: Image of Strategic Air Command shield. Right: Cover of Clinton-Sherman Air Force Base directory and guide.
http://www.strategic-air-command.com/bases/Clinton-Sherman_AFB.htm (Public domain images, no known restrictions.)

By mid-September our six-month TDY was winding down. Our replacements from Fairchild AFB, Washington, started to arrive, and we flew our last missions. I received my orders to return to Clinton-Sherman. Again, I loaded all my stuff on one of our tankers (I had a lot more stuff to bring back than I came with) and flew out for the states. Same as the flight over, we stopped in Hawaii to refuel. Of course it was dark this time when we arrived as well. I wandered over to the same window and looked out at the same lone palm tree. Two trips to Hawaii, one palm tree. Ah, what memories!

After we all got back to Clinton-Sherman we returned to business as usual. We received our "new" bombers, 1954 "C" models. They smelled real bad inside. Shortly after, while my plane was on alert, we were hit with an O.R.I. (organizational readiness inspection). All the bombs were downloaded from the alert aircraft, but the planes remained on the pad, waiting for the horn to sound. When the horn sounded, the crews scrambled, fired up the engines, and took off for a twelve-hour mission. Everything was as if we were at war. They all navigated to a certain destination and made a simulated bomb run, received their scores, and continued on their mission. When the planes returned, our part of the test began. Everything we did to ready our planes to return to the pad was graded.

My plane came back really broke (lots of write ups in the forms). I worked 48 hours straight to get it ready to go back to the pad upload weapons, and be re-cocked. My plane was one of the first to return to the pad. No sleep yet, we had to help park the rest of the planes as they returned to the pad. When every one of the original aircraft returned to the pad, the exercise ended. We all, flight and ground crews, passed with flying colors. The 2nd Air Force conducted the inspection. They awarded the first four flight crews and crew chiefs back on the pad, the Golden Bomber Crew Award. This was the first time that crew chiefs ever received that award. I was truly honored. It was not just a feel-good thing, it really did carry some weight. All four of us were promoted the next cycle.

I am truly grateful for all the opportunities that opened to me. I flew combat missions in the biggest, most unique aircraft the Air Force had at the time, a plane that was entrusted to my care. I routinely ran jet engines, what a feeling controlling so much power! I flew over both oceans. I visited places I never would have seen otherwise. Where else could an incredibly shy and unsure of himself kid from a small town do so much in such a short time? I once read somewhere that often young men in war did the most important things of their lives by the time they were 21. How true, how very true.

The question remains, did we really make any difference? I like to think that what we did saved American lives. I know that we tried. In the end South Vietnam fell to the communist forces. Butch, Bobby and over 58,000 young Americans are lost forever. Their lives taken way too soon. Did I get my revenge? I don't know. How much is enough? I will always feel the terrible loss of my friends. I still shed a tear when I visit Butch's grave. I hope I always do. I never want to be so hardened by life that seeing Butch's grave doesn't affect me.

Why did we get involved in Vietnam? We got involved because several well meaning presidents did not learn from history. They learned nothing from the Chinese, Japanese, and the French. They all left Vietnam, defeated. The French warned us not to get involved there. No one listened. Eventually, we just left Vietnam after a ten-year war. Did we as a nation learn anything from Vietnam? Not a damn thing! Do recent events look familiar? It should be an iron-clad law that every president, and all those in the highest positions of power in this country, be required to learn the history and culture of any hostile country we could become involved with. Really learn it before being allowed to send young men and women into harm's way. For sure, there are times when military action is required for the security of our country. However, all the best, not the most convenient, intelligence must be available before the decision is made to commit troops. They deserve that. Their lives depend on it.

Tony (back row 1st on left) and fellow airmen of the 47th Tech. School, at Chanute AFB, Illinois. Jan. 1966. Courtesy of Tony Gurak.

Jim Creagan's War Stories

My hope would be that the accounts of events that I have written for this book do not make the reader feel as though I am bragging. These events actually did occur. I did not cause them, but only took part in and wish to share them. Boasting is for those who are unsure.

Let none worry nor grow skeptical if society should either care, condone, abhor or just ignore their accomplishments. A smooth road to humility is to be humbly proud of one's own actions and decisions and hope that society may only, at some point, understand.

Right: Jim with a smoke and ready to fly. Courtesy Jim Creagan.

It's Not Always the Enemy: Watch Out!

Early in the year 1967 the 336th AHC at Soc Trang South Vietnam initiated the "Firefly" mission in the "Delta". This was a new concept of interdiction and disruption to the Viet Cong. I was assigned to the 336th upon graduation from flight school (Warrant Officer Candidate School) 11/31/1966 and a month later I was a FNG in the 336th at Soc Trang. In a few weeks I was selected to be a member of the Firefly operation. This operation was done entirely at night using three Huey helicopters - one "slick" UH-1D unarmed, except for door gunner and crew chief equipped with .30 cal. machine guns, and two Huey UH-1B gunships. The object of the mission was to locate and/or intercept Viet Cong movement along the myriad canal and river systems of the Delta area, approximately one quarter of South Vietnam.

Company patch. Courtesy of Jim Creagan.

The equipment was simple. The slick would carry a lighting device composed of seven large spotlights that could be hung outside the aircraft while the pilot would try to keep it focused on waterways below, looking for enemy movement. This was done at an altitude of three to five hundred feet above the ground, the "deadly zone" for helicopters that might be receiving enemy fire. The gunships would follow at a little lower altitude with their exterior lights out, waiting for targets of opportunity exposed by the light or to attack when the lightship, the easiest target in Southeast Asia, was fired upon.

Because I was so new to the unit I was always the first pilot (FP) and flew Firefly with a few different Aircraft Commanders (ACs). In civilian terms, Aircraft Commander means pilot and First Pilot means co-pilot. Get it? Some of the ACs let me fly the aircraft which was a little brutal at first because you had to keep your head turned out the side window and looking down to keep the light fixed upon the meanderings of the rivers. Apparently I was good at this as it became the rule rather than exception that I would pilot the lightship while the AC would watch for enemy movement or ground fire and stay in radio contact with the gunships. Canals were a snap - they were straight.

One particular AC, one that I had flown Firefly with often was a real, for lack of a more appropriate term, ASSHOLE. He, in his own mind, was some kind of rotary wing phenom. Bullshit!! After a few missions with him I learned some basic means of survival. One particular night he wanted to be on the controls and run the light and I was pretty sure he didn't have the gift. It wasn't long before I knew he was fucked up, not on drugs or booze, but with spatial disorientation, or as most folks know it, vertigo. I asked him to let me take the controls; he refused. I asked again, louder, as we were on a collision course with Earth and still got no response. There was something I remembered from flight school about this kind of situation and the most expedient method of resolve. I reached for the billy club (normally carried for this express purpose) between the cockpit seats, and I whacked that SOB hard, once on the back of his helmet and again across his forehead. He let go and I pulled the aircraft up from about 50 feet above the ground while the crew chief and gunner, after turning off the light, cheered. The gunship escort couldn't figure out what we were doing and thought we had been shot down so they started shooting at everything and anything until they saw us pull up again. I explained on the radio what had happened and we called it a night.

Whenever I hadn't been assigned to a daylight mission, I knew Operations would be coming to find me in the afternoon with orders for Firefly. It was simple. I would go to the Officers' Club about 2:00 PM and order a drink, maybe a rum & coke, maybe a gin & tonic, whatever, and I would ask the sexy little Vietnamese bartender to put at least four more drinks in front of me. When the operations guy (our Radar O'Reilly) would toddle in to inform me I had Firefly duty that night, I would ask who would be the AC and if he said "WO Asshole" I would consume all the drinks in front of me in under thirty seconds and apologize for being too intoxicated to fly. He understood.

You realize, in combat, that the enemy is trying to kill you and you adjust. You may not realize there are so many other ways to get dead. The pilot I described earlier went on to cause the deaths of five helicopter crewmen in an extremely stupid effort to show off how close he could fly in formation. His chopper's rotor blades overlapped another ship's blades - then they came in contact - "WO Asshole" and his aircraft and crew somehow managed to land but in such disarray that one crewman jumped out in fear and was decapitated by damaged and wildly turning rotor blades. The four crew members of the other helicopter in this mid-air crash were all killed. The AC of the ship that crashed was a living legend in the 336th with less than one month left on his tour. I was fortunate to have only one bad and less deadly experience with the guilty pilot's ego. WO Asshole was immediately transferred to another unit before a "lynch mob" formed and I'm glad I can't remember his name today.

Aerial combat is just the same as ground combat when what matters most is reliance from and of your peers. Human egos have no place there. Fighting units have to work as one. There is a huge difference between bravery and bravado and we hadn't even come up with the phrase "I got your back" yet.

❀ ❀ ❀ ❀ ❀ ❀ ❀ ❀ ❀ ❀ ❀ ❀ ❀ ❀ ❀ ❀ ❀ ❀

A Belated Valentine

WO Jack Grimmer was my Aircraft Commander and I was the First Pilot of an Army UH-1D Huey Slick (unarmed) helicopter. We were flying in a standard V formation of seven or maybe nine Hueys loaded with ARVN Vietnam infantrymen to be dropped at a Landing Zone somewhere northwest of our home base of Soc Trang, RVN. Jack was giving me all sorts of information, as to what may or may not happen, since this was my first Combat Assault mission.

I had been in the Republic of Vietnam about one month, flying resupply and a variety of other non-combat missions and was still considered a FNG. No indication had been sent via radio as to the temper of the LZ - hot or cold. That is, whether to expect a hostile reception or not. It appeared, like much of the Delta, as flat rice paddies in every direction with a variety of canals and small natural waterways and small tropical forests.

I remember our gunship escorts (UH-1Bs) flying a close perimeter defense for us just prior to touchdown. They were called the T-Birds and our call sign was Warrior. Just before touching down to off-load the troops we carried, there was radio chatter from the T-Birds about hostile fire and it was heavy, coming from a deep tree line to our front, probably forty to fifty meters away. We were to the right and slightly behind the lead aircraft piloted by Capt. R.C. Stewart (AC) and a Major (FP) who I'll refer to as John Doe. Our crew in back, both crew chief and door gunner, were busy trying to evict some of the infantrymen who had not voluntarily left the aircraft and attempt to use door-mounted machine guns to return enemy fire, which, by now, had become intense. The radios went wild with excited messages

Above: Image of a Huey. Courtesy of Ron Hilfiker.

from slick and gunship pilots reporting fire and injuries to crew members and aircraft.

My eyes were fixed on the lead ship to our front which started to turn right on takeoff. I saw a large splatter of blood hit the inside of the left front windshield and as the ship settled roughly to the ground and rolled onto its right side. Capt. Stewart had been shot and killed instantly. As we attempted to take off, our Huey lost power. We hit the ground but remained upright. Now the concern was to get out and stay low since there was no immediate cover available, other than two Huey fuselages and a small rice paddy dike nearby between us and the enemy fire.

I was trying desperately to grab the M-14 rifle hanging from the back of my pilot's seat when the crew chief, now prone on the ground outside the aircraft, yelled that he had wired it on to keep it secure during flight. Probably thinking it would never need to be used, he had done an excellent job. At least I had an armored seat to hide behind while I got the rifle free, all the time listening to bullets crash through the cockpit and cargo areas. I was the last to leave our downed chopper and low-crawled to the dike line to find our crew intact along with the three remaining members, one severely injured, of Capt. Stewart's ship and several ARVN soldiers.

The ARVNs were in complete disarray - some attempting to return fire from the dike line, most trying to retreat via a shallow ditch to my right, and some lying dead or wounded in the field where they had been hit. Those retreating were at least kind enough to leave behind their grenade harnesses and even some of their weapons and ammo. I'm still not sure whether these acts of generosity were to help us or just to lighten their load in flight from the scene. At least they had provided us with weaponry as we had damn little. We used it to keep up fire while Grimmer crawled back to the crashed Huey to get a First Aid kit for the wounded crewman. He needed bandages and morphine, both contained in the kit.

What we really needed was a radio. I'm not sure how, but Grimmer managed to find one, probably on a ARVN corpse. We were probably 25-30 yards from the enemy. Close enough for a NFL pro to kick an easy field goal. You couldn't stand up or even get into a kneeling position to do anything so we did our best to keep firing over the dike. I rolled onto my back and began to toss grenades the best I could from this position. I think I had the distance right, but where they landed is still a mystery. Our support from the Huey gunships was down to almost nothing due to mechanical problems from the hits they were taking, wounded pilots and crewmen, as well as fuel and ammunition shortages. Grimmer had made great progress on the radio and was able to make contact with an Air Force Forward Air Controller (FAC). We were desperate for air support and now only numbered seven (one wounded) soldiers. Major John Doe was useless, lying on his back or side, blubbering about certain death while even the wounded crewman did what he could to help. So let's say there were six of us and a handful of ARVNs.

You could see, in the tree line, muzzle flashes and wisps of smoke and these were our only targets of opportunity. While firing at these "targets" I felt a burning sensation on my right arm. Looking to see what it was, I realized it was a white kind of powdery substance and knew it was insulation from my flight helmet, which I was still wearing. Feeling the side of the helmet with my hand confirmed this. Thinking I would be safer with a steel helmet, I thought I might borrow one from the dead ARVN guy next to me. That was a bad idea because as I removed it from him I fround he had unfortunately left most of his brain in it. It wasn't until several hours later when I finally took off my helmet that I saw where the bullet had actually entered at the forehead, passed between the helmet interior padding and exited over the ear, leaving a heart shaped hole in the fore brow of the helmet. It was February 15th 1967 - perhaps a belated Valentine's gift.

While five of us did what we could to keep up a scant amount of return fire, Grimmer was organizing air support. We searched bodies for smoke grenades to mark our location as well as for more weapons and ammunition. Our original personal weapons had long since run out of ammunition, and it was far too dangerous to return to the two downed ships to get more. I don't know how long it took, it seemed like forever, but at last, support came from the sky. I have no idea why, during the absence of air support the VC never rushed our position. They could have in a few moments killed or captured us all. I guess you could say we were outnumbered a little bit. After all, the body count the following day revealed 331 enemy dead. One of the largest single day tallies of the war to that point and a front page headline in the *Stars and Stripes* newspaper. We had come face to face with a large unit of the U Minh Battalion, a well-known VC fighting unit in the Delta and one I would meet too many more times. Perhaps they were just as scared as anybody might be in a close ground engagement or maybe it was the harsh defensive fire we were issuing. Yeah, I can't buy that myself either. Whatever the reason, I was then and still am today, thankful for their decision.

First on the spot to help us from the sky was the RVN Air Force, flying prop-driven, WWII-surplus, small dive-bombers. A1-Es, Grimmer told me. They were dropping high-explosive-type bombs right on target and we all had bumps, bruises and mud stains from the raining debris. Major J. Doe was still blubbering. Soon the USAF was with us delivering a combination of ordinances I had never seen nor knew of. If one has never heard the sound of 20 mm cannon fire, or felt the wind of napalm bombs pulling combustion air across your back, it's a new and unforgettable experience. We all had what looked like severe sunburns, but they were actually burns from being that close to exploding napalm. All, that is, except Major J. Doe: he was still lying face down and quite pale.

I can't be certain how long the Air Force barrage continued, but after a while the enemy fire appeared non-existent although we were still leery about getting up and moving around. Later choppers from other units came in to extract us and that certainly made us smile and reassure ourselves that we still had places to go and things to do. Later in the day we learned about those who had been wounded and eight other aircraft that had to make emergency landings after leaving the LZ. Out of two companies of helicopters - approximately 70-80 aircraft - there were only about 10 flightworthy the next day. Warrant Officer Grimmer was awarded the Distinguished Service Cross for his heroism, sharp-witted performance and leadership. Without him I'm afraid the rest of us could or would have been KIA, WIA, MIA or POWs, or any combination of these. The rest of us were awarded the Bronze Star with V device for heroism in ground combat. The Major received the Silver Star. One can't fault the military for not honoring tradition and rank.

Above: Stars and Stripes, 2/18/1967 with headline feature story of when Jim Creagan's helicopter was shot down along with nine other U.S. helicopters. Image provided by Jim Creagan.

Tet 1968

The evening of January 29, 1968, more commonly known as the eve of the Tet Offensive, I was preparing to take a light fire team airborne for a routine Airfield Security mission. I had talked to some U.S. advisory officers about recent military events in the local area and things seemed normal and fairly calm. It was just starting to get dark and the local South Vietnamese troops were already beginning to celebrate the Asian New Year. Weapons were being fired off into the air and I was hopeful that the spent rounds would not return to Earth where our aircraft were parked. Many of the celebrants were quite drunk and their understanding of the effects of gravity somewhat diminished. I can still remember the sound of the spent bullets hitting the metal runway as they fell back to the ground.

A light team means two aircraft the lead and a wing man. We were flying AH1-G Huey Cobras that, at the time, were considered the best the US Army had to offer in aerial, rotary wing, armed attack aircraft. I had transition training in-country (Vietnam) after flying Huey UH-1B, C, D and H models for about six months and found the new sleeker, faster and much more heavily armed Cobras to be much to my liking.

The transition training came with a price tag. Any pilot volunteering for this would have to extend his combat tour of

AH1-G Huey Cobra. Courtesy of Jim Creagan.

duty another six months. I found that fair enough as it also included a thirty-day free leave and meant I could be a lot more effective against the enemy.

Airfield Security meant keeping two ships flying near to the airfield during all the hours of darkness to defend against any ground or mortar attacks that might occur directed towards our field at Can Tho RVN or any of our immediate neighboring RVN camps and villages. It was usually pretty boring. Often one of us would practice GCA (ground controlled approaches) communicating with the airfield tower. It was great training for us as well as the guys that worked the tower as they didn't have any more experience than we did. It helped prepare pilots and control tower personnel for instrument flying in bad weather. The security mission was done in two-hour shifts and my team was the second team up this night. It was on one of these flights that I heard the US Lunar Landing with astronaut Armstrong's famous

"Giant Leap" quote. It was cool as we could see the moon that night but that was over a year later.* This night was far different.

Excepting the constant sight of tracers flying through the dark, shot by the New Year's revelers the night seemed fairly serene. We just had to fly a wider orbit to avoid the "Friendly Fire." Soon things started to change. The airfield at Soc Trang, about twenty minutes to the south, reported they were under attack. I knew they didn't always have security "birds" in the air at night, as I had previously been stationed there before Cobra school. I took the initiative to take my team south hoping to help the besieged airfield, still the home of many friends I had made there in the past.

Only a few minutes into our mercy flight came report after report of airfields all over the country being hit and hit hard. I had to reflect on how well the enemy, which we all thought was an almost primitive military, was putting this startling campaign together and with complete radio silence. I'll avoid the controversy as to whether or not the Pentagon had any previous knowledge. I'll also avoid the word "Intelligence."

After thinking this over for about half of a second, I headed my team back towards Can Tho. It was, after all, our primary duty to protect our base. Nothing there had happened yet but it wasn't long before the action picked up. Soon many RVN outposts nearby were being overrun and a few of them that had sober people still on duty were calling for help and we would rush to give them fire support but, typically, the Viet Cong would cease firing as soon as they were aware Cobras were in the area. There was, however, one persistent enemy gun position that began firing at us. Judging by the size and volume of their tracers we were sure it was at least a dual mounted .50 caliber anti-aircraft gun. We started our attack. As lead ship I went first with my lights out so as not to give away my position until I fired a few pairs of rockets and a whole lot of machine gun ammo.

As I climbed back up to a safe altitude and turned my lights back on and my wingman went dark and started his attack dive. The .50 cal. had stopped for a few minutes but soon they were back in action but not as accurate, mostly shooting behind us and my wingman, who was still dark, moved closer to my ship and off to my right. We attacked again as we had before, "go dark and dive" and again the ground fire ceased. While we went looking for other targets of opportunity that .50 cal. started up once more. This time it was ludicrous, they were firing all over the place but seemingly at no particular target so we decided to double the attack. We were becoming annoyed by this gun position but were almost laughing at them. After our last attempt to quiet them there was no more trouble from that gun. A few days later we learned from agent reports that our first attacks had been effective in killing the gun crews and the third destroyed the weapon. This explained why the

*Refers to the Apollo 11 lunar landing on July 20, 1969 when astronaut Neil Armstrong, the first man to step on the moon's surface proclaimed, "That's one small step for a man, one giant leap for mankind."

accuracy level kept diminishing. The replacement gun crews had little or no experience.

Meanwhile my company, the 235th AHC, had launched more Cobras and I was running low on fuel and ammunition. Once refueled and rearmed, we were back in the air and I was trying to coordinate with other flight crews and our Operations office as I had been the first to see where some of the attacks were originating from. To the nearby north a munitions depot had come under attack and though we tried to give support, the force of exploding ammunition, grenades and bombs made it almost impossible to control our aircraft and the brilliance of the flames and explosions made it difficult to spot enemy ground fire and soon it was a complete loss.

Company patch. Image provided by Jim Creagan.

As dawn approached the action lessened greatly. In the morning we would see almost every small outpost in our area abandoned and flying the Viet Cong flag. Can Tho had suffered mortar and small arms attacks but no breaks in perimeter defenses. There was some damage to aircraft and structures but we generally felt lucky as compared to many other bases we had heard about. I don't recall any casualties among the many flight crews that flew that night from Can Tho.

I stated earlier how in awe I was concerning how well the enemy conducted the beginning of this great Tet Offensive. They deserved praise. But was it sad to see the dead bodies of young boys (Viet Cong) hanging lifeless in the Concertina wire around our perimeter. Some of them carried certificates that guaranteed financial rewards when their war was won. Others carried cannabis, I suppose, as support. Still sad, but at least their war was over. The Tet Offensive was an overwhelming statement of purpose but only a momentary victory for the Viet Cong and North Vietnamese. In the days and weeks that followed the rules of engagement changed drastically and our unit as well as others dealt heavy casualties to the Viet Cong and NVA military.

I now have three sons, two are 22 years old the oldest is 27 and I still constantly worry as to whether they should drive in poor weather or if they live in a safe neighborhood or if they're choosing the right education or profession etc., etc.. I was 21 when January 30th, 1968 occurred. It might have been a privilege, and I know it was an honor and an adventure, to be coerced to grow up so fast, but I'm happy and proud to say I did - but my sons don't have to.

Helicopter Pilot On Furlough From Vietnam

Warrant Officer James Creagan, of Caledonia, who has just completed 11 1/2 months of service in Vietnam is spending a 30 day furlough visiting his mother in New York and friends in the Genesee Valley. He was shot down on his first mission. His helicopter received a bullet in the cockpit, and has been hit 48 times. He attended Geneseo State University for one semester. Creagan, who at one time worked at the Seldon Angus farm in Greigsville has received the Bronze Star. His cousin, Larry Utbert of Perry, runs the Dairy Bar in Geneseo and his grandmother, Mrs. Meade, runs a diner in Caledonia. He is a friend of Ron Scott of Geneseo. Creagan will return to Viet Nam for about six months more duty.

Mt. Morris Enterprise, 1/10/1968.

❀❀❀❀❀❀❀❀❀❀❀❀❀❀❀❀❀❀❀

Mountain Trip

The Mekong Delta is flat. You've seen Kansas flat, Iowa flat and all those other Midwest US states flat. The Mekong Delta is flatter. One exception is an area referred to as the Seven Mountain Range. These small mountains just popped up, out of the flat, for no apparent geological reason. Unlit, they were a flight hazard on night missions as our usual cruising altitude was 2000 ft. and some of these were a bit higher than that. They lie to the west of the Mekong River and just south of the Cambodian border. Each mountain had a name but this writer cannot remember them.

It must have been in August or late July of 1969, when my fire team was "scrambled," a term for an emergency unplanned mission. As fire team leader of a pair of AH-1G Cobra helicopters I was given the usual information, geographical coordinates, radio frequency and call sign of the unit needing our help. At this time I was more than familiar with the territory and knew from the coordinates given me that we were headed to the mountains.

On route I made radio contact with the distressed unit. A small group of South Vietnamese infantry, probably a platoon, led by a US Army advisor had managed to get themselves pinned down on the south side of the largest of the Seven Mountains. The details were hard to understand as the advisor would only whisper on the radio and asked me to do the same as they were so close to an enemy position and did not want to make any noise which could jeopardize their safety.

After a 30- to 40-minute flight we had arrived at the target area and it wasn't too long before I made visual contact with the unit in trouble. Unable or unwilling to use smoke grenades to identify their position they were relatively easy to spot being that there were many wounded wearing white bandages, stained with red. They were in a terrible position on a rather steep slope with a rock outcropping above them concealing them from the enemy, only a short distance away. To put in perspective, it was as if the enemy was occupying the top floors and roof of the Miceli's Deli building on Main Street, Geneseo while the good guys hid under the awning below. Precarious didn't fairly describe their plight. They were in deep shit up to their chins. Don't make waves I thought. Just above them was a cave entrance with a tripod mounted .50 caliber machine gun manned by Viet Cong plus several more small arms positions scattered around the mountain face. There was no good escape route for the poor souls below that gun.

We began making passes at the cave without firing our weapons to scare the bad guys away, but to no avail. I took some hits in my aircraft and my wingman took enough to completely wipe out all his armament systems. I directed him to leave, return to our home base in Can Tho, pick up a new ship and return. I radioed my Operations officer to get more help but none was available. It was another busy day in the Delta. That left me on my own with the good guys still in a hopeless mess. The US advisor was pleading with me not to use my firepower to distract or defuse the enemy as he was certain his group would be part of the carnage I would leave behind. He was just too damn close. This guy had no idea he was talking to a cocky, but confident, 22-year-old Cobra pilot who already had over two years of aerial combat duty experience. I tried to assure him that I was the best shot in the Delta and could easily take out the .50 cal. position but he continued his plea. So I switched to the theory that he and his group were doomed without my help but could possibly escape if my fire was extremely accurate. He still didn't like the odds and I began to realize I hadn't ever fired this close to "friendlies" before. Then again they were doomed if I didn't and only maybe doomed if I did.

Making the decision wasn't easy but my confidence was high. At that time the Cobras were equipped with a flip-up prism style rocket sight. These were surplus WWII bomb sights which were mounted directly in front of the pilot and could be folded down flat for normal flight and we regularly adjusted them (sighted in for accuracy). However, it was not uncommon for more experienced gunship pilots to merely put a grease pencil mark on the canopy (windshield), get into a "sweet spot" or sitting position and fire accurately, especially at short range. This was the method I was using on this mission, "grease mark and sweet spot". Going head-on towards the mouth of the cave I released two pair of 2.75-inch rockets with 17-pound explosive warheads, making them about equal to a 105mm Howitzer shell.

Huey dropping troops off into the field. Courtesy of Ron Hilfiker.

My copilot and I were both certain the rockets found their mark but now I had no wingman to back me up on this. Quickly I radioed the man on the ground to see what he thought, but there was no reply. I had prided myself for never bringing harm upon our own troops. It was rare that a gunship pilot, even with a lot less time in the cockpit than I had, could brag about this. Friendly and civilian casualties were all too common. I guess now we call that "collateral damage." I couldn't stomach this idea no matter how it's spelled. Now I was, seemingly, on the other side of the fence although almost sure my rockets had been precisely on target. All sorts of emotions were starting to pop into my once-confident ego. Self-doubt, self-pity and pity for those poor guys on the mountain were some of the things I was feeling but I continued the attack on the cave.

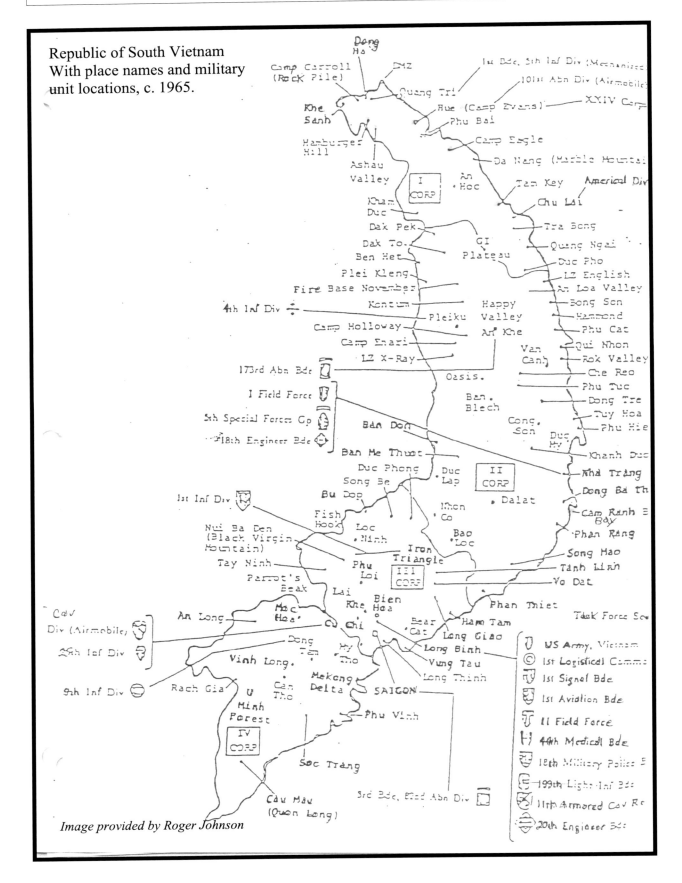

Republic of South Vietnam
With place names and military
unit locations, c. 1965.

Image provided by Roger Johnson

By now we were picking up more and more small arms fire from a variety of positions on the mountain and I flew a little further away for a respite. I was wondering if my wingman was OK, and on his way back and wondering about what I may have done to those guys I had been sent to help. There was an Air Force FAC (forward air controller) in the area who had been watching our small show. He suggested an Air Force air strike and I said I was still concerned about the status of the people on the ground. I hadn't heard a thing from them for nearly twenty minutes. We had flown back by the .50 cal. position and were glad to see that was no longer a threat. Within minutes two **Air Force fighter** jets were on the scene and about the same time I got a radio call from a very out-of-breath US advisor whom I was now certain I had terminated. After listening to my tirade about not answering my radio messages, he explained that he was just too damn busy getting his men down the mountain to a secure place and that the strike was perfect. How do you spell relief? "Why not, bring it on baby" I radioed the FAC.

Now it was USAF's turn. I put a few more rockets at the cave entrance to mark it for the FAC and he in turn used his WP (white phosphorous) rockets to mark it for the F-4s. On the very first run by the lead aircraft the pilot dropped a bomb on a horizontal run just over the top of the mountain and the damn thing went right into the cave opening, it was like watching a Roadrunner cartoon. This shit just never happens in real life. Now, I know what an orgasm feels like but I'm sure that Jet Jockey was feeling something much better after that shot. He put on a one man Thunderbird show right there above us while his wingman made a few more runs on the south face of the mountain. I wanted to watch more of the show but was seriously low on fuel and had to fly to the nearest refueling port I knew of. From there we went back to Can Tho as I learned there was a new fire team on its way to relieve us. There were explosions from within the cave for over two hours after that beautiful bomb drop, I was already back at our airfield having a cold one when I learned this from the other fire team that had relieved us.

The USAF was happy, I was real happy, and that US ground advisor was ecstatic, after his long worrisome silence, now he wouldn't shut up. Guess what? The US Navy was happy too. My wingman, en-route to Can Tho for a replacement aircraft, encountered a Navy riverboat under attack in the Mekong River. As he had no fire power he simply flew his Cobra between the Viet Cong and the boat, distracting the VC enough for the boat to get out of harm's way. He was later awarded the Navy Cross for heroism by the USN. Not bad for a farm boy from Iowa. Wish I could remember his name.

Weeks later on another mission supporting ground troops the "mountain man" who again was the advisor to an ARVN patrol called on the radio and asked if I was the same Dealer 23 from the mountain mission. I confirmed I was and he explained again how thankful he was and that he, personally, had written me up for the Silver Star Medal. My discharge came up early, quite by surprise, and I was out of the military only a few weeks later - but not before being shot down for a second time. I still wonder what happened to that paperwork and to him. Hope he got home safely.

I guess my point, in this story, is the fact that young men from all over the country and all kinds of backgrounds found themselves involved in situations where, beyond courage, decision making is paramount for success. These decisions often include who lives and who dies and that's a major responsibility for a seasoned combat veteran, much less young men in their late teens and early twenties. As in every phase of life and living, making any decision, right or wrong, is usually far better than making none at all. This day I was lucky and made the right choice and had the aptitude to successfully carry it out. As far as I know there's no military training for this, perhaps not even a manual. I saved my bad decisions for other times.

❀ ❀ ❀ ❀ ❀ ❀ ❀ ❀ ❀ ❀ ❀ ❀

Jim Creagan and crew mates. Courtesy of Jim Creagan.

Tibbetts

You meet a lot of people in the service just like you meet them in school or civilian employment. Some of them are forgotten, or at least become blurry in your mind and a small few are truly unforgettable, burning or branding a spot in your brain forever. WO Hoye D. Tibbetts was that kind of branding iron. Texan, gambler, bullshitter and most of all a reliable and courageous pilot. Tibbetts was a little older than the average Warrant Officer helicopter pilot. He had been in the service back in the fifties and served in Germany in the same platoon with Elvis Presley. He had nothing but good things to say about "the King" and the rest of us loved the stories. After his first military tour of duty Hoye returned to Texas where he became a Texas State Trooper. His stories from this episodic drama of his life would enthrall us younger guys and we didn't care if it was true or not. Hoye was just a great story-teller, and it's more fun to believe. We were young and great listeners. During his time with the Texas Troopers, Hoye found out about the US Army Helicopter Training and reenlisted.

This big, self-confidant Texan was also a real gambler. I mean at a poker table, not necessarily with life and death but I'll get to that later. Hoye was a smart and proficient card player. In a short time he had amassed a small fortune of MPC (military pay certificates) and he kept it in his foot locker. MPC was worthless unless you could spend it in-country (Vietnam). You couldn't send it home unless you thought it would make interesting wall paper or souvenirs. Damn Tibbetts, he had a better idea. When some of the guys were short on cash they would go and see the "Bank of Tibbetts" for a transaction. He would actually cash personal checks, written against a GI's bank at home, for officers and enlisted men. He would then send those checks home along with his entire military paycheck for his wife to deposit, thus turning MPC into American cash. He did, at one time, confess to me that only about one third of the checks were good and that was only because he took them from enlisted men. The officers' checks hardly ever bore fruit. Still, when you have $15,000 in your foot locker and it's really only paper, getting one third of it home is a good day's work and $5,000 in real money, in the bank. At the time an average Warrant Officer helicopter pilot was earning about $7,200 a year including flight and combat pay. Oh yeah, that's before taxes. I don't think the infantry guys were even close to that.

I'm not really sure how Tibbetts and I bonded, I was a Yankee from New York and he was a real Texan. Hoye never wanted to be a fire team leader but he wanted to fly wing on someone he could trust and I wanted a wingman that I had faith in. It just worked out that he was my wingman on so many missions that we both knew intuitively what the other was thinking. Once when we were working with a squad of Navy SEALS who had managed to get themselves in over their heads and needed extraction. This operation was carried out from a Navy ship in the South China Sea anchored a few miles south of Phu Quoc Island. The ship was small enough that one helicopter would have to land, shut down and tie down the rotor blades before the second one could land. We were there to provide air support for the SEAL unit if they got in trouble or diversionary fire so they could accomplish whatever sneaky little things they were doing. Supposedly they were on their own as far as transportation. Now they were in trouble and needed to get off the island. A little-known fact about Cobras is that the front ammo bay doors could be opened to provide an external seat. One on each side and even had a seat belt. We didn't have time to call another helicopter. When I called Tibbetts to explain that we would have to land one at a time and pick up two each of the squad members and if he thought that was a good idea he replied "We don't have a choice do we?" as calm as if I was talking about getting a haircut. I knew he'd say that. We each took some small arms fire on our landings and pick-ups but the other Cobra could suppress that.

After I had my passengers Tibbetts went in to get his guests and I covered him but could only use the front-mounted machine gun (mini-gun) as I wasn't sure what those two outside riders would do seeing rockets fly by two feet in front of their noses. I didn't want my ammo bay full of SEAL poop and it probably wouldn't have been safe either. We got our "crazy boys" safely back to the ship but a few minutes after I got shut down, Tibbetts had landed first, #1 SEAL approached me telling me we had to take him back to the LZ where we just picked them up. At first I thought he was joking or nuts or both but he was adamant. It seems that they had forgotten a weapon and that weapon may have been not quite kosher with the Geneva Convention and if you don't know what that is, it's just like the NY SAFE Act, only for wars. So back we went. Tibbetts gladly volunteered to carry the man on his ship as he told me he thought that little clearing in the tropical forest was "kinda purty." With no extras on board, my co-pilot, WO Bob Cook, and I could use all the weaponry at our disposal. We let loose with rockets and mini-gun fire while Hoye made his landing, weapon retrieval and departure. On our short flight back to the ship, Tibbetts calls me on the radio to complain about how Cook and I had made too much noise while he was on the ground and also he wanted us to land first on the ship so he could further torment his passenger for being so stupid and forgetful.

I learned so much from this man, mostly serenity and common sense. In the middle of a fire fight his voice was just as calm as when he raised a bet in a poker game. No panic ever, never. His confidence was so overwhelming. Any given evening in the Officers' Club Hoye might say he was a little short on beer money, then get some tokens for the slots stating he needed to make a bank withdrawal. He'd put a few tokens in the same slot I had been playing all evening and all those little pictures would line up and pump out twenty dollars for him. I'd be broke. On another occasion he and I were sharing drinks and lies at the OC (officers' club), when our airfield came under mortar attack. Everybody fled the club for the safety of bunkers strategically planted around our base. The OC was now empty except for me and Tibbetts as he was explaining to me the logic of odds. Odds were a mortar round might not hit the two bar stools we were sitting on. Odds were if we ran for the bunker we might run into a mortar and be killed. After that we calmly walked towards the bunker because Hoye said it wasn't cool to die in a panic and all sweaty like in the bunker where they would complain about our cigarettes. How can you not love this guy and his logic?

On another evening Tibbetts was my wingman on a normal harassment and interdiction (H&I) mission near our air field at Can Tho. H&I meant go fly around until you get shot at and then shoot back. We also had "Spooky," but we preferred to call them "Puff," as in the Magic Dragon, working with us that night. Spooky was an Air Force AC-47 aka DC5 loaded with thousands of rounds of 7.62 minigun ammo and flares. After Puff had raked an area with machine gun fire they dropped flares so my team of Cobras could make an aerial observation to see if there were any visible enemy losses. There were no visible enemy losses but there certainly was visible enemy activity.

We came under some pretty heavy ground fire. I took a few hits but Tibbetts took more including one through his cockpit. It grazed the back of his neck and in that same old Texas calm he said, "Hell, Jimmy, I've had worse bug bites. Let's git 'em" and we did. On another night mission I wasn't sure what was going on, we hadn't run into any bad guys and the weather seemed normal - it was just weird. No matter where I looked, it appeared the ground was covered with snow and that's just not gonna happen in Southeast Asia. After we were back on the ground I confessed to Hoye about what I thought I had seen and wondered if I was finally "crackin' up." Tibbetts said, "Jimmy, I seen that same shit too but was afraid to tell the story." It's like all the UFO sightings. Who's gonna believe you? It was weird though, neither of our co-pilots saw it. Wonder what it was?

I wish I knew where Hoye D. Tibbetts was today but he just seemed to disappear. I do know he got out of Vietnam alive and that's good enough for me. What a guy.

Note: After Jim Creagan wrote this essay he learned that Hoye D. Tibbetts passed away on March 26, 2012 at his home in Granbury, Texas at the age of 73.

<u>Shot Down Again</u>

Our mission for the day was to escort US Navy river boats on a search and destroy mission in the myriad canals and natural waterways of the western Mekong Delta. I was leading a light team (2 aircraft) of AH1G Cobra helicopters. On the typical escort mission we were obligated to protect the patrol boats if they became involved in a fire fight or otherwise engaged with the enemy and also provide reconnaissance in the local area. The Navy river boats were well-armed and when they encountered the enemy it was usually at close range and by surprise. They were always grateful to have armed helicopters for support as we could scout ahead and detect enemy movement or other dangers that may exist out of their range of observation. The natural waterways, more so than canals, were lined with heavy tropical vegetation and were full of bends and curves so that it was difficult to detect danger to either side, front or back. I think the guys on the boats said port and starboard, fore and aft. That probably didn't matter much to me that day.

This particular day the Navy was working with South Vietnamese (ARVN) Infantry units, perhaps two companies of men, some of which rode on board the boats but most who swept opposite shorelines behind them. I was the fire team leader but had chosen to take the front seat or co-pilot's position this day to give a fairly new guy more experience in the "back seat"- a coveted spot for FNGs. The front seat of a Cobra had fewer gauges and instruments, abbreviated controls and a lot less room. Although the pilot in front could communicate on all four radios provided in the aircraft and the intercom, the guy in back had control of setting the frequencies or channels. There was also a device known as a "scrambler" in the rear cockpit. This device prevented the enemy from listening in on our radio conversations. It was removed from the aircraft daily and reprogrammed by our operation's office for use the next day. It was easily removed or reinstalled in seconds.

The progress along the river was slow as the boats could only cruise as fast as the infantry behind them could travel by foot and occasionally they would fire machine guns into the shoreline vegetation just to provoke enemy response but there were no results or retaliation so far this day. Often they would ask us to lay down some fire to their front though I was being frugal with my ammunition just in case we might get into a real firefight. I still had over an hour before a new fire team would relieve mine. It was our second session of coverage and we had just gotten back on station while the other fire team had left to refuel and reload munitions when, while having just crossed over the two gunboats at low level from right to left (or starboard to port), we saw them. In the tall grass maybe two or three hundred yards from the riverbank there were about a dozen armed Viet Cong just below us and to the right. I could see them as they stood and opened fire at us but our ship was too close to return fire.

My wingman had seen them and opened fire before I could even radio him

him that we were taking hits. While trying to tell my inexperienced pilot in the back seat to swing around to attack the guys that had shot at us we were receiving bad news from the instrument panel. If you look closely at the front and rear Cobra cockpit photos attached to this article you might notice in both a rather blank area at the bottom right of both instrument panels, this is the systems warning panel. This panel was usually blank but my new pilot and I agreed that there were not many warning lights unlit. Most disturbing were the two that said "Hydraulic System 1 Failure" and the other saying "Hydraulic System 2 Failure". This was serious. I had immediately grabbed the controls when I realized we were not flying a smooth and level flight and did the best I could do to establish something close to that goal. My wingman was wondering what the hell was going on and I radioed him that we were in deep trouble. He wasn't sure as to how much damage he inflicted on the shooters but had managed himself to escape unscathed.

It was at this point I knew that we couldn't get home or even to the closest landing strip while trying to fly a 14,000-pound machine without hydraulic aid. I reflected back to a flight school classroom session about basic component failures. If Hyd. System 1 failed do this, if Hyd. System 2 failed do something else. Either way one or the other did not spell disaster. One of my fellow students asked what to do when Systems 1&2 fail simultaneously. The instructors reply was, "Whatever you do will be unique." This was not at all a welcome memory.

Although I was looking at a downwind landing, inherently dangerous of itself, I didn't have enough confidence to try and turn this now very cumbersome machine around. There was a long flat grassy area ahead and I announced to my co-pilot and wingman this was my choice spot for an emergency landing and I would attempt to slide in. Hovering was impossible. As we came closer and closer to touchdown my FNG co-pilot says on the intercom "Do you want me to help?" Now I go ballistic. I thought he had been helping all along. He was at least as big as me so I just assumed I had only been helping him with my controls about the size of the joysticks on our current video games. I screamed most of the obscenities I knew and made a few more up and informed him that if he hadn't been helping before, don't start now. We wobbled down to the ground, I cut throttle and we slid about fifty yards to a safe and level landing. I guess that was "unique" enough.

It gets a little goofier now. Normally I only carried a .38 caliber revolver (not a great weapon for jungle warfare or escape and evasion) in the aircraft, but this day I happened to have a small automatic rifle on board. It may have been an AR-15 or CAR-15, I never knew much about weapons but I'm sure it must have been an assault weapon. I'm already out of the helicopter and shouting at my new guy to cut the fuel and shut it down and get out. I guess I kind of shoved him a little to get to the weapon which was stored behind his seat but he didn't complain and I set out to see the scenery. After a few seconds I looked back to see how he was doing and realized that he's actually trying to remove the four radios and still sitting in the

the cockpit like one great big target. Making up a few yet unused expletives, I jumped up onto the step to the rear cockpit, reached in and yanked out the scrambler and told the poor guy, "just spin the F'n dials on the radios." He hadn't been out of flight school long enough to know that you don't have time for removing radios like they teach you to, at least not in a hostile environment. Spin the dials to errant frequencies and grab the scrambler for security reasons. When it gets more serious, shoot the scrambler before you and it are captured.

By this time I was a little confused as to exactly where we were in relation to the position of the VC that shot us down. Handling the aircraft had been so difficult I wasn't paying much attention to geography. I just wanted to get safely on the ground. I figured if we survived the crash that I felt was certain, we could worry about the bad guys then. If we died in the crash, why worry? Once out of the ship I had the new guy keep an eye on one side of our downed Cobra while I kept watch on the other. Now I could hear excited Vietnamese voices coming toward us through the tall thick grass. I signaled to the other pilot to come over and get ready to start shooting.

Now I was unable to talk to my wingman via radio but he was making a very low pass right over the area the voices were coming from and he wasn't shooting. When I looked again toward the voices I could see many Vietnamese men in uniform and, more importantly, Americans with them. *Whooooopee!!* They had left the river mission and come to our defense, setting up a secure area for the extraction of our wounded bird and ourselves. Meanwhile my wingman had coordinated efforts to get a new fire team on the way, a Huey to pick us up and a Chinook (CH-47) heavy lift helicopter to extract the Cobra and take it back to our base at Can Tho about 100 miles away. Everything went smoothly. Thanks, wingman.

Chinook 'heavy-lift' helicopter. Courtesy of Ron Hilfiker.

Monkhouse, Jim's crew chief (kneeling) pointing to a hole through the main push/pull control rod to the main rotor. Jim Creagan writes, "Had the rod been severed this picture would never have been taken nor would I be writing this. The Huey was so badly shot up it was sent stateside for reconstruction, the engine seized as soon as I cut power after landing." Also pictured Don Raczon, the door gunner. Courtesy of Don Raczon.

Jim relaxing in the back seat of his helicopter. Courtesy of Don Raczon.

By the time we got back to Can Tho I had a terrible thirst and hoped we wouldn't be delayed too long at our Operations Office explaining the recent events. Ops was cooperative and only kept us a few minutes, just long enough that as we left the office we got to see the Chinook bring in our wounded "Snake" and literally drop it off. It was a much harder landing than its last one.

Next stop was the Officers' Club, naturally, and word had already been passed around about our exciting day. We got handshakes and back slaps and a few free drinks for as far as anybody knew no pilot had ever had a successful landing of a Huey or Cobra without hydraulics. I was basking in the glow of being a legend in my own mind and lying to my co-pilot about what a great job he had done and that I would never think of him as a FNG again. Why not, he was buying. That's when Captain "Nofun," our maintenance Officer came in and destroyed my rosy disposition. Apparently the Chinook's hard drop of the ill-fated Cobra had done significant damage. The irate captain took me to task for not flying the aircraft home and preventing the further damage as could normally be done with a single hydraulic failure. I advised him that both systems were out but he continued screaming that was impossible because we had a safe landing and were still alive. Later he returned, humbly, and apologized, admitting after inspecting the damage, that indeed both systems had been struck as well as engine and transmission oil lines that certainly doomed the ship. I courteously accepted his apology, shook his hand and informed him it was his turn to pay for my cocktails. By this time poor old FNG had a sudden urge to sleep and was unable to share in the gloating.

Statistically the first three months and the last three were the most deadly for a soldier in Vietnam. I had been shot down the first time just seven weeks into my tour. I often wonder if I kept extending my tour only to put off those last three months. It was almost exactly when I had just three months left that this incident occurred in September of 1969. About a week later our Executive NCO advised me if I wanted to leave Vietnam tomorrow he had my orders waiting but I would, of course, have to pass on my upcoming R&R to Bangkok. The army had a new program that would release personnel with 90 days or less in their military obligation. Wow, tough choice, I was a civilian three days later. Bye-bye.

P.S. Sorry I cannot remember the names of crewmen involved. They all, even FNGs, performed magnificently.

Pilot honored for service

Geneseo man receives Conspicuous Service awards

BY COURTNEY VEAUNT
For The LCN

Jim Creagan, who flew helicopters during the Vietnam War, was recognized with two awards from New York State this month — more than 40 years after he served.

Creagan received the New York State Conspicuous Service Cross and Conspicuous Service Star on Aug. 3 during Geneseo Veterans of Foreign Wars Post 5005 annual veterans' picnic at the National Warplane Museum.

Frank Hollistar of the Livingston County Veterans Services Agency was also honored at the picnic.

The Conspicuous Service Cross is a awarded by New York State to members of the military who have also been awarded any of the following by the United States: Medal of Honor, Distinguished Service Cross, Purple Heart, Distinguished Service Medal, Silver or Bronze Star, Distinguished Flying Cross, Legion of Merit, among others. The Conspicuous Service Star is also awarded by the State to veterans who are recipients of at least one of the following unit commendations arising from combat Distinguished Unit Citation/Presidential Unit Citation, Joint Meritorious Unit Award, Valorous Unit Award, among others.

Creagen, who served from 1967 to 1969 in Vietnam, earned more than 30 air medals flying Cobra gun ships.

The Conspicuous Service

Award presentation. Geneseo's Jim Creagan, right, stands at the front of the room as Frank Hollister, director of the Livingston County Veteran Services Agency, announces the awarding of the New York State Conspicuous Service Cross and Conspicuous Service Star to Creagan. Roger Johnson, left, shows the awards to attendees of the annual veterans picnic earlier this month.

Michael Johnson/Livingston County New

awards, he said, are designed to recognize those "who did more than their share" while in the service.

Roger Johnson, who was an infantry soldier during Vietnam, noted the importance of these pilots.

"They were angels on our shoulders," Johnson said. "They were the guys that got (the infantry) in and out."

Hollister, of the Veteran Services Agency, called Creagen "a very courageous man" whose actions in Vietnam "saved thousands of American and allied lives."

After Creagan's time in the service, he "came back to Geneseo ... and has stayed here ever since."

Hollister was also recognized at the picnic. He had

previously been named recipient of the state American Legion Service Officer of the Year award.

The mission of the Veteran Service Agency is to provide entitlement information and advocacy assistance to military personnel, veterans, and their dependents in matters relating to veterans' law.

Johnson acknowledged Hollister's efforts by stating, "He is an amazing person to have in that position. We are blessed to have someone who fights for us."

Prior to the awards ceremony, the group also recognized, with special gifts, Emerson Johnston who hit the beaches of Normandy during World War II's D-Day invasion in 1942.

Michael Johnson/Livingston County News

Also honored. World War II veteran Emerson Johnston was recognized at the annual veterans picnic for his part in the D-Day invasion.

Clifton Donald VanDerveer

❋ ❋ ❋ ❋ ❋ ❋ ❋ ❋ ❋ ❋ ❋ ❋ ❋ ❋ ❋ ❋

Cliff "Don" VanDerveer describes some exciting as well as mundane adventures he experienced after he was sent to Duc Pho in Vietnam to join the 174th Assault Helicopter Company, 23rd Infantry, Americal Division.

CLIFTON VAN DERVEER

Mr. and Mrs. Clifton A. Vanderveer have received word from Major Richard A. Brown, Infantry Commanding, that their son has been assigned as a member of the 174th Aviation Company (AML) 14th Combat Aviation Battalion, APO San Francisco 96217, located at Duc Pho, Republic of Vietnam. "The 174th Aviation Company was activated at Fort Benning, Ga. Oct. 1, 1965. On March 15, 1966 the unit departed Fort Benning and arrived in Qui Nhon Harbor March 16, 1966.

"This unit was initially assigned to the central coastal area of Vietnam. It was later moved, early in 1967, to Duc Pho, and we continue to support the 11th Light Infantry Brigade and the Americal Division.

"At present our company has flight platoons, The 'Slicks' (UH-1H Helicopters) are the troop carrying aircraft and are called the Dolphins; the gunships (UH-1C Helicopters) are called 'Sharks' and have permission from General Robert Lee Scott, jr., Post Commander, China Air Task Force, to use the famed shark-mouth of General Claire Chennault's Flying Tigers, painted on their aircraft. We are proud of our unit and each individual."

Nunda News, 3/27/1969.

I was unceremoniously off-loaded and pointed toward what I soon enough learn was the P.O.L. Point (Petroleums, Oils, and Lubricants) or "Refreshing Point." As I picked up my duffel, and started walking 25+ yards toward the company area, "Charlie" decided to welcome me to the A.O. with a short mortar and rocket attack. These attacks occurred almost 50% of the time that I was in-country. Seldom accurate, but irritating as hell! I dropped and low-crawled to a nearby ditch. Ten minutes later I reported in to the company commanding office looking and feeling very filthy. My brand new no-iron khakis were pretty much covered with the remnants of the wet ditch that I had just crawled out of. Oh, what a wonderful start to my year in Duc Pho with the 174th!

After a couple of days of settling in, I was assigned flight missions as a co-pilot (technically the Army term is 1st Pilot), the more well-known nickname was "Peter Pilot." My first mission was on "body recovery." The name is self-explanatory and yes, it was grisly, and shocking to a brand-new Peter Pilot!

My time in Vietnam was made up of missions that were 75-80% boredom. Days filled with command and control, resupply, administration runs and non-combat troop movement (stand-down) extractions, low priority sick or wounded, etc. Some resupply and extraction missions could be quite stressful due to the terrain and jungle canopy. Some the of the LZs were small (literally the size of the aircraft), double and triple canopy, pinnacle areas where the chin of the aircraft is over a drop-off of several hundred feet. The weather often played a role in the way we performed and completed our missions. Whether high temperatures and humidity or monsoon rains we strove to the point of obsessive-compulsive behavior to support the troops in the field and complete our missions.

There were areas that we flew over that were devastated by saturation bombings and areas that were unbelievably pristine. Along Highway 1 there were villes and district headquarters that showed the sign of combat and rebuilding. The main village of Duc Pho was a bustling community of shops, craftsmen, farmers and public markets. There was a Catholic orphanage that a lot of us volunteered at. During the day you could fairly safely go about the area. It was known that at night the area was infested with Viet Cong and NVA. I personally believe that little happened close in by Duc Pho because both sides "let sleeping dogs lie."

In the latter part of May 1969, our company was involved in a muti-unit, heavy combat assault that cost us the loss of a fine crew of four and a lift aircraft. Plus, many other aircraft to small arms hits. Early that morning before 6am, our company commander ordered all of the available aircraft (approx. 18 lift ships and 8-10 gunships) to be loaded. After loading eight troops on each lift ship at the staging sight, we climbed to about 2000 ft above sea level and formed up in a V shape of three formation. Usually no farther than 20-30' apart at 100-120 miles per hour. We had total of 18-20 aircraft. This would be considered a 'heavy lift.' After a supposedly accurate heavy artillery prep of the LZ and surrounding area, we were given the OK to conduct the combat assault.

> **Warrant Officer VanDerveer Receives Air Medal**
>
> DUC PHO, VIETNAM (AHTNC) —Army Warrant Officer Clifton D VanDerveer, 21, son of Mr. and C VanDerveer, 17 State street, Nunda, received the Air Medal near Duc Pho, Vietnam May 22.
>
> WO VanDerveer earned the award for meritorious service while participating in aerial flight in support of ground operations in Vietnam.
>
> A pilot assigned wth the 174th Aviation Company near DucPho, WO VanDerveer entered the Army in December, 1967 and completed his basic training at Ft. Polk, La. He was last stationed at Ft. Rucker, Ala., and has been serving in Vietnam since February 1969.
>
> *Nunda News, 6/26/1969.*

Because of the location, size, and shape of the landing area, the whole heavy lift approached into a valley with high hills on both sides. The gunships were flanked both left and right as we approached in tight formation. Whether by poor intelligence or bad luck, we were attempting to land in an area heavily defended by VC and NVA forces. From rear to front the aircraft began taking fire from Chicom .51 cal. machine guns and rifles. The trail aircraft, flying less than 30 feet from my aircraft, took hits that must have caused fatal damage. It rolled onto its side and fell from 2000 ft. to its destruction and the deaths of the infantry men and four crewmen on board. As they were going down, Flight Lead radioed, *"Abort, abort! Proceed to secondary LZs!"*

I was flying co-pilot that day. I'll never forget that helicopter breaking apart and men falling out as they plummeted to their destruction and fiery deaths. I was only 21 years old. Unfortunately I watched them fall all the way to the ground. I did not know the grunts but I had become friends with both pilots and had worked with both crewmen. From then on through the rest of my tour I passively rejected direct responsibility as long as I could. I had been due to become an Aircraft Commander by the end of May. I had the hours, experience and knew the AP. I let my platoon leader know that I would fly any mission but that I did not want to be in charge! Evidently that did not sit well with him or the Operations Officer. I was scheduled to fly almost every mission that needed a Peter Pilot for the next 4 1/2 months. I knew that I was being kept out of the 'Good Ole Boys Club' for not being gung ho. It did not matter for me. All I wanted to do was 1) fly; 2) do my tour; and 3) get the hell out of Vietnam alive! Mid-October I was promoted to Aircraft Commander. Trust me, there was no celebration.

Throughout the remainder of my tour I never shirked my duties, refused a mission, or foolishly jeopardized any of my crews or passengers. During my tour we lost other crews, aircraft and unit members to enemy action, accidents and other causes. I know that while flying support mission I was able to do emergency medevacs when waiting for 'dust-off' would have been deemed too late. Also, there were times when Battalion Commanders balked at giving up their command and control aircraft to these emergency missions. But usually after fast-talking and prom-ises, they would release us for the 45-60 minutes needed that was taken away from their scheduled use of the aircraft. It was not that the commanders did not care about their troops. They did, very much so. But on most occasions due to equip-ment, time, and scheduling constraints, they could lose our availability for the rest of the day. A sad but true fact existed, red tape and bean counters ruled!

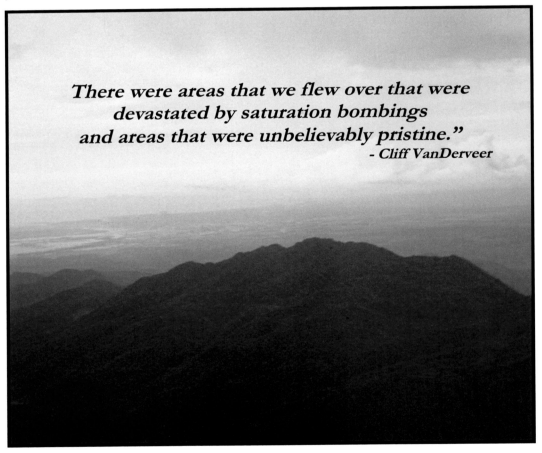

There were areas that we flew over that were devastated by saturation bombings and areas that were unbelievably pristine."
- Cliff VanDerveer

Photo courtesy of Roger Johnson.

During my tour I was able to make contact with a few Geneseo and Nunda schoolmates. Most cases it was a quick "Hey, I know you!" or "Aren't you from Geneseo?" I was told that I made contact with Chuck Freese one of the times that my aircraft was involved in an emergency medevac when he was wounded. Chuck said that he recognized my name on the back of my helmet while lying on the cargo floor. If it was me, I'll always be proud and honored that I was in the right place at the right time!

There are so many memories that I could write about but will only add one more. Late in October 1969, a few of the pilots contacted family at home and asked to have special costumes sent ASAP. On Christmas morning our unit flew resupply as usual. Except that hot chow of Christmas dinner and 'fixins' was the order of the day. The pilots with special costumes flew as many of those supply missions as they could. That morning the "Dolphin" call-sign was replaced with "Santa!" The smiles and thumbs-up with never be forgotten by me!

Welcome home Brothers and Sisters, I'm proud that I served with you!

C. Donald VanDerveer,
CW2 USAR Ret.
"Dolphin 27"

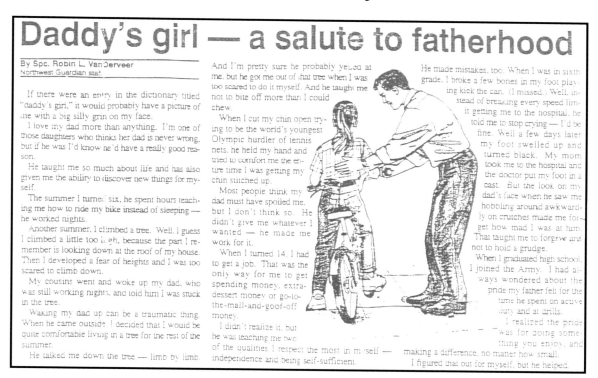

Daddy's girl — a salute to fatherhood

By Spc. Robin L. VanDerveer
Northwest Guardian staff

If there were an entry in the dictionary titled "daddy's girl," it would probably have a picture of me with a big silly grin on my face.

I love my dad more than anything. I'm one of those daughters who thinks her dad is never wrong, but if he was I'd know he'd have a really good reason.

He taught me so much about life and has also given me the ability to discover new things for myself.

The summer I turned six, he spent hours teaching me how to ride my bike instead of sleeping — he worked nights.

Another summer, I climbed a tree. Well, I guess I climbed a little too high, because the part I remember is looking down at the roof of my house. Then I developed a fear of heights and I was too scared to climb down.

My cousins went and woke up my dad, who was still working nights, and told him I was stuck in the tree.

Waking my dad up can be a traumatic thing. When he came outside I decided that I would be quite comfortable living in a tree for the rest of the summer.

He talked me down the tree — limb by limb.

And I'm pretty sure he probably yelled at me, but he got me out of that tree when I was too scared to do it myself. And he taught me not to bite off more than I could chew.

When I cut my chin open trying to be the world's youngest Olympic hurdler of tennis nets, he held my hand and tried to comfort me the entire time I was getting my chin stitched up.

Most people think my dad must have spoiled me, but I don't think so. He didn't give me whatever I wanted — he made me work for it.

When I turned 14, I had to get a job. That was the only way for me to get spending money, extra-dessert money or go-to-the-mall-and-goof-off money.

I didn't realize it, but he was teaching me two of the qualities I respect the most in myself — independence and being self-sufficient.

He made mistakes, too. When I was in sixth grade, I broke a few bones in my foot playing kick the can. (I missed.) Well, instead of breaking every speed limit getting me to the hospital, he told me to stop crying — I'd be fine. Well a few days later my foot swelled up and turned black. My mom took me to the hospital and the doctor put my foot in a cast. But the look on my dad's face when he saw me hobbling around awkwardly on crutches made me forget how mad I was at him. That taught me to forgive and not to hold a grudge.

When I graduated high school, I joined the Army. I had always wondered about the pride my father felt for the time he spent on active duty and at drills.

I realized the pride was for doing something you enjoy, and making a difference, no matter how small. I figured that out for myself, but he helped.

The article above was written by Cliff's daughter who followed in her father's footsteps a few years ago. Courtesy of Cliff VanDerveer.

Ron Hilfiker's
War Stories
❀❀❀❀❀❀❀❀❀❀❀❀

I was drafted and inducted into the Army on Oct. 24th, 1968. I received my Basic Training at Fort Dix, New Jersey and Advanced Infantry Training at (Tigerland) Fort Polk, Louisiana. Given MOS-11 Bravo.

In Vietnam, I was assigned to the 101st Airmobile at LZ Sally in northern I Corps-Quang Tri Provence and served as a company clerk, member of LZ Sally Security Platoon and finally Alpha Company 1st of 501st Infantry. After 13 and 1/2 months in RVN, I was granted an early out with Honorable Discharge on May 26th, 1970, Ft. Lewis, Washington.

THE MISS

Part of my duty at LZ Sally is in the camp security platoon. I pull night bunker guard duty to protect the perimeter of Sally from the Viet Cong. I also run Recon patrols through the local villages as a show of power and to look for any signs of enemy activity. One patrol is to conduct mine sweeps on a gravel road alongside a railroad track that no longer is in service as the bridge had been blown up. This is the way it works. First down the road are the soldiers with the metal detectors sweeping them back and forth to locate any mines. Next in line is a deuce and a half truck loaded with stone backing down the road. The idea is that if the back wheels roll over a mine the force of the explosion will be taken up by the stone in the bed with the driver spared. This is somewhat redundant but effective and I have heard of one case where the mine sweeper had missed the mine and the explosion had occurred under the truck.

I was in the group that walked alongside this operation to secure the situation. There are established paths along the road/railroad bed to walk on. One thing that I encounter is the punji traps that are easily visible as some of the covering vegetation had wilted. A punji trap is a pit dug into the ground about 2 feet deep with sharpened bamboo sticks pointed up in the bottom. The points were smeared in human excrement and the top of the pit camouflaged with a lattice of twigs and vegetation. This is a primitive but very effective trap as it takes the wounded soldier off the battle field as well as others to assist in treatment. It causes severe infection and is demoralizing, as the enemy is defeating you with only the materials at hand. This caused the military to develop a combat boot with a steel plate in the sole to control punji stick penetration.

About a half hour later we are on a berm along the railroad when I hear the crack of a bullet above my head and then the sound from an AK-47 going off. I fall to the ground and look to the hedgerow from where the shot had come ready to shoot my M-16. Mind you, a bullet travels faster than sound! The platoon leader says, "Hold your fire" as there is a "friendly" village on the other side of the hedgerow. A Loach helicopter arrives and picks up the platoon leader to see if anything can be spotted from the air. No enemy is spotted. It was my lucky day as I was the tallest target on the berm; thus, an easier target.

The sniper missed (which I am very thankful for).

Top:
Command bunker at LZ Sally.

Left :
Railroad bridge undergoing repair after being blown up by the Viet Cong.

Courtesy of Ron Hilfiker.

ACCIDENT OR INTENTIONAL?

I received word that I was being transferred from LZ Sally's security platoon to a line company that works out of LZ Sally, 1st of the 501st Alpha company. This is the real deal in that you are in the field searching for the enemy to engage 24 hours a day. I arrive and am put in 1st Platoon and a company formation is called with everyone lined up in army fashion. A shot rings out and I still remember the platoon leader I am facing cursing. I cautiously look over to the adjacent platoon and a circle of soldiers had formed.

All of a sudden the circle opens and a river of bright red blood flows out. A soldier had dropped his M-16 with the bolt to the rear and the magazine in place. The impact of the drop causes the bolt to go forward and chambers a round and fires the rifle. The bullet hits the head of the man next to him in the formation. He is dead when he hits the ground. A jeep arrives and removes the soldier who had dropped the rifle. He was screaming something I did not understand. Those two involved did not get along. Welcome to Alpha Company!

DAZED AND CONFUSED

We are flown into a LZ on a hilltop that has been cleared and used previously. It has been raining hard for days and is still raining. The platoon leader and I have a strained relationship probably because I challenge authority. He instructs me to 'walk point' down the hill. I lead the company down the hill and pick up a path. Anything could have created. There are no footprints, animal or enemy, as they would have washed away. Vegetation is so wet and soggy that I cannot see on either side of the path. After about a mile of following the path I come to the stream crossing and observe.

The moss on the rocks in the center of the stream bed is worn away like someone is using the center of the stream as a path. The foliage on both sides is disturbed and is visibly pushed back as if large objects like timber or mortar tubes have been carried up the stream. There is a GI helmet strategically placed in the stream such that one would step on it to cross the stream to keep your feet out of the water and dry. Why was the helmet there? Was the helmet booby-trapped? If you step on it will it cause an explosion? I halted and called the platoon leader to see my discovery. To my amazement he calls command and we retrace our steps and move to a grassy area overlooking the wooded area we had come from. An observing Loche helicopter and Cobra gunship show up and fire rockets into the area. The platoon leader comes to us and states there might be some people appearing "dazed and confused."

This is long before the movie "Dazed and Confused" but I often think back on this to wonder what would have happened if I had stepped on the helmet in the stream bed. I believe the platoon leader made the correct decision to withdraw as I expect there was an NVA bunker complex ahead on the path.

Right: Alpha Company sign.

Middle: Loach observation helicopter coming in for a landing.

Lower: Cobra gunship parked between barriers.

Courtesy of Ron Hilfiker.

AIRBORNE

GERONIMO

A COMPANY
1ST BN.(AMBL) 501ST INF.
COMMANDING   1SG
CPT. ZAPERT   RUSSELL
GERONIMO, SIR!

ARC LIGHTNING

The Hueys drop us off about a mile from the mountains. It is a beautiful night and we are fully resupplied and even have air mattresses. Alpha Company is positioned so that we could ambush any enemy from the mountain to the low lands. Darkness comes and I am comfortable on the air mattress but it starts to rain. I feel the earth tremble and see what looks like heat lighting on the other side of the mountain. This is Operation Arc Light and is really B-52 air strikes on the Ho Chi Minh Trail. I cover up with my poncho and lay on my air mattress which keeps me surprisingly dry and then I hear "phsssssssshh....phsssshhh" as a hole develops in my air mattress. Now I am laying in a puddle but my body heat keeps the puddle warm so I can sleep.

In the morning we are dawn busters and I strip all my clothes off. Another soldier examines me for leeches and finds two, fat and happy, engorged with my blood. You cannot pull them off so he lights up a cigarette and touches the leeches with a hot tip and of course, the leeches release their attachment. You really do not feel them or know they are attached. During this, I notice a huge, unexploded bomb ten feet from where I was sleeping, mired in the mud. I tell my leech inspector to quickly get the Commanding Officer. He comes and realizes the danger of the situation and moves the whole company out of the area while someone detonates the bomb. I hear a huge explosion and the shrapnel singing through the air.

CHOPPER COUNTING

What is going on now? We are loaded up in cattle trucks and transported out of LZ Sally to the edge of the forest where we sit and wait. Two hours later the Hueys take us to a hilltop in the mountains.

One of the 'Shake 'n' Bake' sergeants goes out in an ambush and kills an NVA coming down the trail. He keeps the enemy's belt buckle and family photos but cannot sleep for a couple of nights. Later in his tour the sergeant is obsessed with ambushing and killing. I ask him why he has changed. He says he "relishes the look in the enemy's eyes when he sees me just before I pull the trigger for the kill shot."

The sergeant I speak of sold musical instruments before going into the Army and married into a Mormon family before going into the war. Such a transformation into a killing machine!

I get dysentery - or is it from the malaria suppressant pills? – orange large pill once per week – a little white one once a day. I am so sick I do not eat and run out of the perimeter at any moment. The medic is out of the medicine he needs to control it so I wait for the medicine until we return to LZ Sally.

The choppers return and pick us up leaving one platoon in ambush. The same number of choppers removes us and we hold up silhouette persons to look as if the chopper is fully loaded. Evidently, the enemy was receiving the chopper information from LZ Sally. So, we trick them into thinking that all of the troops had been removed. The NVA will always come up to the LZ to salvage anything we leave behind. That is what happens and the ambush is successful. The choppers go back and pick up the remaining platoon. End of mission!

Right:
Ron Hilfiker (first on left) with platoon mates.

Below:
Helicopters deployed on a mission.
Photos courtesy of Ron Hilfiker.

MAN'S ONLY FRIEND

The choppers drop us off at the base of the mountain and we start up a path through low forest. We are eating lunch when I hear mortar rounds being shot from the mountain top. There is about a five- to ten-second delay before they hit the ground and explode. Ron has no place to run and no place to hide but the mortar rounds miss the mark!

A chopper flies in with a scout dog (Labrador retriever), point man, and slack man. A point man is the first man leading the others and it is very dangerous as he is the first to engage in an ambush or detonate a booby trap. The slack man is next in line. The dog leads the way followed close behind by the point man, slack man, and the first platoon towards the location where the NVA fired the mortar. The dog scents the trail to the backside of the mountain. We all tag on.

The NVA usually locates their camps on the backside of the mountains away from our fire bases - or in this case LZ Sally. The high trajectory artillery is very inaccurate as it must shoot over the mountain to hit their camps. It is also more difficult to monitor the enemy's movements as they cannot be seen directly from our fire base. The dog continues to trail the enemy down the backside of the mountain and encounters two NVA soldiers. The point man shoots one and the other flees.

Our Kit Carson Scout recognizes the dead NVA as a fellow teacher before the NVA came and forced him to become a soldier. A Kit Carson Scout is an NVA soldier who has defected to our side and is very valuable as he knows the area and is fluent in Vietnamese and English.

The rest of the company move down the trail. As I walk down the path I realize that the vegetation above has been trained to conceal the corridor from helicopter observation. Then I freeze as we are standing in front of a completely camouflaged NVA bunker complex, but the enemy has fled. We explore around and uncover a cache of AK-47s and ammo camouflaged in their latrine area.

My company moves out, going a different way to the hilltop LZ. A few soldiers remain behind to blow up the bunkers before catching up with us. The choppers arrive and take my company to the next mission. The scout dog goes back to camp for a well-deserved meal as he prepares for his next assignment.

My luck holds up once again with a little help from man's only friend.

Right: (top left) Scout dog, "Rex" with Ron Hilfiker in background; (top right) Scout Dog orderly room; (middle) compound where dogs were kept when not working; (lower right) Scout Dog walking point with handler; (lower left) Van Longe, a Kit Carson Scout.
All photos courtesy of Ron Hilfiker.

PACHYDERM SCAT

The sortie of helicopters drops us off at the base of a mountain range after a long flight time. There is a large expanse of grasslands to the front and a low- growing forest that we take refuge in to avoid the heat. Someone says we are in Cambodia or Laos but I cannot confirm. It made sense because President Nixon is bombing in these countries to stop the NVA coming down the Ho Chi Minh trail. Anyway, I ask the company commander what the mission is. He states we are going up the hill to make a LZ on its top. I ask him what plan B is and he states there is no plan B.

One of the platoons starts cutting a trail up the hill with machetes. I and another guy are warming our C-rat with heat tabs that are provided. Someone from back home sent me some hot sauce that adds variety and flavor. We pretend we are back home at our favorite restaurant having a gourmet meal. It works to mentally take your mind away from the current situation.

I explore the immediate area and notice that the tree bark is all torn up and branches are broken, creating a trail. I follow it for a while wondering if the enemy was using motorized vehicles here. Then I come across huge piles of dung similar to horse dung. Elephants! That night I have trouble sleeping because I have the thought of a herd of elephants using the trail and trampling us to death.

Morning arrives and we are dawn busters with the 1st platoon cutting trails. Then the 2nd platoon falls in moving up the hill. Then the headquarters element, 3rd platoon, and 4th platoon...The sun comes out and it is extremely hot, probably over 100 degrees. Soon the medic is sending soldiers down the hill with heat exhaustion. We never made the top of the steep hill and choppers eventually arrive to transport the unit to a new area and mission. It must be plan B.

SKINNY DIPPING

The helicopter drops us off in a valley with a river flowing through it. The Hueys cannot set down on the ground as there are stumps hidden in knee-high elephant grass. We jump the remaining six feet not knowing what or where we are going to hit. Once we start setting up in a perimeter it becomes evident that there is higher ground on three sides. I talk to the commanding officer and want to know where he went to military school as this is a disadvantageous situation. He said it looks like we are being used as bait and 20 minutes later a platoon on Recon near the river encounters the enemy swimming in its water. They fire up the enemy but do not hit them. The naked enemy is running down the trail along the river.

The platoon radios in and the company commander tells them not to proceed as he fears an ambush is set up. Fire power is ordered by the CO and soon F-105 smaller bomber jets appear. We lay down hugging the ground and I hear the guy next to me start to whimper, "the bombs are falling on us." I look to the sky above me to see jets releasing bombs overhead before peeling off to circle around for another run at the hill. I explain to him that the speed of the jet will cause the trajectory of the bomb to carry into the side of the mountain. He says, "I sure hope that trajectory stuff works." Thank goodness for the laws of physics!

No enemy shows itself but we are on 100% alert for the night. In other words, no one sleeps. My eyes stay open. They close and I force them open. I see movement but it is only my foot and I am glad I didn't shoot it. The next day we are pulled out of the area!

Left: Ron heating up C-rations. Courtesy of Ron Hilfiker.

Right: Mountain scene. White puffs of smoke in the background show area being prepped with artillery.

Courtesy of Ron Hilfiker.

WHITE CLOUD MOUNTAIN FISH

Back at LZ Sally after the rain stops we are assembled in a company formation. Top - 1st Sergeant - explains that we are going on a very important mission to be a blocking force in the Rung Rung Valley. Top states he knows we have drugs, marijuana, opium, etc. and he does not want this going to the field. He turns his back to the formation and says he will not court-martial anyone if they give it up now. Some came forward and drop it at the ground behind him.

He turns around and says, "Must be you don't understand I am going through your gear and if I find drugs I will court-martial you." He turns his back again and more come forward and deposit their stash. Top then burns the pile in front of everyone and starts going through everyone's gear. He finds drugs and is true to his word.

Geared up to go out on a mission. Courtesy of Ron Hilfiker.

Being at LZ Sally we are given cold sodas and beer. I have been drinking all day and am drunk. Not thinking clearly, I pack some beer and ice in a rubberized bag. So when I load on the Huey I carry my M-16, combat rucksack with radio and the bag full of refreshments. The Huey lands on a hilltop LZ and to my amazement a General is there directing the situation. I never have seen this before or after but I sober up fast. We hike down the hill and I pass the beer around to the other guys to get rid of it.

In the morning we hike up another hill and our temporary CO is a 50+ year old from the National Guard. He is having trouble physically with the heat and the hill climb and says to me, "Do not off-load ammo or water – only food." I gladly take his unwanted C-ration. We are short on water because of the heat and we hike down to the stream and follow it up to a canyon. At the end there is a beautiful waterfall and pool at its base. This reminds me of Rainbow Cove on Seneca Lake where some of my buddies and I stream fish for trout. The air temperature in the canyon is cooler and the water is fresh and cold. Some of us lap it like a dog and others suck the water as if we are elephants. As I peer into the pool I see some small fish that I recognize from when I had a tropical fish aquarium growing up. These were White Cloud Mountain fish that are native to Vietnam.

MALARIA OR FROSTBITE?

It seems like it is raining forever with high winds. We are soaked. Our area of operation is a forested mountain top and the wind does not let up. I am so cold. How can I be cold in Vietnam? Trust me, as the wind evaporates the water from your clothing, it also takes the heat from your body.

Soon we have no radio communication; we are out of food for three days and we have no chance for a new supply. One of the men is diagnosed with appendicitis so it is decided to hike down to lowlands for medical help. I help carry him in a makeshift stretcher. Once we are on the lowlands stream crossing becomes an issue. On one crossing the man immediately ahead of me falters in the water and cannot swim. I grab him by the rucksack so he can regain his footing.

We hike to an area where the cattle truck transports us to LZ Sally. Once at the base camp the man with appendicitis is re-diagnosed with constipation. Constipation delivered us from the monsoon rain and cold! Yeah!

I recall that in Advance Infantry training at Fort Polk, Louisiana, part of our training was to watch a movie on malaria. When we went to the classroom we were shown a movie on frostbite and then this is repeated again and again. Finally, someone asks, "Shouldn't we see the malaria movie as the majority of us are going to Vietnam?" The response is, "Oh, the malaria movie is broken so we are showing the frostbite one instead." Given how cold I was maybe the training did make sense after all.

UBI UBI ESTNE SUB UBI

It was the week before Thanksgiving and we have been rained on for two weeks. The clothing is literally rotting on our bodies and the seams are splitting open. While the line of soldiers is slogging down the path all I see are bright white asses peeking out of the split-seamed trousers. We do not wear underwear as the groin area will remain moist. When the sun is out the sweat will collect there and when it is raining there is a double layer to hold the moisture. This is the perfect environment for "crotch rot" a fungal infection that if not treated, can infect the rest of the body and is most difficult to treat in the RVN humidity situation.

On Thanksgiving Day, Striker the Battalion Commander appears in a Huey helicopter loaded with dry clothes and socks as well as hot Thanksgiving dinner compete with dressing, mash potatoes, and gravy. I wash off in a cold stream and notice I can peel my skin off my feet (looks like dishpan hands.) The dry clothes are instantly wet but do not smell and the seams are not split. Good as it gets!

Oh, I need to tell you about "Ubi Ubi Estne Sub Ubi." In high school I was required to take some language so I took Latin. The teacher was a quite older woman but our American history teacher was very lively and came up with this group of words. Which, if you use a literal translation means, *"Oh where, Oh where is my under where?"*

GOOK HUNTER

I was a "short-timer" driving jeep in the rear and not in the field at the time this happened, but it is one instance of friendly fire.

A chopper was outside its area of operation and decided to go "gook hunting." Gook is slang that refers to anyone of Asian origin and in this case means the enemy or NVA or VC. Referring to the enemy with these terms also dehumanizes them. So, when you waste one you are not killing another human being like yourself. I expect that the chopper pilot or door gunners might have been high or drunk. They saw movement on a hill top and fired it up with M-60 machine guns. The movement was a squad from our company and two men were hit with .30 caliber bullets from the machine guns.

As reported to me, one took two rounds through the lungs but his death was averted by sealing the entrance and exit wounds so his lungs did not collapse. The second man was not as lucky as he took a round to the groin that severed the femoral artery. The position of the wound did not allow the medic to apply a tourniquet and I expect he bled out in minutes. "Top" (our 1st sergeant) went over to the chopper squadron and spoke to the warrant officer in charge. I am not sure if anyone was ever court-martialed or not.

VOLLEYBALL

The last two months of my tour I was a jeep driver in the motor pool for our company. One day the 1st sergeant has me drive him to the hospital to visit some company members that are healing up. As we arrive we spot other members of the company standing on the helicopter pad. There are also body bags lining the pad. We walk over and see that they are wounded and shivering with fear, probably either from anxiety attacks or shock.

This picture is burned into my mind forever - the door gunner washing out the helicopter with a garden hose causing a bright river of blood to run onto the pad. Later that week we drive over to identify the bodies. As we pull up, some soldiers are playing volleyball and one leaves the group to open up the walk-in cooler. One at a time he unzips the bags so we can identify the bodies inside. We sign some paperwork and he goes back to the volleyball game.

Left: (Top) Image of Huey out on patrol.
(Lower) Close up of door gunner's M-60 gun barrel. Courtesy of Ron Hilfiker.

Charles "Chuck" Freese's Story

❀❀❀❀❀❀❀❀❀❀❀❀❀❀❀❀❀❀❀❀❀

Army Infantry – 11B

I arrived in Vietnam mid-July, 1969 after flying from New Jersey to California, to Hawaii, to Okinawa, and then into 'Nam. It was a charter flight with all new recruits to be assigned various duties in Vietnam. Once in 'Nam I was assigned to the Americal Division, which was based in Chu Lai. Chu Lai is located in the northern sector of South Vietnam, which was the operating area for most of the North Vietnamese army, along with the Viet Cong. It was a large base with an airfield, hospital, supply depot, and all the support personnel to keep a large field force operating.

The procedure for new soldiers was to get a couple days of training and get used to the heat and humidity. Then I was flown south about 100 miles to Duc Pho, home of the 11th Brigade, my outfit to be. I landed in a KC 130 plane with sandbags on the entire floor. I was told they stopped some of the smaller caliber shots from getting in when we landed or took off at the end of runways. Then I was airlifted into the field where the line company was operating (line company being a combat group of about 150 men or fewer). I got a helicopter ride out with the mail and other supplies; now I was in Delta Co. and knew right away this was not going to be a good year.

Delta Co. was part of a battalion called 1st/20th - a battalion consists of four combat line companies. When Delta Co. was not in the bush or field, they were at their home firebase. When at the firebase, we were the base security. Life on the firebase was such that a squad of men stayed in a perimeter guarding bunker, slept on cots, took turns watching the wire, and keeping a 24-hour guard. Only time we got hot meals, took a shower, or had a cold beer was our time at the firebase. The line companies rotated in and out of the base about once a month, so for three weeks or so you had no good food, you slept on the ground, you smelled really bad and you constantly fought off bugs,

Landing zone LIZ with observation post on hilltop. Located about ten miles NW of Duc Pho, LIZ was home to artillery battery, mortar support team, and recon platoon of the 1st, 20th Battalion. Courtesy of Chuck Freese.

leeches, snakes, and the pesky enemy. The weather was also a big party killer - either too hot, too cold at night, or constantly wet during monsoon season.

In late August while on the firebase, I volunteered to go in the Recon platoon. I had to pass a few tests, and a two-day question and answer session with their commander and 1st Lt. My first night was not so good, as Recon assigned me a small bunker (two-person hole in the side of the hill). When I went to the mess hall to eat, my now unmet roomie came back to base from a Recon patrol and as I walked up to the bunker I saw my gear being tossed out the door. This was not a good start, we had a little scrap, and a couple guys separated us. My "to-be-roomie" was not a people person, and I was sent to another bunker with other Recon guys. "Mr. Battle," my ex-roomie, lived alone, I guess I passed the last test, so I was told.

Our Recon platoon was an interesting mix of characters. I learned to trust them all, and I learned a lot. Our missions were a wide variety of types: night ambushes to restrict the Viet Cong's movements and disrupt their communities; observing NVA troop movements; scouting out villages; following suspected Cong and looking for tunnels. Most of our work was done at night – we hid and slept during the day. One such day I was sleeping and was gently awakened by a buddy to tell me not to move, as a bamboo viper was curled up and sunning itself on my chest. Bamboo vipers are light green, small and thin, but very deadly. He left when the sun's rays moved off me. Did I mention I hate snakes big time? His last session of sunbathing was that one.

One day while observing a village from a distance, we saw several NVA troops beating a couple old villagers. Our orders were to move in and possibly capture one or more of the NVA soldiers. We made a plan, and a couple of us moved around to the backside of the last hut. Jungle cover helped me and a buddy to get in close. When the shooting started an NVA and a tall guy in a different uniform came running around the hut and right into our guns. The NVA tried to fire but my buddy shot him. I was locked in eye to eye with this young, tall guy. He had a pistol half drawn, but not out of its holster. He was looking back out front when he rounded the corner. He put his hands up quickly, even before I spoke.

We had a prisoner, but what the heck was he? Turns out he was Chinese. They were demanding the villagers get and store rice for them to use during a coming offensive in the area. This guy was with us a couple of days while we were on patrol. He never spoke to us and was no trouble. One night he heard us talking about the war and something set him to speaking. We were in shock - he spoke perfect English. He told us his rank – a Major in the People's Republic of China Army, and he had attended college in California for 2 ½ years. When we got back from patrol we never saw him again, but we got two nice bottles of liquor from the brass.

This observing of villages paid off another day as we watched about 20 Viet Cong jump down a well in the middle of this village to avoid a line company making a sweep of the area. The line company came into that village and found nothing until we radioed for the OK to proceed into the village and link up with the line company. Together we found a tunnel complex that was huge; the wall had a hole under the water that came up like a beaver's house. Very clever enemy we were dealing with.

Time and days seemed to stand still, but I remember one day while hiding and napping that it was almost Thanksgiving Day; that meant that Christmas was in the near future. Christmas was going to be here, and right afterward I was going to Australia on R&R. The thought of R&R was a big deal, and I was so excited to see Australia. It turned out not to be. About 3pm on December 21st, I was on a patrol and following some NVA troops and was wounded along with five other guys. On a hilltop someone or something set off a buried 105mm artillery shell right in front of me and six of us found ourselves lying where the blast had tossed us.

On this particular patrol we had seven guys (rather than the usual five or six men), lucky for us one man (Bob Gee) was unhurt. He was on the radio fast calling for a dust-off or medevac helicopter and was checking on us and propping us up if we could still shoot. He pulled me up so I was leaning on my backpack with my rifle in my right hand. The NVA were still close by and we were expecting the enemy to emerge at any second to finish us off.

Several minutes passed and a helicopter landed on this hilltop, the only clear space anywhere near us. The helicopter was carrying a full-bird Colonel and he loaded me and a couple others on his helicopter and he stayed with our survivor to guard the other wounded until another helicopter could come in. This Colonel was risking his life for us, and was a short-timer also.

We were airlifted to Duc Pho where the nearest medical facility was located. I was medicated and wrapped in bandages, given blood, and flown to Chu Lai where the Army surgical hospital was at that time. I was in and out of consciousness. My first real memory was the next day as the head surgical nurse explained my injuries and the time frame of my care. The nurse told me that the doctor who operated on me was very busy, and had been in surgery for over twenty hours straight when I was brought in around 11PM.

My surgery lasted four hours and he took extra time to attach my left thumb, which another doctor wanted to take off. He thought it would not be of any use to me. Well my thumb is working great, no knuckle in it, but it is great. How lucky I was to have such a great doctor work on me, he did work some other magic also, but to be as tired as he must have been, and to take extra time on me says it all for the dedicated medical people we had. My stay in Chu Lai was about a week, and then I was flown to Cam Rahn Bay where I spent the night, then I was flown to Camp Zama in the middle of Tokyo, Japan. I had surgery on my left foot while there and stayed there for about a week. Then I was flown to Baltimore with a refueling stop in Anchorage, Alaska.

Top: A copy of Chuck's Purple Heart award.
Lower: Paper unknown, dated 2/11/1970.
Images courtesy of Chuck Freese.

THE UNITED STATES OF AMERICA

TO ALL WHO SHALL SEE THESE PRESENTS, GREETING:

THIS IS TO CERTIFY THAT
THE PRESIDENT OF THE UNITED STATES OF AMERICA
HAS AWARDED THE

PURPLE HEART

ESTABLISHED BY GENERAL GEORGE WASHINGTON
AT NEWBURGH, NEW YORK, AUGUST 7, 1782
TO

SPECIALIST FOURTH CLASS CHARLES FREESE

FOR WOUNDS RECEIVED
IN ACTION
On 20 December 1969 in the Republic of Vietnam
GIVEN UNDER MY HAND IN THE CITY OF WASHINGTON
THIS TWENTY-SECOND DAY OF DECEMBER 19 69

ALTON F. GROSS
MAJ, MC
27th Surgical Hospital
Commanding

Stanley R. Resor
SECRETARY OF THE ARMY

CAMP ZAMA, JAPAN - Army Specialist Four Charles R. Freese, left, 20, son of Mr. and Mrs. Kenneth Freese, Sr., Nations Road, Geneseo, when a patient at the U.S. Army Hospital, Camp Zama, Japan, received a visit from U. S. Representative Martin B. McKneally (R - N.Y.) on Jan. 6. Freese is now at St. Albans Naval Hospital in New York City and visits his parents some weekends. Spec. 4 Freese served as an infantryman Company E, 1st Battalion, 20th Infantry Brigade near Duc Pho, Vietnam. He entered the Army in February 1969 and completed basic training at Ft. Dix, N.J.. The specialist holds the Purple Heart. He is a 1967 graduate of Geneseo Central. (U. S. Army photo).

Once in Baltimore I was taken by hospital bus to the Naval Hospital at St. Albans, New York on Super Bowl Sunday (mid-January, 1970.) At St. Albans I had a couple surgeries and physical therapy until March 30th and then was given leave to come home for a couple weeks. My next Army stay was at Ft. Riley, Kansas where I had therapy every day and worked in a supply room for the incoming replacements.

My care was great and helped me recover well, my wounds numbered over forty - face, both hands, both arms, stomach, both legs, and left foot. I consider myself one lucky guy, doing OK. I've been through some trying times over the years, but I can't complain. Lots of guys never got a chance to heal or complain. This was harder to do than I thought it would be.

"Gaza Strip Operation Clears 8900 Acres of Harsh Terrain Near Duc Pho"
Southern Cross newspaper, 11/7/1969, p. 4-5

I was standing right back here about 30 feet

Takes Land Or Water With Ease

A rare amphibious landing in the tradition and excitement of World War II recently took place on the Gaza Strip northwest of Duc Pho.

The land clearing project was a joint Army-Marine mission involving about 220 men, to start a massive 8900 acre land clearing operation. Tracks and infantrymen from the 11th Bde. debarked support landing crafts to provide the engineers with the needed security during the operation. Working on a 30 day timetable the engineers are required to clear the rugged terrain of pine forests, jungle foliage rice paddies, and beaches.

Twenty bulldozers, taking only time for brief coordination, immediately started the operation by moving "en masse" clearing everything in their path.

"It is our third operation with the Army engineers, we work well together," said CPT Richard Schoaf (Atlanta, Georgia.) However, said the Marine, "It's the infantrymen, they are outstanding, they give us great security."

The two month old provisional company immediately faced an area full of booby-traps, mines, and other anti-personal devices. But pre-planning paid off as a nine-man demolition team was landed with the engineers and troops to destroy or disarm any discovered devices.

When the clearing operation is completed the enemy in this area will be deprived of a sanctuary, vulnerable to attack, and powerless to continue their terrorist tactics.

Chuck Freese provided this article and notes his location on the news photo above.

CERTIFICATE OF APPRECIATION

CHARLES ROBERT FREESE   SPECIALIST FOURTH CLASS   UNITED STATES ARMY

24 February 1969   thru   23 February 1971

I extend to you my personal thanks and the sincere appreciation of a grateful nation for your contribution of honorable service to our country. You have helped maintain the security of the nation during a critical time in its history with a devotion to duty and a spirit of sacrifice in keeping with the proud tradition of the military service.

I trust that in the coming years you will maintain an active interest in the Armed Forces and the purpose for which you served.

My best wishes to you for happiness and success in the future.

Richard Nixon

COMMANDER IN CHIEF

DA FORM 1725

DEPARTMENT OF THE ARMY

CERTIFICATE OF APPRECIATION

In recognition of the active service of

CHARLES R. FREESE 085 38 4600 SPECIALIST E-4   AUS   INF

The United States Army presents this testimonial
of esteem and gratitude for
Faithful Performance
of duty

23 February 1971
DATE

W. C. WESTMORELAND
General, United States Army
Chief of Staff

DA FORM 3822

Military certificates provided by Chuck Freese.

Roger Johnson's Story
✿✿✿✿✿✿✿✿✿✿

Above: Roger having a somber moment on "stand down." Photo courtesy of Roger Johnson.

<u>Introduction</u>

Time had passed so quickly since the Spring of 1965 when after gym class at GCS class advisor and friend Butch Rosebrugh told me that he had enlisted in the Marine Corps. The smile on his face and the excitement in his voice halted me from asking him why. He was most certainly happy and very proud of his decision.

Again at school in October of 1966, I heard that Butch had been killed in action in that far away place called Vietnam. It was very difficult for me to comprehend his death after seeing him so happy telling me of his enlistment. It was even harder seeing him being laid to rest at the Lakeview Cemetery.

Graduation came for me in June of 1967 and it was then that I started my career as a clerk/carrier at the Geneseo Post Office. In December, I learned that a family new to Geneseo and living on Oak Street had just been informed that their husband and father Charles Wilkie was killed in action in Vietnam. While delivering the mail there I was fearful that if someone had come to the door I would not have known what to say.

In January 1968 the darkness came once again to Geneseo when the notice of Bobby Henderson being KIA in Vietnam arrived. I had known Bobby - not that well, but it mattered not as he too was in school with us at GCS and had walked amongst us in the town.

The deaths of Butch, Charlie, and Bobby impacted me deeply, but I was not brave enough to enlist on behalf of their memories. I would wait for the draft to serve in this small and far away place called Vietnam; I would not have to wait very long.

Our flight originated from Sea-Tac airport in Washington State, October 1, 1969 and its only stop so far was in Guam where we re-fueled. While we were taking off I looked down to see US B-52s lined up in their "reventment walls" - it was quite a sight. The flight was very long and I had dozed off; as I awoke I looked out from my window seat. I saw bright flashes and my mind ran away with the thought that, *"My God, that must be Vietnam below us."* As my mind cleared I came to realize that what I was watching was in reality flashes of lightning as our airliner was passing over a storm.

This whole thing was surreal to me as only a bit over four months ago I had been drafted into the US Army and now I was only a few hours away from landing in South Vietnam. Our aircraft touched down at the sprawling US military base at Cam Ranh Bay. As the plane doors opened and we exited, the heat and humidity that greeted me was oppressive. As we moved towards a staging area where we FNGs were to go for our next set of orders, we became very aware of those soldiers who were getting ready to leave Vietnam after having served their tours. They appeared so much more mature or seasoned, and they let us know that they had been "there" and we were about to find out what war was really about.

We were housed in a large metal billet where we were to stay while orders to our units were being cut. I had my afternoon meal and went back to our quarters for the night. I had just nicely dozed off when suddenly something hit my chest ,waking me. The GI next to me said, *"Did you see the size of that F------ rat that just jumped across your chest?"* What a freaking place.

The next day my orders came down and I was going to be assigned to the 5th Battalion, 46th Infantry, 198th Light Infantry Brigade of the Americal Division based in Chu Lai in I Corps. We were loaded into a C130 aircraft where we sat on the floor and had straps from both sides of the plane act as seatbelts. The plane started the engines and the craft shook and rattled and after about 15 minutes I stood up to see how high we were, only to find out that we had not left the ground. I think that is why they called us FNGs.

Platoon mates Bravo Co.
5/46 HQ.
Courtesy of Roger Johnson.

We arrived in Chu Lai and were quickly sent to our units. I was now a member of B-Company, and began the process of meeting the supply SSGT and gearing up for the field. He was a pleasant fellow and filled me in on my being a replacement for the losses just suffered by the company. There had been two or three KIAs and more WIA so they needed new guys in the field. That same day I was on a chopper heading to my new platoon.

Riding to my unit right out of the box in a Huey was a new experience in itself. The guys on the ground 'popped smoke' and the chopper quickly dropped to the ground, we unloaded and the chopper was on its way. A good sized Buck Sgt. approached me, introduced himself as Sgt. Depuy and welcomed me to his squad. I was on the ground and scared as hell.

Sgt. Depuy walked me around to meet the other squad leaders, Cremer, Popovich and Kelly. They seemed like great young men and offered their advice: pay attention, listen closely to what they told me, and maybe we all would get to go home one day. As darkness fell on our NDP, a lone shot came from the wood line above us. I ducked, while the others did not seem too bothered; now I knew I was a FNG.

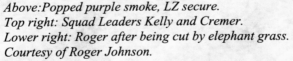

Above: Popped purple smoke, LZ secure.
Top right: Squad Leaders Kelly and Cremer.
Lower right: Roger after being cut by elephant grass.
Courtesy of Roger Johnson.

In the first few days with my platoon I quickly learned how much ground we could cover and how extremely heavy my rucksack was. We typically carried four to seven days of C-rations, two to four grenades, two or three bandoliers of M-16 ammo, normally one hundred rounds of M-60 ammo, smoke grenades, a claymore mine, trip flares, no less than two or three canteens of water, and whatever else we may need. Often after taking breaks to rest, we would have to help pull each other up rather than take the rucksack off.

As seen in the movie *Platoon*, where the new guys walked point, our unit never put the new guys on point as their inexperience could very easily get them and those close to them killed. It was a month or better before I was positioned at point and even then it was a frightening job. We covered open rice paddies as well as mountainous areas. Jungle areas that were so thick you could not see five feet ahead of you. It was one of these areas, with elephant grass of eight or nine feet in height, that I took the wrong split in a trail and became separated from the rest of the platoon; scared the hell out of me. Later on, the razor edges of that elephant grass cut me so badly I was bandaged up from neck to waist.

Our AO was north and west of Chu Lai as well as south and west to the mountains and to the southeast to include the Quang Ngai province. It was in the Quang Ngai province near the village of Son My where there were six small hamlets named My Lai and each were identified by a number, 1 through 6. Our companies and my platoon worked in and around all of the six My Lai hamlets and it was in My Lai 4 that I had my first experience with the horrors of war.

We combat-assaulted into the edge of My Lai 4 with a platoon-sized force. There we hooked up with a Marine CAP team of four men working with the residents of the hamlet. We were informed by the Marines that the entire area had a very strong presence of Viet Cong and their sympathizers as well as being the AO of the 48th Viet Cong Local Force Battalion of the National Liberation Front (NLF). This enemy force was a battle-hardened, well-entrenched force that our troops were constantly chasing and doing battle with. They were a very dangerous enemy and were made much more difficult to find as they so easily slipped back in amongst their families in the villages and hamlets. The Marines needed to move from hootch to hootch so that they would be relatively safe from any attack. Our first night on the outskirts of the ville all hell broke out as the Viet Cong attempted to kill the Marines in the village and tried to cause any sort of hell for our platoon. I remember all of the tracers flying towards and over our position. That turned out to be my first real firefight. It only lasted for about 10 to 15 minutes, but it was more than enough to help season me as a grunt. My CIB was earned that very night.

After a long and nervous night, morning came and we learned that no one in the CAP team had been injured in the attack, but they had killed one of the "dinks" that had attacked them. Some of our guys, including myself, were asked to walk up to the ville to talk with the Marines and see the results of the attack. As we neared I

Top: Huey on CA mission over "Fat City." Lower left: Roger geared up. Right: Platoon mates at the ville they protected called My Lai 4. Courtesy of Roger Johnson.

saw the body of a person dressed in the "black pajamas," a term we had heard of since basic training. I saw a motionless body and from behind his ears, his skull was gone. The sight rattled me, but I then knew this was what I needed to get used to.

During that day patrols were sent out around the village looking for any and all signs of the enemy, but all came back in without any contact. As darkness fell on the area I was told I would be going out on my first ambush to cover a trail used the night before by the VC that had attacked the ville. Ambush teams were comprised of 4 to 6 men and were used as an early warning of enemy movements at night. They were also used to destroy enemy units moving while near our area.

We left the security of the platoon and headed towards our ambush site. As we were preparing to set out our trip flares and Claymore mines to cover the trail, the stench was horrible. I had no idea at first that our ambush site was in fact the villagers' dung field. I can't begin to express how disgusting the smell was and the very thought of being set in the middle of such a foul location. There was no contact that night and I could not wait to get back to the platoon.

The next day we were back on the Hueys heading back to our LZ. Our brigade headquarters was in Chu Lai, but we spent most of our time between missions at one of two LZs. One was called LZ Gator and a second called LZ Bayonet. Gator was where most of our CA missions left from. While there we would take re-supply, pull bunker guard, have hot chow and enjoy a hot shower. Those were great treats as our platoon and company would often be in the field three to five days, and up to two weeks at time.

While pulling bunker guard one night at Gator, I was paired up with one of the guys whose job was in the rear at Gator. We grunts never were too excited about that type of pairing as the rear guys never were as focused as they needed to be. After I finished my shift, I woke this guy up for his shift. The next thing I knew I was being awakened by one of the night officers who told me that the man I had put on guard was found sleeping at his post. That could have gotten us either both killed by the enemy or given Article 15s by the commander of the base. I had a conversation with the officer and he accepted my claim. You might say I spent the rest of that night telling the guy found sleeping just how little I thought of his actions.

Most stays at the LZs or in Chu Lai were short in duration, one to three days as a rule, for clean-up and re-supply. They also were our opportunities to unwind or to decompress. While on our missions we had to be on the edge, always on full alert you might say, never allowing ourselves to drop our guard. That is just the way it had to be.

While in Chu Lai we enjoyed hot meals, cold 3.2 beer and watched movies. Mostly being there, where we did not pull any sort of guard duty, we actually got reasonable sleep. What a treat. In the field, sleep was very hard to get as you were pulling watch every two or three hours.

Above: Aerial view of LZ Gator. Lower: On patrol near Police Call Hill.
Courtesy of Roger Johnson.

I had been in the field nearly two months when our platoon had completed our sweep and mission and was lucky enough to get into LZ Gator for Thanksgiving. Oh man what a treat - turkey and all the trimmings and out of the field to boot. It was great but was tempered by a conversation I heard between a junior and senior officer. We had not yet known that one of our sister companies had been in some 'shit' a day or two before and sustained some KIAs and WIAs. The junior officer said to his superior that he was sorry about the losses. The senior officer then stated that it was all right as he had replacements coming in. I felt that his words were so out of place for having just lost some of our troops. So cold and matter of fact, his words still remain in my mind even today.

I was getting more comfortable with my platoon mates and I am sure they were more accepting of me as I was always hanging on their every word. As a grunt everything was a learning experience. I got to see the old "punji pit" traps that were so very lethal at the beginning of the war, but that had become somewhat less effective because of better combat boots with steel plates in the bottom of the soles and heels. The booby traps were everywhere: wired to trip wires on the ground, on paddy dikes, trails, and even hanging in the trees; so very deadly, and a constant worry.

While on patrol one time I was second in line following a squad leader nick-named Dixie when he hit a trip wire connected to a juice can. I was looking right at him when it exploded. I was about 20 feet behind him and I momentarily froze as we did not know whether we had walked into a mine field or what. When the smoke cleared, I yelled for the medic and got to Dixie as quickly as I could. He was yelling in pain but at the same time he was telling me that was the third one (third Purple Heart) and that he was going home. His fatigue pants were full of small tears where the shrapnel had created his wounds. I am sure that there must have been 50 or better wounds in his legs and lower torso but he survived and was going back to the 'world.'

One of our other platoons had been set up in a different area and received orders to relocate and patrol. Mission completed and they returned to the location they had left days before. Their platoon leader decided that he would set up in the very same spot that he had placed his gear before. Setting his gear down he tripped a trip wire and his right arm was blown off. Those freaking booby traps and mines had neither heart nor soul and they would haunt us again in the near future.

At times we really enjoyed ourselves. When we had mail call in the field it was almost like a mini Christmas. We all shared the highs and lows and the packages. A package filled with baked goods, canned goods, hard candy and most everything else was like enjoying a 5-star restaurant. Everyone shared in the wealth. Sometimes they included 'luxuries' such as film, toiletry items and batteries. We also shared news from home, good and bad. The most feared letters were those notifying everyone of the loss of friends and relatives or the dreaded "Dear John" letters.

We all leaned on each other to help with the many different letters received. One I remember well was received by one of the guys I felt very close to. We were in the field and all who had received any sort of letter or package was busily going through their treasures. All of a sudden my friend started to rip up his letter and its contents. Our first thought was that it was the dreaded "Dear John." As we tried to console him he told us that was not the case. We questioned him further to try to comfort him and he told us that he had told his girlfriend that he wanted very much to have a picture of her in the nude and by George she had fulfilled his request. We asked what the problem was and he told us that now he had no idea who had taken the picture. We were all so close, we laughed together and we cried together. That is what got us through it all.

Our missions continued into the mountains and the rice paddies. I can't even guess how many 'klicks' we would cover every day trying to find our elusive enemy. Many days we would not see any villages or Vietnamese. We would find deserted villages and nothing more. When we did find active villages and questioned the residents, we found them unwilling to share information. The Viet Cong did not treat any villager who shared information with us kindly and I soon became aware of the tough spot we put them in. We could not be there to protect them. There were times when we made great strides in working to help such villagers with medical care, sharing food and treats. I loved working with the kids. For the most part they were like the kids back home, full of life and smiles even with the war all around them.

In one village we spent time in, a 'mama-san' invited me and another guy to share her meal. The basic meal was rice, a type of potato, and fish heads. As it was cooking, it smelled like the most vile food I had ever been near or eaten. I did not want her to feel humiliated so we ate it. One helping was more than enough and then we thanked her and went on back over with our guys.

We often encountered "soda girls," young girls that appeared as soon as we worked into an area. They seemed to have an endless supply of ice–cold Coca Cola and we saw them as future entrepreneurs. They were very friendly and always a treat to be around. After I got my rear job later in my tour, one of these "soda girls" got a note to my platoon still in the field and my guys got it to me in the rear. Her writing was quite good and I was very surprised to have heard from her.

Our chopper combat assaults took us to so many different locations in our AO. One assault took us into an area where an Armored Unit, M-60 tanks, and APCs had turned a rice paddy area into pure mud, most likely to destroy the food source of the enemy. The door gunner yelled to me that they could not set the chopper down and that we would have to jump from four or five feet above the ground. That would be a first for me but when they gave the OK, out I went. When my first leg hit the mire I tried moving forward to keep my balance and fell face first into the muck. I could hardly pull myself out of the mess. As I looked back towards the chopper I saw the Warrant Officers laughing like crazy. I guess that they were enjoying the mess

Top: Chinook after dropping supplies. During monsoon season support became limited.
Lower left: Squad Leader "Dixie" smiles through the pain after being wounded by a booby trap because he knows he will receive a 3rd Purple Heart and be sent home.
Lower right: My-Lee, a young "soda girl." Photos courtesy of Roger Johnson.

Mountain view from LZ Gator tower. Courtesy Roger Johnson.

Patrol using rice paddy dike.
Courtesy Roger Johnson.

that they helped me get into. Once we secured the area, it took me quite a while to get my M-16 cleaned and able to fire. What a mess.

To this point I had not really been that close to injury or death, but that would soon change. We broke our NDP and headed out through some very heavy cover. We were in a platoon-size group and it was quite slow-moving. It was mid-morning when the lead members reached an opening where the cover broke into a rice paddy. It was decided that we could make somewhat better time if the platoon crossed the paddy. That typically would be ill-advised as it would expose the entire platoon to an attack. The decision was made to make the crossing and the platoon started moving once again.

The rice paddy was narrow, probably about one hundred yards wide and five to six hundred feet long. Most of the platoon was nearly halfway across before I reached the opening. I was second to last in the platoon and a young black kid called "Houdini" was in the rear. I remember how quiet and still it was, when all of a sudden a splash of water about two feet to my immediate left was followed by the sound of a rifle shot. As I turned towards the cover where the shot had come from, a second round hit again to my left. I was trying to get behind the paddy dike, when my rucksack strap broke and knocked me off balance just as the third round fired and struck again, hitting just to the left of my feet.

When I got to the ground I began firing at the location where I thought the sniper may have been positioned. Both Houdini and I laid down fire but the enemy shooting had already stopped. The medic started running towards me and I yelled to him to stay there as I had not been hit but most certainly had been rattled. How lucky I had been that the shooter had under-shot me, and misjudged the range. When I got my composure, Houdini and I caught up with the remainder of the platoon and my first request was for a smoke. I was shaking so bad I needed to do something to calm my nerves.

There was never a lot of time between missions and soon after my near-miss we were in the choppers again back to My Lai. This mission included a second platoon and one of the guys was a fellow that I had gotten to know quite well at LZ Gator. He was like us all, young, full of life and was quick with a smile. On this particular morning this young friend was on a patrol a few hundred yards from the village where my platoon was when a single shot echoed across the open ground between where we were set up and the wood line where the patrol was working. Within moments our radios started crackling the request for a medevac chopper to be dispatched to our location as a 'pack' was injured and needed immediate medical care. Names were never used in the field but all soldiers were given what was called a pack number to identify them.

We heard the response from the medevac chopper that they were airborne when a second transmission on the radio told the medevac chopper that they would not be needed as a second chopper would extract the wounded. A few minutes later we heard the in-bound chopper as it approached. Valuable minutes were passing as the Huey arrived only to circle high above the pick-up location. The unit whose man was seriously wounded asked frantically to get the chopper on the ground to extract their wounded man, only to be told that the extraction could not take place until the area was secure. Guys in our platoon, including me, were saying that was total bullshit as the attack that had wounded our soldier appeared to have been a single sniper attack and that the enemy soldier was long gone. Still the chopper circled high above for many more minutes without any attempt to land. After what seemed to be an eternity the chopper finally touched down and the wounded soldier was carried off to the hospital where he died shortly after arrival.

When the involved platoon hooked up with us shortly thereafter, I found out that the wounded soldier was the young man that I had gotten to know at LZ Gator and my heart sunk. We were all broken up as we had just seen one of our own wounded. That news was made worse when the other platoon members told us the reason that the extraction had taken so very long had been because the Brigade Commander was on that chopper and they did not feel that the LZ was safe enough to land. His chopper had waved off the "dust-off" chopper, and then wasted countless time high in the sky while a young American was fighting for his life on the ground. The actions of the Brigade Commander had gone against the grain of everything we had been taught and had learned in all of our training about mission; helping and protecting each other in the field, completing the mission, and being timely and on schedule.

The last straw came when later on that day we were informed that the young GI had died of his wounds. We all were so distraught over what we had witnessed that there were no words but plenty of bitterness and contempt. A friend, Sgt. Brown and I decided that we had to write letters to the head of the Senate Arms Services Committee in Washington to inform them of this officer's actions. We never thought that there would be a response. Later when a response came, the result would cause me pain for the rest of my life.

I had been in-country nearly three months now and I was starting to see the transition of some of my platoon mates to either rear jobs, or even better, those guys whose tours were winding down and getting ready to go back to the "world." They were guys that helped me in my first few weeks in-country and had become trusted and very good friends. I couldn't have been happier for them but their leaving was bittersweet as I knew I would probably never see them again.

By this time, because of the need to be doing many different jobs, patrols, ambushes and walking point, I had the chance to carry every type of weapon (M-60 machine gun, M-79 grenade launcher, my M-16 rifle) as well as the PRC-25 radio. I also found that I was not really man enough to carry the M-60 all that easily - the weight kicked my ass - but I did my best. I had gotten used to using C-4 explosives in helping to clear chopper drop areas and to destroy enemy material.

Left: Roger with a "grunt's taxi."
Right: Aircraft leaving after bombing mission.
Below: A "tunnel rat."

Photos courtesy of
Roger Johnson.

I also took on the responsibility along with a small group of my platoon brothers of learning how to become what was known as a "tunnel rat." I can't really explain that move but I am sure that I felt that whatever I learned and did would help my platoon brothers. We shared that responsibility and I did everything I could to learn it well. I never found any extensive complexes or weapons, but certainly learned how these tunnels, spider holes and bunkers were a main-stay for the enemy; they were everywhere. When I entered these in-ground areas, my gear was a flashlight and a .45 caliber handgun. There was not enough room for anything beyond that. I always had to watch for booby traps and any type of explosives, along with an enemy soldier who may have been waiting in ambush or simply hiding from us. This "tunnel ratting" would come to a very sudden halt on an upcoming mission.

There was beauty in Vietnam; the bright blue water of the South China Sea, the mountains to the west, and the landscapes including the rice paddy areas, although sometimes we were just too busy and focused on our missions to appreciate it. While in the choppers going between locations, I remember taking in the sights from a couple thousand feet above the ground, sometimes higher, sometimes lower. The best ride was sitting on the outside edge of the chopper with my feet hanging outside of the door. Though it made me more vulnerable to hostile fire it was the quickest chance to exit the chopper as well. Those views were quite beautiful, watching the farmers working their rice paddies, but hoping like hell that someone else there on the ground wasn't getting ready to try to shoot us out of the sky. This was something that we faced on every mission.

We were in the field when orders came down to us that a segment of the ghost-like 48th VC Battalion had been spotted in the open during the day not too far from My Lai in the Quang Ngai Province area. We were immediately picked up by our chopper unit and headed towards that location where we expected to do battle with the VC. I know that my own adrenaline was in high gear as our unit, since my arrival, had not encountered any large enemy force. When we arrived at the drop area, the choppers made a wide swing into where we were to hit the ground. I could see the landing zone was a large, somewhat open area surrounded by tree lines and heavy brush and cover. The choppers were in their approach when the door gunner yelled to us that it was a "hot" LZ and the gunner near me opened up with his M-60 machine gun.

I immediately felt something burning on my neck and thought that I had been hit. When I reached into my collar I found a spent round casing from the M-60 and no blood; it was then that I knew I was OK. As we jumped from the chopper I ran into a defensive position only to find myself looking into cover so thick it could have concealed the entire North Vietnamese army and I would not have been able to see them. I don't mind saying I was scared as all hell.

As the assault choppers rose into the air the entire LZ became deathly quiet. We had no idea what the enemy was doing or exactly where they were. We expected they would hit us any moment, when all of a sudden a large explosion to my right caught everyone's attention. The large plume of smoke rising from the ground and the screams calling for the medic told us that at least one of our guys was hurt. We held our positions, still waiting to be hit by the enemy, as the medevac choppers swooped down and extracted three of our men. Houdini (who I mentioned earlier when I came under fire from the sniper) had stepped on a land mine and reportedly lost both legs and one arm. Two others had been hit by that same shrapnel and were rushed to the hospital in Chu Lai. I was never able to find out how Houdini turned out with his injuries, but the two other guys were treated and soon rejoined our unit. We never saw the enemy and they did not hit us that day either.

Our platoon now was working with a new commanding officer. His name was 2nd Lt. Michael Foutz, a young man and he was on his first assignment. He truly was a likeable officer, a good leader with the special gift of good communication skills, which in many cases was a gift a lot of junior officers did not have. He was always making contacts with the platoon members, asking how they were and what was on their mind. It was easy to see that he was a very good leader and that he truly cared for the men who served with him and we would have followed him anywhere.

Christmas was nearing and it was the first time that I had ever been separated from my family or away from home, just like most of the guys I was serving with, and it was quite difficult considering where we were. But the care packages from home started arriving and they certainly were helping. A friend of my mother's had knitted a little Santa Claus and sent it along with all of the other goodies and I quickly attached my Santa onto my rucksack. One of the other guys had received a small artificial Christmas tree which he carried on his rucksack as well; it wasn't home but they helped. A couple of days before Christmas an armored unit was assigned to us and having them with us was always comforting. We worked together and had no contact with the enemy, sometimes rode on the tanks or APCs and saved on the shoe leather. It also allowed us to cover a lot of ground rather quickly.

On Christmas Eve there was a declared ceasefire for the holiday which really did not mean much to us as the enemy had a bad habit of not respecting many of the truces. As nightfall settled in the tanks and APCs formed a circle and our unit filled in the holes. In the darkness the only visible lights were the small glimmers of light escaping from inside the APCs. Right around midnight the fellows in the APCs turned on the radios and we listened to a wonderful sound: the playing of Christmas carols. I will never forget it.

It was now the New Year, January, 1970, and thanks to the lessons taught by the old guys, I am still alive. Some of my older platoon mates have

Huey departing after combat assault drop. Courtesy Roger Johnson.

gone home and their replacements, the FNGs, continued to arrive and with them came a new attitude. With the Paris Peace Talks being conducted some of the new guys had the belief that the dangers had lessened and those were attitudes that could get us all killed. I along with the short-timers paid little or no attention to the talks as long as we were still in the field. We actually received an order from the rear stating that we were not to fire unless we were fired upon. Needless to say that order did not go over very well with us grunts and was never followed. Then we were getting news from home that there were massive protests against the war and that returning veterans were being spat upon and being verbally abused.

I thought, *what the hell was going on? Here we're trying to stay alive and they were in the streets back home. Why aren't they supporting us?* It was bothering us but there was nothing we could do. I felt strongly that the protests were giving our enemy a shot of confidence and ultimately would cost us more lives. I still believe that today.

Our missions remained the same: search and destroy and do everything we could to kill the enemy without being killed. It is nearly impossible to explain to anyone who has not been there of how totally black it got at nightfall in Vietnam. The nights were the most frightening as we grunts knew that the enemy owned the night. That was when the enemy moved supplies and men, as well as set up attacks on American troops without being detected. When there was no starlight you could not see anything at all when in the field, especially in the jungles. This would cause one particular night to be scarier than most.

We had been on patrol in what was known as a free-fire zone, an area with no villages or civilians and considered an enemy - only location. It was an area of double or triple canopy jungle and we moved to a high ground location to set up for the night. Because of the cover there was no room and we had to set up our trip flares and claymores much closer to our positions then we normally did. We dug ourselves in the best we could and prepared for the night. Not long after, we began to hear the enemy talking below our position. We could tell they were moving back and forth and it really put us on edge. It was obvious they knew our location and whatever they were saying had to be about us. This went on for quite a while when all of a sudden there was a crashing off to our left and one of the guys yelled there was a "dink" in the perimeter. That caused sheer terror as we may have had an enemy soldier among us and we could not see him.

We were so sure that this breach was the start of an attack of one sort or another and we did not know what to expect next. It became deathly quiet and there was no sign of any movement within the perimeter. We thought that whoever breached our lines had immediately turned around and left, *"or had it been an animal?"* We were not sure. The enemy continued to talk below us, when all of a sudden above myself and my buddy Joe, we heard something crashing through the limbs. We both yelled, *"Grenade!"* and covered the best we could. We blew the claymore mine in front of us and it was so close that we both were hit with the backblast.

As the seconds passed, we waited for the explosion but it never came. Our platoon was being probed and apparently the enemy for whatever reason never attacked. As the sun rose in the morning, Joe and I found the baseball-sized rock that they had thrown and it had landed right between us. This was truly a night of terror.

As all units did in the field, we often returned to certain locations many times. One of these places was My Lai. It was always found as one of our "hot spots" but this time it was something else. The rumor mill was that something had gone on there and that our platoons were rotating in and out of that area as security and protection. It was also the first time that I had gotten to see our Brigade Commander; the very man that I had earlier complained about because of his actions when his chopper had failed to quickly pick up a fellow wounded soldier who later died. Our squads had just come in from an ambush and patrols when he called us into formation and to attention and inspected us. He levied complaints to us over unshined boots as well as being unshaven. We were not in the rear where spit-shine and shaving was expected; this was in the field where we had just finished walking through thick cover and rice paddies. *You freaking gotta be kidding me, and this guy is in charge of a combat brigade.*

There were many times when our missions were easier and without contact. These were times that we were thankful for; spending time getting to know the new guys and sharing our stories with all of the guys. One such mission was on January 20th when we left LZ Gator and choppered down along the coast. The Hueys made a wide circle not far from the South China Sea and turned inland and dropped to let us unload and then they were off. We gathered and then worked our way into an old village area. After working around the area that day, we set up our NDP near the old village. As we were preparing for the night we had the chance to enjoy our c- rations and talk about what we would be covering tomorrow.

Like always, our Lieutenant Foutz was sharing our conversations and went from man to man talking, joking and asking everyone what was going on in their lives back home. He sat down beside me and asked what I had done back home. I shared with him that I had come from a small college town and that after graduation from high school I had applied for a job at the local Post Office and had become a part time clerk-carrier. He was quick to say that sounded interesting and that he himself might look into that when he got home. Some more conversation and some laughs and the Lt. moved on to one of the other guys. We always felt close to the Lt. and we all liked him and were proud of him as well.

The next morning, we broke our NDP and again headed inland. We had covered quite a distance, I was second or third behind the point man and the Lt. was behind me when we came across US-made commo wire lying across the path. The commo wire was way out of place for this area, it simply should not have been there, and this made us very uneasy. We followed this wire to a nearby tunnel, when I asked the Lt. if he wanted me to check it out, and he said yes. He said, "keep two men with you and we will continue on, when you finish meet us up ahead." He handed me his .45 and his flashlight and they moved forward. I dropped my rucksack and slowly entered the darkness of the tunnel.

This whole thing seemed very scary and I was more than on edge. I listened closely for any and all sounds that may have alerted me to any voices or movement, when all of a sudden all hell broke out up on top. I at first did not know if the two guys with me made contact or if it was the platoon. As I got back to where I had dropped into the tunnel, I saw that the guys waiting for me were in a defensive position, so I quickly got out of the hole and got into a defensive position as well. The fire-fight was the heaviest that I had heard so far in my tour, and at that moment I knew that we had to reconnect with the rest of the platoon as soon as we could. I started following the same path I had last seen the platoon follow and moved as cautiously as we could. Less than a hundred yards away, I started yelling to our guys not to shoot at us as we hooked up with them. The firing was still going but at a lesser rate when we got to our guys. The first guy we talked to told us that they had walked right into an ambush. The VC had attacked the platoon from the left flank and had hit the Lt. first. He had turned and was heading towards our medic yelling that he had been hit. He had been shot in the chest and died shortly afterward. Our machine gunner had also been hit multiple times and was in serious condition.

The fire-fight was so heavy that we hadn't heard the medevac chopper come in to extract our dead and wounded. I picked up a couple of belts of 60 ammo carried by our wounded machine gunner and threw them over my shoulder and around my neck as we created a perimeter around where the enemy had launched their ambush. I then noticed that my utilities had gun powder on them and saw that many of the rounds in the belts were damaged from the enemy fire and were no longer serviceable. With the enemy still hidden in their positions, we were ordered to fall back and set up positions west of the ambush site as an air strike was being called in. We dropped back about 150 yards and set up a defensive position to protect our platoon from any additional attacks.

We soon heard the jet screaming in from the north to the south. As the jet approached it unleashed a 250 or 500-pound bomb that appeared to hit dead on the ambush site with a horrendous explosion and concussion that rocked us. The fighter-bomber made a big arc over the sea and came back in for a second run and as it dropped a second bomb, the tail on the big explosive clearly separated from the bomb and the bomb hit the target with a thud. When the bombing run was completed we slowly made our way back into the site to mop up. The big explosive had done the job and we started to clear the area by pulling three dead Viet Cong bodies from the tunnels and holes they had launched their ambush from. It was only then that I realized that we had been acting on adrenaline and fear, but now we were coming to grips with the fact that we had just lost our beloved Lt. Foust. He was killed and a second platoon mate and friend were seriously wounded. The pain was

Top: Roger's buddy Joe. Below right and left: Burning enemy hootch in free-fire zone. Courtesy of Roger Johnson.

impossible to measure as we tried to cope with what had just happened. There were tears of loss and such contempt for the enemy soldiers who sprang the terror upon us. As the enemy bodies were laid out on the ground, there were no feelings of loss of their lives at all, just contempt and hate.

As the mop-up continued I began to think that maybe if I had not been in the tunnel and had been in front of the Lt., maybe I would have seen or heard something or heard anything that may have averted the Lt. from being hit. I also thought that if I had maybe heard or seen something while in the tunnel, things would be different. Then again, had I been near the lead, I too could have been shot and killed. *Too many thoughts, too many questions with no answers.* With all of that running through my mind, it was also the last time that I entered any tunnel or anything below ground. My nerve was gone and going below ground would have brought back too much emotion and pain.

We were still mopping up when we were informed that our platoon was being pulled out and replaced by another platoon. Apparently the Command needed to get us off the site for whatever reason and it did not settle well with my platoon as we wanted to finish this mission. It was our fight and we wanted to be the ones to complete it, as much for Lt. Foust as for us. It mattered not as a replacement platoon soon arrived and we were choppered out to the rear. January 21st, 1970 was a horrible day that will live with me as long as I live.

It was not long after Lt. Foust's death that I received a letter from my parents telling me of more bad news. Chuck Freese, a dear friend and fellow classmate from Geneseo Central, had been severely wounded by an enemy booby-trapped 105mm artillery round. He too was in the Americal Divisions 11th BDE and was working south of our AO. I did not know at the time, but he had been transported to the medevac hospital in Chu Lai and then back to the states.

My platoon did not have much time to absorb the pain of loss as we were back in the field almost immediately. I guess for good reason. Our missions were many and often, from the LZs and firebases to the mountains and flatlands, we were pretty much always on the go. As more FNGs joined our unit, there was more talk of the unrest at

Cong Mine Wounds Soldier from Geneseo

GENESEO — A Geneseo soldier has been wounded in Vietnam by a land mine.

The telegram reporting the wounding was received by Mr. and Mrs. Harold F. Freese of Lima Road about three weeks after they had received a letter from their son, Charles about a previous brush with the Viet Cong.

Spec. 4 Freese is a "point man" in an Infantry squad clearing booby traps and mines from the path of an advance.

In his letter he described spotting two booby traps shortly before an explosion which wounded a buddy in the hip. Freese gave his friend first aid and stayed with him until help arrived.

He became a casualty in the same type of action within the past week. Fragments from the exploding mine wounded him "slightly' in legs,arms, and abdomen said a telegram the Freeses got Sunday.

Paper unknown (likely Rochester Democrat & Chronicle or Times Union.) Dec. 1969. Provided by Roger Johnson.

home as well as more talk of the on-going peace talks. The peace talk crap did not mean much to those of us who now had been in-country for four to five months, we could have cared less. But the unrest at home was more than troublesome. The feeling was that every bit of protesting in the states was providing great support for the very communists that we were fighting. While we were looking for the support of those back home in our efforts, we were seeing the protestors seemingly aiding and abetting our enemy. To this very day I believe that any actions such as those protests offer an advantage to the enemy.

By February or March 1970, I had been in-country between five or six months and I started to pay more attention to the absence of vegetation around our LZs and firebases. I also noticed barren areas in our AO in the jungles and along the waterways as well. Vietnam was awash in green everywhere, but around where our units had bases or where we patrolled in, and around certain jungle areas it was completely barren. We would be in areas so thick with vegetation we could hardly

LZ Gator. Evidence of vegetation killed by chemical defoliant Agent Orange. Courtesy of Roger Johnson.

Top: Roger in jungle mission in the "rocket pocket."
Lower: Crewman and 4.2 (4 deuce) mortar tube, "friendly fire".
Courtesy of Roger Johnson.

move, then walk into the next area where there was nothing but dead plants, bushes and trees. At the time it wasn't an issue as we worked patrolling, setting up trip wires and claymore mines. In areas where we could not take re-supply, we were sometimes drinking the water and bathing in those barren areas; this would cause us horrible problems later in our lives. Agent Orange was lurking in those areas without vegetation. The military felt that this chemical would save American lives by eliminating cover for the enemy, but mostly what it did was poison us. It eventually caused us cancers, diabetes, and horrible birth defects in our children. I will never forgive my government for what it did to us all and especially to my son Wesley.

Friendly fire was something we all faced as well, whether from airstrikes, gunships, or artillery; a person only needed to be in an area where someone called in the wrong coordinates or it could be a result of some "cowboy" on a firebase. While our platoon was on LZ Bayonet our infantry platoon helped pull guard duty with those stationed on the base. That was fine, but often a grunt bunker would be next to a bunker with guys who never had much weapons training. One night I was on guard duty and the joker in the bunker next to mine began to "H & I" with an M-79 grenade launcher. After launching two or three rounds out in front of his position he lobbed a round right near my position. It exploded and a piece of shrapnel caught me in the back of my head. Damn it hurt like hell but it was only a surface wound and caused no real injury. The perpetrator caught all kinds of hell from me though.

My next experience with friendly fire could have been so much worse. Again at LZ Bayonet, one of our squad leaders named Kelly was called on to take an ambush out west of the base. Kelly picked me along with three other guys for the ambush. When on an ambush only a couple hundred yards off the base we always traveled light: weapons, ammo, claymore mines, and trip flares used for illumination, and a radio for communications. We would start out right at dusk, set up at our ambush site, set claymores and tripwires and call in our coordinates. Then we would take turns on watch for enemy movement. Around three to four hours later we could hear the mortar platoon on Bayonet "H & I-ing." This was a measure to keep the VC from trying to get in too close or make them aware that they may have been located. After hearing a few rounds impact some distance away, it became quiet.

Then we heard the thump of the mortar tube firing again and all of a sudden the rounds started landing all around our ambush site. Kelly began screaming on the radio to *"cease fire, cease fire!"* as the rounds continued falling all around us. The impacting of the rounds sent bright flashes, shrapnel rocks, dirt, and whatever else all over us and we could feel the awful heat when they exploded so very close. We were sure that some or all of us would be wounded or killed before the rounds stopped falling. God must have been watching over us that night as the half dozen or so 81mm mortar rounds landed so close to us but did no more than scare the living hell out of us. I don't believe anyone slept the rest of the night as we were pretty rattled over the near miss that we had just experienced. I know the next morning when we returned to the base Kelly did some serious ass-chewing to whomever had set up the fire mission that could very well have wiped our ambush out.

Halfway through my tour I thought I had a pretty good chance of getting promoted to E-5 (Sergeant). My name had been put in twice but both times I missed the E-5 boards because no choppers were available. We were in the field when my third attempt came up and I was ready to go when my platoon Sergeant informed me that they could not let me go in as we were just too short-handed. I was pretty disappointed but decided I really didn't care any longer about the rank and I let it go. Shortly after the downer, one of the squad leaders told us that we had a re-supply chopper coming in and I was to be a part of a small bunch of guys to descend the high ground to secure the LZ. Most times our choppers were inbound on a reasonable schedule but this inbound bird was nowhere to be found for at least an hour or two.

It was a beautiful day and we had gotten quite comfortable while waiting for the Huey. All at once we heard the thump of an enemy mortar tube. The VC had set their sights on the hill where our unit was set up and apparently had no idea that our small group was that close to them. We quickly moved closer without giving up our position and started laying down some pretty heavy small arms fire. The VC managed to get three or four rounds off before we quieted them and they were gone as quickly as it had started. They had no time at all to zero in on the hilltop where our unit was. No injuries, no wounds, no problem.

I remember when I first got to Vietnam, I questioned myself on how well I had listened during my training. *Did I miss anything that may save my life later on during my tour?* When I was assigned to my unit I hung on to every word spoken by the squad leaders. They said, "Listen close to what we tell you and maybe we all will get to go home," and believe me, I listened. Sometimes it did not matter, when someone was in the wrong place at the wrong time, their time was up. This was the case with a new guy who was assigned to one of our company's other platoons. I had seen him a few times in the rear but never really had the chance to meet him. He had been in-country less than three weeks when his platoon came under attack while in their NDP (night defensive position.) A "Chicom-grenade" was thrown and landed in his foxhole and he was killed instantly. *War is Hell. It did not matter whether you were a new guy or on your last day in the field. Thank God we never knew if and when it might happen.*

A new program began assigning what was known as the Kit Carson Scouts to our infantry units. The Kit Carsons were Viet Cong soldiers who defected to the South Vietnamese and Americans. We also called them "Chieu Hois." I have no doubt that many of those Kit Carsons became loyal fighters for us and I hope they

Left: Chieu Hois, also called Kit Carson Scouts, who worked with Roger's unit.

Below: Front and back of a safe-conduct surrender pass widely distributed by the U.S. military as propaganda to encourage Viet Cong and North Vietnamese defection.

Courtesy of Roger Johnson.

GIẤY THÔNG-HÀNH

SAFE-CONDUCT PASS TO BE HONORED BY ALL VIETNAMESE GOVERNMENT AGENCIES AND ALLIED FORCES
이 안전보장패쓰는 월남정부와 모든 연합군에 의해 인정된 것입니다.

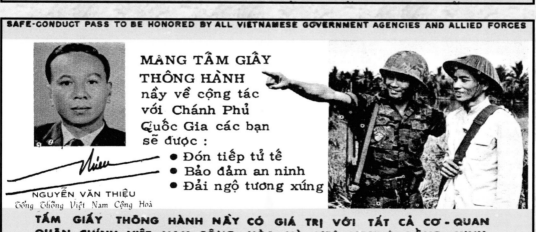

SAFE-CONDUCT PASS TO BE HONORED BY ALL VIETNAMESE GOVERNMENT AGENCIES AND ALLIED FORCES

MANG TẤM GIẤY
THÔNG HÀNH
nầy về cộng tác
với Chánh Phủ
Quốc Gia các bạn
sẽ được :
● Đón tiếp tử tế
● Bảo đảm an ninh
● Đải ngộ tương xứng

NGUYỄN VĂN THIỆU
Tổng Thống Việt Nam Cộng Hoà

TẤM GIẤY THÔNG HÀNH NẦY CÓ GIÁ TRỊ VỚI TẤT CẢ CƠ - QUAN
QUÂN CHÍNH VIỆT - NAM CỘNG - HÒA VÀ LỰC - LƯỢNG ĐỒNG - MINH.

had an opportunity to escape Vietnam and come to the US when South Vietnam fell in 1975. Had they not escaped, I am quite sure that they would have been killed as traitors. I also will say that those scouts who worked directly with us in the field never made us feel that they could be trusted. Case in point: whenever we entered an area where we thought that we may get hit or attacked, our Kit Carsons disappeared, they simply left us only to return when we found ourselves in a more secured area. They did not try to build any sort of trust between them and us, and while they worked with us we constantly kept our eyes on them.

In between the times of terror, there were some peaceful moments when you could re-read your letters or write one. It was one of those times while I was penning a letter back home, when off to the west beyond the nearest mountains I heard the exploding munitions being dropped by B-52 bombers. Later on that same day I was listening to Naval gun fire, hearing the track of the fire resonance over the sea and then over the land as it searched for a target. It set me to thinking of how many different American military units were out there trying hard to save our asses on the ground. Each and every time I heard an air-strike, gunships, or the B-52 strikes, I prayed that they would kill the NVA or VC that tomorrow may kill me or my brothers. That often was enough to bring me some additional peace.

Bomb crater bathtub. Courtesy of Roger Johnson.

We experienced other quiet times in the field. When we located a bomb crater or a moving stream it was our version of bath night. Guys would set up defensive perimeters and the rest would soap up. After days in the heat we must have smelled pretty foul and a quick bath always helped. When we finished, the first thing we had to do was to check ourselves for the ever-present leeches. These slimy little suckers would crawl up onto us and bury their heads into our flesh and we would never feel it. I dealt with them up to five or six inches long and had to be careful in removing them without breaking their heads off in my flesh or it would quickly lead to an infection. We would just put a lit cigarette or hot match on their back near their head and they quickly pulled their head out, then we killed them. They would attach themselves anywhere on the body including one's "personal equipment" so it became very important for us to check ourselves carefully.

By now I was in the second half of my tour. I was halfway home and showing some wear and tear. I dropped from around 180 pounds to about 160. Ninety-to one-hundred-plus degree temperatures nearly every day along with nearly non-stop missions helped me become slimmer, stronger, and fit. I got used to eating C-rations and actually I enjoyed them. Some sort of canned ham, fruit, and pound cake were my favorites, certainly more enjoyable than fish heads and rice.

The letters from home by my mother were telling me that my dad was not dealing very well with my being in Vietnam. He was very supportive of me but was in constant turmoil and worry over his fear of my not coming home alive. I felt terrible over his pain, but the only comforting thing I could do was never to say anything in my letters home other than simple hellos and ask how everyone was and what was new. I never said anything about what I was doing and what I was dealing with, I left it at that. The one thing that I asked my family to do was to tell my brother Stanley to join the National Guard. There was no way that I wanted him to end up over here.

As our operations continued, we visited the same areas and villages many times. The connections with some of those villages led us to a Viet Cong tax collector. A number of the residents in different villages pointed him out to us multiple times. We would interrogate him and then send him into HQ for further questioning, only to find him back out in the villages during our next mission. The residents who had pointed him out to us risked so much as the Viet Cong would find them guilty of helping us. Those people could not win as the Tax Collector would take what little money they had to support the Viet Cong. Then the Viet Cong would treat them as traitors for helping us. The Tax Collector was a white-bearded old man who turned on his own people and we despised this abuse.

The final time our platoon encountered this Tax Collector, my life nearly took a very dark turn. Once again seeing this bearded old man stealing whatever he could from the villagers became too much for me and one of the other guys to handle. We were simply fed up with the fact that he continued to be interrogated, and then sent into the rear only to have him released and sent back to continue his task. The frustration had become too much to handle and two of us secured a rope, created a noose, and threw it over a limb. Then I placed the noose around his neck and we began to hoist him up. We had him about three feet off the ground when some of our platoon mates stopped us and we lowered him back to the ground. Everyone was telling us that they felt the same way. That old man certainly deserved this fate, but it was wrong and we simply could not end it this way. They were right; we nearly did a horrible thing. I knew then that the horrors of warfare could turn a young man into something he was not, and a soldier into something that he would never want to be. The strength of my fellow soldiers helped me avoid becoming a monster, a person that I would have never been able to forgive. The Tax Collector was released once again to continue his evil work, and I was able to move on without the weight of that horrible moment to deal with.

We always tried to make some difference with the Vietnamese people. They had so little and we did as much as we could to help them. I loved working with the kids as most of us were no more than kids ourselves. The Viet Cong used the children to get to us as well. In one instance one of our companies were paying the kids for un-exploded grenades and munitions. A little boy approached one of our guys with a grenade in his hands. The grunt was about to secure the grenade when the little boy dropped it at the feet of our guy and it exploded. It killed the little boy instantly and severely wounded the GI. This was an opportunity for good that turned deadly in a heartbeat.

We were very aware of the rewards being paid to the Viet Cong and their sympathizers for the killing of Americans or capturing of American weapons. Shooting down a chopper and the dismemberment of its crew earned a rather large reward. It was very easy for us on the ground to hate those who would commit such savagery.

We were beginning to see the draw-down of some of the bases in our AO. The first to be noticed was LZ Gator. When I first arrived there it was huge, maybe a half-mile square. Now it had been retracted to the high ground, leaving a considerable open area to cover and to protect the command post. We found this out on April 1st, 1970 (April Fools Day) when our platoon was on LZ Gator. On the evening before I had been told that I would lead an ambush south of the CP and above the small village below. We went out at dusk and covered the few hundred yards to an abandoned American bunker and set up our claymores and trip-wire flares towards the village thinking that would probably be the route of entry if there was to be an attack.

It was around midnight when the VC hit the command post area with a barrage of small arms fire and explosions. Apparently the enemy had decided to hit the LZ from the north where there were lots of huge boulders which gave them pretty good cover. Where we were set up it was so wide open it would have exposed their attack to those at the command post as well as my ambush. We never saw any of the attackers and had none of our trip flares or claymores encountered. We were more than ready to hit them but it never happened. All we could do was watch what was happening on the high ground at the command post. We found out the next day that there were many attacks all around the area. We did not suffer any injuries or losses but one of our platoon mates had been struck with terror and fear and they could not get him out of the bunker. No charges were filed against him. God only knows we all felt the same feelings of terror at times.

The next morning our ambush worked its way back up to our unit command post to report. There had been no injuries, and no real damage reported so we quickly started to police the perimeter for wounded enemy and equipment. We found quite a few unexploded handmade grenades and explosives scattered around the perimeter. We set small explosive charges near the weapons and blew them in place. It appeared that the enemy had tried to do considerable damage with the many weapons we found, but apparently they were turned away by some pretty heavy fire laid upon them. Our guys hit them pretty hard.

After Lt. Foust had been killed, we received a new platoon leader, a very brash 2nd Lt. with a chip on his shoulder and a know-it-all attitude. He quickly made himself very unpopular within the platoon as he refused to listen to the advice of anyone, especially the squad leaders who had been in-country for months. His only experience was what he had learned in OCS, and believe me that was not enough. We had heard that his father had been a career officer and apparently he thought that was enough to make him a good officer as well; *he thought wrong*. He was volunteering our platoon for every available mission.

One time we had just completed a mission and arrived back in Chu Lai for stand down when we immediately were informed that we were to take re-supply and head back out to the field on a follow-up mission for which he had just volunteered our platoon. We had not even had time to hit the showers and get clean fatigues. We all assumed he was trying to get himself promoted or get to pin additional medals on his chest (on the backs of his soldiers) before the war ended. This was not a plan that we had much respect for and we all hoped it would not end with some of us being killed. I respected the good officers that I had experienced but had little respect for those who did not have the same respect for their men.

Left: Platoon questioning Vietnamese. Right: Roger preparing to destroy enemy Chicom grenade. Courtesy Roger Johnson.

As I mentioned earlier, while in the field our platoons would rotate in and out of the LZs and firebases in our AO to pull perimeter guard. We were pulled out of the field to an artillery base/LZ named "Fat City" to help protect their guns and crews. This was the first time that we pulled duty protecting an actual artillery base and on our arrival at the base we had to meet with the gun crews to get our orders as well as to learn what our duties would be. We had no idea of the duty or the consequences. We received our orders to be located on the side of the base where a battery of 155mm Howitzers was positioned. We were then placed on each side of the big gun barrels right near the muzzles. Those positions would help prevent enemy troops from placing charges known as "satchel charges" either in the gun barrels or close enough to destroy them. Being that close to the guns' muzzles also put us right where the horrible blast would be the loudest. I can't explain how deafening the non-stop firing of those guns was.

When nightfall came, the fire missions of the artillery batteries never stopped - one round after another all night long. I knew how important protecting this artillery was in the protection of our infantry units in the field, but I truly wanted to cry out loud because of the deafening noise. By sun-up I could hardly hear at all and it was days before any of my remaining hearing came back. A friend and schoolmate who was in an artillery unit told me that his gun crews would bleed from their ears after firing those nonstop fire missions. I did not suffer that experience, but later back in the "world" my hearing exam showed that I had lost 90% of my hearing in my left ear and 60% in my right as a result of the artillery noise and the sounds of combat.

We continued to do our job, always on the move from one area to another, chasing what sometimes seemed like the shadows of our enemies. We were always trying to work with and assist those in the villages we encountered. We were always trying to gain the people's trust and in turn trying to locate those who were our true enemy and in most cases it was useless. The main exception was our work with the children. We always held out hope to reach the kids and show them that we were their friends and were trying to make things better for them. Maybe we made a difference, maybe not, but we tried.

Often while writing home or while on a firebase or LZ my mind would wander and I would think about the things that I had experienced so far in my tour. Often I would look back on the letter I had written on the actions of our Commanding Officer that I believed had ultimately caused the death of a fellow soldier earlier in my tour. The incident had brought me much unrest and contempt, but after more than five months had passed, I had come to the conclusion that my words had fallen on deaf ears. I was so wrong and that was about to bring me some of the greatest pain of my life.

Two or three days prior to April 21, 1970, we were sent to the mountains west of Chu Lai where we had worked before. It was an area covered with heavy jungle and extremely difficult to work in. Hard to traverse as we often had to literally cut

Roger in "a quiet moment" next to a 155 mm Howitzer. Courtesy of Roger Johnson.

our way through with machetes. As hard as it was, the real danger was the fact that you could walk right into an ambush and would not have a chance. On the 20th we had been in the jungle cover all day and had located a spot where we could set up our NDP and protect ourselves the best that we could. The jungle was a terrible location to defend and we all hated the prospect.

My squad leader SSGT Carl Bauer called me over to inform me that I was to walk point in the morning. It was my turn and my job and that was what I would do in the morning. After my meeting with Sarge, I continued setting up our defensive lines when our platoon radio crackled with a request to have "PAC number __ ready for a pick-up to the rear." I thought that it was my PAC number called but was not sure. The radio crackled again and this time I knew it was mine. *But why?* I wondered. SGGT Bauer yelled to me to gear-up and get ready to be picked up and extracted. I heard the inbound LOH (Light Observation Helicopter) and started to move towards a slightly open area when SSGT Bauer yelled to me and said very clearly, "Roger, I will walk point for you in the morning." I said, "Thanks Sarge" and moved to the chopper, boarded and was on my way.

I arrived back at our company area, went to our HQ, and there I was instructed to report the following morning to the Battalion HQ's Board of Inquiry concerning a letter I had written earlier. *Damn, somebody did care enough to respond to my accusations and I was to have my opportunity to tell my account of that day.* The next morning I dressed in my best fatigues and reported to Battalion. I was called into the office of an Army Major where I saluted and was told to sit down. At that point he discussed with me the seriousness of my charges, and asked me to explain what I knew of the event.

When I had finished he then seemed to turn the tables on me explaining that my Commanding Officer had a stellar record and had acted in accordance with procedure. Then he told me that according to the medical staff that treated the soldier who had been shot, the wounded soldier would not have survived because of the wound and that sickened me. I again said that the time wasted waiting for the medevac to do the extraction was vital. He told me that would not have mattered and at that moment I knew that my charges were dead on arrival, justice was not to be served. He asked me to sign a form of release of charges and I saluted him and angrily left his office. It was then that I truly became aware of the politics of the military.

My day was about to get much worse. As I arrived back in my company area one of the men of my company approached me and asked if I had heard. *Heard what?* And then he said that my Squad Leader SSGT Bauer had been shot in the head and killed by a sniper hidden in the thick cover of the jungle as he walked point. I nearly fell - I could not believe what I was hearing. *This can't be!* I immediately heard SSGT Bauer's voice saying, "Roger, I will walk point for you in the morning." All I could hear was his voice over and over again, "Roger, I will walk point for you in the morning." I think I was in total shock. Shock may not be the word, but I once again had to deal with this sort of pain, guilt and bewilderment.

I could not rid my brain of all of the feelings and emotions that I was trying to deal with. I was supposed to be walking point, SSGT Bauer was dead and it was my fault. I was supposed to be there, not him. This all happened because I tried to correct a wrong that had cost a soldier's life earlier. Then my absence caused a second death, that of a squad leader and friend. *What the hell have I done?* I truly have no memory of what I did the remainder of that day other than to continue to ask why and to blame myself.

I geared up the next day and went back to my unit where I was to learn of the details of SSGT Bauer's death. It was early that morning that my platoon broke their NDP and again started out in that terribly heavy jungle cover with SSGT Bauer at point. As mentioned earlier, the cover was so very thick you could hardly see any distance in front or to the sides, just a very dangerous position to be in. Apparently the sniper had positioned himself very close to the platoon and was able to stay easily concealed. SSGT Bauer had barely left the NDP when the sniper fired a single shot, striking the SSGT in the head and taking his life immediately. The sniper was gone in an instant and return fire was futile. The telling of the details of SSGT Bauer's death sheds light on the painful details but has brought me neither comfort nor peace. I could not change what had happened and it was my cross to bear. I still do to this day. I quickly had to find the strength and courage to be able to put SSGT Bauer's death behind me before my lack of concentration in the field caused any more pain. Not paying attention in the field would get you or your buddies killed.

It soon became business as usual, pain or loss did not stop or alter what orders came down, where we were to sent or what missions we were to be involved in. We continued to work with the Vietnamese villagers in our area, tried to find the very elusive VC and NVA and destroy them and their supplies. Other than some sniper fire, destroying booby traps, and always being on the move, things remained the same. The days and weeks passed slowly, but our platoon did not suffer any more casualties, no thanks to the continued ego of our platoon leader.

Huey after another combat assault. Courtesy of Roger Johnson.

Our real refuge continued to be our visits to the rear where we were able to get away from the dangers of the field. While there, we would have the occasional rocket attacks, but for the most part we had hot meals, showers, wrote letters home, enjoyed the company of our platoon mates, and drank our fair share of cold 3.2 beer. We had to deal with a few of the guys who had rear jobs and those whom Jim DeCamp would call Rear Echelon Mother F------. They were fighting the war in the rear for whatever reason and they were mostly jerks. There were occasional fights, but we pretty much tried to stay clear of them. On one occasion while we were on stand down one of these REMFs had been ordered to the field by the commanding officer. I am pretty sure that he did not want to follow the order so he wired up a hand grenade and trip wire to the commanding officer's billet. Fortunately, it was discovered before anyone was hurt, and the REMF was court-martialed and was sent to Long Binh Jail, a military stockade in South Vietnam. He got what he wanted: a record.

It was now June, 1970, time for my R&R and I was very excited. I was leaving Vietnam for seven days and traveling to Hawaii where my girlfriend Linda and I were to be married. We were married on June 25th at the Army base Fort Derusy. We ate wonderful food, toured the island of Oahu and enjoyed what must be one of the most beautiful places on Earth. I tried very hard to put Vietnam out of my mind, but it was nearly impossible. One evening Linda and I were sitting upon a concrete retaining wall along a manmade canal when someone set off some firecrackers nearby. Had it not been for Linda I would have dived into the canal. It was very obvious that the habits of an infantry soldier do not change quickly. Our time in Hawaii passed quickly and before I knew it I was saying goodbye to my wife and boarding the airplane to return to Vietnam. Leaving Linda and the tranquil Hawaiian island was more than painful, it was a scary feeling heading back to a war zone, but that was my duty and there was no choice.

Arriving back at my company area in Chu-Lai, one of the soldiers I knew in the rear area informed me that the job of Company Mail Clerk was going to be available in the near future as the current clerk was leaving for the states; his tour done. Man what a shot of adrenaline that was for me, having just gotten married and becoming more and more concerned with the changing attitudes of the replacement soldiers along with the new platoon leader putting us all in harm's way. I thought this could be a dream come true.

I soon found myself on a Huey being transported back to my unit in the field. My first order of business was to approach my platoon leader to ask if I could be considered as the replacement for the mail clerk position for the company. I shared with him that my being a letter carrier and having had a mail clerk's experience back home would make it an easy transition. His initial response of needing seasoned men in the field was a sincere kick in the gut for me. He made it clear that I was better suited in the field rather than in the rear. As our meeting ended, I felt that my request had fallen on deaf ears and that I was about to spend the rest of my tour in the field. My spirit hit the floor.

It was only a few days after my meeting with the Lieutenant that my squad leader approached me and said that I had been chosen to be the new Company Mail Clerk. Again I nearly hit the floor but this time it was a feeling of pure joy because I was getting to hell out of the field. I had now spent nearly ten and a half months in the field, had done everything asked of me, and felt that I had done a good job. The only guilt that I was feeling was that of leaving the guys that I had been serving with. But now it was my good luck that I could finish my tour in what most would say was a much safer place.

I went to the rear and worked with the old Mail Clerk, learning the many ropes. Many of the duties were exactly what I had been doing back home. Sorting all incoming mail and packages to the various platoons, getting mail to the airfield where the Hueys could get it to the guys in the field. I also was assigned to doing the paperwork on incoming troop replacements. I remember two of these guys being placed in our company. One was a young black fellow who had just been reassigned to our company from Korea. He was a wonderful guy who I had been able to talk to a number of times before he was sent to the field. Less than a month after joining our company he was killed by a command-detonated 105mm artillery round hanging in a tree. The second young soldier, on arrival to my office, informed me that he was from western New York. I asked whereabouts and he replied he was from Nunda, NY. I had taken his address so that I could get in touch with him when we both got home, but unfortunately when I got back to the "world" at Fort Benning, Georgia, I had my wallet stolen and along with it was my address book.

My duty was a very busy one but I was not about to complain. I had three hot meals a day, showers every day, and a dry and comfortable place to sleep. I got to spend time with my unit buddies when they came in for stand down. We would gather at the EM club or take in a movie; we still had the chance to stay in touch. As mentioned earlier, in the rear the largest danger was the occasional rocket attack. One evening while taking in a movie, the film ended abruptly when two or three rockets came sailing in and damaged some of the surrounding buildings. Other than that, there were no serious incidents.

The only hardship that I had to deal with while I was in the rear was malaria. One morning while in the office, I started having chills, followed by shivering and my teeth chattering. My condition got more severe and a couple of the guys loaded me into a Jeep and rushed me to the nearby hospital. I was very lucky that I was so close to treatment and the staff at the hospital told me that it was in fact malaria and I would be treated accordingly. I remember feeling a lot worse before starting to feel better, but thanks to the care given me I was in good hands. I spent about a week in the hospital before being sent back to my company. An irony for sure, while in the field for ten and a half months with all that I contended with and I hadn't gotten sick until I was in the rear.

After a full recovery, I remained very busy with my job and the time passed quickly. It was now the middle of September, 1970, when orders to be shipped back home came down for me and the other men who came into country when I did. My words cannot explain how exhilarating that was. The excitement was only tempered by the thought of something happening to any of us before our "Freedom Bird" arrived. On September 30th, we all boarded a plane to Da Nang where we then boarded an airliner. I remember how deathly quiet it remained on the plane as the aircraft raced down the runway and became airborne. When we were out and over the South China Sea, the captain said we were clear of Vietnam, and all at once a tremendous roar arose from everyone on board. We had made it and we were on our way home.

When arriving back in the "world," we touched down at the Sea-Tac airport in Washington State and once again had orders cut for a thirty-day leave at home. I was reunited with my wife and family at the Rochester airport. After warm embraces, my folks and brother left, and I left with Linda as she said there was a stop that we had to make before going home. As we neared my childhood home, Linda pulled into the Mt. Pleasant Cemetery to visit the gravesite of a dear family friend, Mort Taft, a World War II veteran who had passed away while I was in Vietnam. After saying my farewells, we left for home. While home with my family I did not speak of my year overseas as my Dad was finally at peace knowing that I was now safe. I did not want to change that.

While visiting friends and getting reacquainted with Geneseo, I was welcomed home by many, but there was only one who thanked me for my service. His name was Jim McCaughey and he worked for the Village of Geneseo. I have always been grateful for his kind words but I became ever more private concerning my service. At the end of my leave I was ordered to report to Fort Benning, Georgia to an Infantry training brigade. I had no desire to play war games with new officers and recruits, so I quickly became a friend of the company reenlistment SSGT and became his reenlistment clerk. While there I finished out my two-year obligation and was discharged from the active military on May 7th, 1971.

I had some difficulties with flashbacks and bad dreams after arriving back home, going back to work, and starting my new life with Linda in our new-to-us home. When these struck me Linda was always there to comfort me and help me work through it. *Thank you, Linda.*

About a year after I got home, I really was able to open up for the first time with good friends and Vietnam vets, Chuck Freese and Jerry Vickers, while at the Vital Spot bar in Geneseo. Chuck had been seriously wounded and Jerry Vickers flew six missions for the Air Force as a Load Master Trainee on C-141 Starlifter aircraft delivering ammunition and supplies. Fellow vets and cold beer gave us all the chance to get loose and let it all out.

We made it!

Top: Tiger Lines, "Freedom Bird."
Lower: Roger (center) and platoon brothers landed safely back in the U.S. at Sea-Tac Airport, Washington State.
Courtesy of Roger Johnson.

During my 365 days in Vietnam I met some of America's greatest young men with whom I shared many good and bad times. (Today I still am in touch with three.) It is so important for me to mention the sort of young guys that I had the honor of serving with. They were from big cities, small towns, the country, and almost every state in the union. Most were high school graduates, had jobs, girlfriends and seemed to be as happy as the times would allow. They were the sons of contractors, hopeful artists, or coal miners, and played in garage bands. They were proud young Americans and believed, as I did, in why we were there. Whether or not any of these young men ever read my words or not, I had the opportunity to serve with some of America's best young men and I could not have been more proud. They were my brothers then and they always will be my brothers.

I had times of tranquility and then times of sheer terror. I saw my friends and fellow soldiers wounded and sometimes killed, and those are the ghosts that will haunt me for the rest of my days. When I left Vietnam, I felt that those horrors were behind me, but after getting home they arose once again with illnesses caused by my being exposed to Agent Orange. My son's birth defects have caused me the greatest pain. He did not deserve to suffer with these problems because of my service in Vietnam. Be assured: I will never forgive my government for doing that to my Wesley.

I have tried to make peace with my wartime experience, but it has come with a price. I am very much a changed person. That special innocence that comes with being a young boy from a small town was lost. I had become a man at the price of his youth. I became somewhat hardened to fear and loss; it remains, but seems to be harder to express. I will carry on and I will strive to remain the best sort of man that I can be - for Butch, Bobby, and Charlie, and the brothers I lost in Vietnam, and the little boy I lost at home.

WESLEY C. JOHNSON
JULY 27, 1978 - DECEMBER 30, 1989

After

✿ ✿ ✿ ✿ ✿ ✿
by Jim DeCamp

Coming home for all but the three local guys who didn't was similar to our "Before" experiences. Most of us re-entered our lives and some went back to careers that had been so rudely interrupted. The visible scars of war were few but the interior ones have lasted. Chuck Freese returned home on a stretcher after being severely wounded. But things turned around for him with the help of a good woman (this book should be co-dedicated to the supporting women and families that surrounded us) and he closed with the commentary, "Lucky is my life story, down but never out."

The proverbial 'welcome home sputum' was rare, but it happened. John Carney, returning home from a TDY to Korat Royal Thailand Air Force Base in early 1973 got a foul welcome:

"I couldn't wait to get home until a long-haired, bearded, dirty Hippie freak spat on me while calling me a 'baby killer' at San Francisco International Airport. He didn't know what I did in the Air Force. I had to dig my hands into my pockets and walk on…"

There were some dramatic homecoming incidents but for most of us it was a quiet event, a few family members and friends. No parades for many years. Although most of us are doing fine now, retrospectively, Bucky O'Neil said, "I don't remember folks being all that thankful for my service. Frankly, I think I was a little ashamed at first, but then changed my mind over the years as I realized what I experienced as a 19-20 year-old kid."

Photo: VFW Post 5005, Memorial Day, May 30, 2002. Left to right; Ray Robinson; Ron Long, Vietnam vet; Bruce Booher, Vietnam vet; Sean Eaton, Iraq; and Lenny Mack, Iraq. Courtesy of Michael Johnson, Livingston County News.

I wasn't welcomed home by a stranger until 41 years after I got back. I was doing an in-take interview at the Batavia VA to qualify for medical benefits and the clerk was handing me off to the social worker, a requirement for all Vietnam vets. As she left me in the waiting room, she shook my hand and said "Welcome Home!" I teared up and then was worried I had to meet my social worker and explain that I was not a threat to myself, or humanity.

Our generation, like veterans of past wars, didn't talk about our war experiences. Most people, and popular culture, didn't seem to care about us once they got past the "crazy killer" stereotype. Pete Williams said, "I never did talk about my experiences in Vietnam. Friends asked questions but I never said much about it. After a while they stopped asking." Or as Donny Peraino said, "I put my Army experience behind me and never looked back."

As mentioned earlier, the military culture was a hard-drinking one and that pattern followed many of us home and civilian society wasn't as receptive to drinking as our military one had been. Bruce Booher characterized those first years back home as pretty bleak, "Black years - booze, drugs, women, bars & fights. I hated uniforms and authority. Couldn't keep a job, worked several."

Tony Gurak concurred:

"I had a real hard time trying to readjust. I was still on a high state of alert, very jumpy. I was used to being in charge and now I had to work for someone else. Some were idiots and I didn't handle it very well. Drifted from job to job, unfortunately I drank heavily, way beyond a good time. Way too many bad choices. It took me a very long time to straighten out and come to terms with what I could not change."

Readjusting for Terry Johnston was also difficult:

"I had a very rough time after I got home trying to adjust to civilian life. Family & friends were very supportive but the less I spoke about war, the better off it was. I didn't want people thinking about it and I still don't to this day. There are things we seen & done that we are not proud of but I did what we had to do, just to return home alive. The only good thing about this war was it made me unscared of everything back in this life."

Courtesy of Terry Johnston.

Drinking and readjusting took its toll on Rod Bowles too: "Went to school, did not have a lot of friends, starting drinking heavily, graduated, worked, got divorced, never mentioned Vietnam to others, went to AA at 29 & stopped drinking." And Roger Johnson painted a clear but disturbing image, "After 40 years, the ghosts still remain" and "I came home with so many kinds of worms in me I thought I was going to be used as bait."

We came back in individual olive drabs and dribs. No decompression boat rides home with the unit you trained with, just a 'freedom bird' airline with 250 strangers whose DEROS dates matched yours. No exit interviews, no counseling, just an abrupt end to what you were doing. During a very strange visit to the outgoing staging area I was asked by the MPs the expected questions of "Do you have any weapons, ammunition or grenades?' I wasn't expecting "Do you have any Vitalis bottles of urine?" Evidently the guys who were "dirty" from drug use had their cleaner buddies contribute some good urine. When we went to the MP guarded "Pee House of the August Moon," you could squeeze your borrowed piss into the cup. They did detain one guy I was with who had an intact skull in a baggie. They didn't stop him from going home, just confiscated his souvenir as if it were a plant trying to cross the border into California.

GENESEE VALLEY CITIZENS FOR PEACE

NO MORE VIETNAMS

According to a March 20, 1975 Harris poll, an overwhelming 76% of the American people think that "we should never again commit American soldiers to such a war as Vietnam." A 71% majority believes that the "United States should avoid all guerilla-type wars," and 67% think that "we should not commit American lives to the defense of corrupt governments abroad." The vast majority also opposes President Ford's request for additional aid to South Vietnam and Cambodia.

The recent developments in Indochina demonstrate conclusively what the United States' anti-war movement has been saying for years: without continuous billions of U.S. taxpayers' dollars and direct military support, corrupt dictators could never have stayed in power in Phnom Penn and Saigon.

It is clear from the Harris poll that most Americans have learned a lesson from Vietnam. They have clearly rejected the policy which killed and maimed millions of Indochinese and hundreds

of thousands of Americans. They realize that the war was never in their interest or in the interest of the Indochinese peoples.

It is to be hoped that those people who say "we should never again commit American soldiers to a war such as Vietnam"

continued above

will soon see the moral correctness of resisting that war and join in the call for Universal and Unconditional Amnesty for those who have suffered so much for their acts of resistance and been sent into exile.

Livingston Republican, 5/15/1975.

> **"Reflection and reconciliation is a horrible enemy to a soldier in combat.
> It will most certainly get you killed. But, it's a most necessary process for a
> human healing from the emotional damage of war."**   *- Jim Adamson*

Jim Adamson explained that his return home from the war included bouts of depression before the healing process began:

"I was as unprepared to come home as I was to go over. Of course I was beside myself with joy to step off the airplane in California and plant my healthy body on U.S. soil once again. The reunion with my family was a huge high and the tomato-throwing slurs of the anti-war protesters only hurt a little bit.

West Point, 1977. After Vietnam, Jim Adamson returned to West Point as an aerodynamics professor. Courtesy of Jim Adamson.

One old soldier in San Francisco Airport even bought me a cup of coffee and thanked me for my service. I'll never forget that man. I wish I had his name. I'd like to thank him today. I had made it back alive and it was time for me to get busy re-orienting my life and return my focus to the most important things for me which were flying and space. Little did I know that the war was not quite over for me just yet.

As I proceeded from peace time military assignments to graduate school, back to West Point, test pilot school, and finally to NASA, I was haunted by overwhelming bouts of grief and sadness. These episodes happened less frequently as years went by but they lasted almost 15 years. I was embarrassed at first because I would sometimes just start crying for no apparent reason. The feeling came out of nowhere and I had no control of where, when, or in whose company it happened. I finally decided that it was simply the bleeding I hadn't had to do in the war coming out slowly and mercifully over time.

Reflection and reconciliation is a horrible enemy to a soldier in combat. It will most certainly get you killed. But, it's a most necessary process for a human healing from the emotional damage of war. Once I thought I understood what was going on I just let it happen...let myself spend some time thinking about things I never dared to think about while I was in-country. It worked, at least for me. I was able to heal slowly."

Jim DeCamp's narrative continues.

Terry Alger was one of the few GCS vets who stayed in the service so his re-adjustment was different. "I did not have to adjust to civilian life since I stayed in the Army and returned to Vietnam a second time in 1970. Between assignments I was at U.S. military posts and therefore isolated from some of the less pleasant events happening in the U.S." The timing of our individual returns, like the timing of our deployments, made a difference. Those who came home early in the 1960s were as ignored as much as the war was then. In the turbulent late 1960s the reception outside one's family might have been as unpopular as the war was becoming. This faded to a benign neglect and indifference in the 1970s to the war and the returning troops.

I came home to do 12 hours of graduate work at SUNY Geneseo in the spring of '71 to become permanently certified as a teacher and was out of step with the 'kids' at the college. But I didn't care as I was back home with wife and family and didn't need anything else. As a group we may tend to be a little

> Neil Thompson's story is a good example of how soldiers remained on "alert."
>
> *"After my tour of duty in 'Nam I had to do a year and a half in Germany where it was very different. I was being processed into my new unit when someone called, 'Hey, Charlie!' The next thing I knew I was on my stomach firing my weapon (which I didn't have) along with 20 other vets. Charlie was the post tailor. Whenever a vehicle backfired I dove for cover. This lasted for quite a few years and even now I occasionally wince."*

'jumpier' than men who didn't serve in Vietnam.

Whether or not our experiences affected our career choices was another survey question. The hire-ability of returning vets is a vital concern in today's downturned market. Finding a job was not too hard for the returning Blue Devils, keeping it was. Many of us had come from positions of trust and responsibility in the military, leading men into and out of life and death situations, flying and servicing million dollar aircraft and submarines. Then we came home to prospects defined by the last grade level we had achieved in school and

JOHN NEIL THOMPSON, JR., son of Mr. and Mrs. Laverne Mc-Kelvey, of 51 North St., Geneseo, has returned from Vietnam where he spent one year, stationed at Cam Rahn Bay. Thompson says that most of the soldiers he was acquainted with felt they had a job to do, and were proud and willing to do their duty. While he wasn't in the center of action, he said the Air Base was hit once with heavy fire, that you could usually hear the mortars, M-60's and M-16's, and at night could see the tracer bullets trail through the air. He expects to leave soon for Germany for the remaining 15 months of his enlistment. Thompson is a 1964 graduate of Geneseo Central School and attended Bryant and Stratton Business Inst. in Buffalo.

Right: Livingston County Leader, 4/10/1968.

were limited by local options. There were few hiring programs for returning Vietnam vets and little incentive for employers to hire us, as we all carried the stigma of an unpopular and unsuccessful war.

I had been teaching high school English before I was drafted and continued to do so for the next 39 years. I was lucky to get back into the school system as I ran into an assistant superintendent who loved Section V basketball. But I still lost three whole years in the New York State Retirement System. Military skills are not immediately transferrable - there wasn't much demand for a mortar crew man in the civilized world. Military training and discipline were definitely assets however, and most of us used these learned habits to advance in our 'world' jobs. Some of the vets transitioned easily into the corporate world, like Terry Alger who left active duty in 1977 and whose IBM customers were often ex-military. Alger stated that "our mutual experiences helped in my experience as a computer salesman."

Many guys saw a tie between the skills learned in the military and civilian occupations.

Chuck Freese spoke of the advantages of teamwork in the workplace:
"Career-wise no real benefit as to type of work; but looking back, the Army gave me a sense of duty and to commit to whatever I was doing. You learn in the military that teamwork is the most important element to success. How to get along with all different types of people, race, religion, temperament, how to blend into other's views, and not try to force yourself onto others."

Often there were numerous jobs in between the "real" duties of a soldier and the duties of a worker in the "real" world. As Tony Gurak said,
"It took me a long time and a lot of jobs to find a job that I liked as much as working on B-52 bombers. Eventually I did, and stayed working in the medical equipment business for 37 years."

Bucky O'Neil also successfully transitioned from the Air Force to a career in the medical field:
"Experience in the military did affect my career choice somewhat. I saw a lot of pain and suffering during my years in the service and other components of my life, so I was headed toward the health care profession early on. One thing I did learn in the service (which I was lacking when I went into the service) was a true sense of discipline and knowledge of how to lead and how to get things done. I have been CEO of one small hospital with 700 employees to a national system with 45,000 employees, so often I am thankful for the self-discipline I learned in the Air Force."

There were limited transitional services to assist veterans back then and few guys had the patience to deal with the bureaucracy, but Lenny Peri was able to take advantage of a program that led to a long-lasting career:

"Yes, my time in the service had a major impact on my decision of a career. I knew I didn't want to return to the salt mine, and I didn't want to go back into farming. While I was stationed in Ft. Lewis I attended a program in the Army called 'Project Transition'(Preparing for Civilian Life). This is I how I got into IBM and stayed with them for 34 ½ years."

Malcolm Stewart attributes his Marine Corps training in helping him become a successful lawyer:

Malcolm Stewart (center) with son Jonathan and daughter Kathryn. 2007. Courtesy of Malcolm Stewart.

"Although my service in Vietnam did not affect my career choice (law), my Marine Corps service certainly did.

Without the training, experience, GI Bill and disability payments, I doubt I would have otherwise had the motivation, discipline, perseverance and confidence necessary to attend law school and become an attorney."

Neil Thompson agreed that his military experience was influential in his pursuit of meaningful work to ensure that others were treated fairly and squarely:

"Yes it did, as I only wanted to help people on welfare get all the help and benefit that they were entitled to. I was a NYS auditor for Social Services and Medicaid for 37 years."

When asked if their experiences in the military changed their attitude toward war and/or government, the questions elicited some of the most interesting responses to our survey. Jim Barber and a few others simply said no. But Jim Adamson stated, "Vietnam did not change my attitude toward war, but it did erode my naïve confidence in government and military 'leadership' as a result of the mismanagement of the war by the Kennedy and Johnson Administrations, which ignored the prudence and restraint of the Eisenhower Administration and resulted in 58,000+ American military deaths." Other responses were more succinct. Don Peraino's consisted of, "Number 1 lesson: Don't trust government unless you know all the facts." And Roger Least stated straight out, "The government will lie to you."

Quite a few were more verbose and reactions went from cautious approval to betrayed outrage. Terry Alger was measured in his response, "War is obviously bad. The major problem is that both sides have to agree that it is bad for peace to work. Perhaps the best lesson is for the government to have a plan on what to do if they win or lose before becoming engaged." Dennis Staley echoed this concern for clarity and support when he said, "The lack of support for all servicemen and women. If the government agrees we should go to war - from that point on let the military do what needs to do be done. Lesson learned."

Above: Doreen and Jim DeCamp on vacation in Vietnam, March 2013. Courtesy Jim DeCamp.

Roger Mustari compared the military unfavorably to a business: "If the military I was part of were a business it would not exist. No accountability in spending, no leadership, no help for those who need help because they thought they were dong the right thing." Al Dietrich was philosophic: "With hindsight, the war probably could have been avoided, but the people making decisions then were living in that time and without the knowledge that came years later."

Wayne Tuttle's views of the U.S. government didn't change after serving in Vietnam. "My military and political views of that time are the same today. I'm extremely patriotic and back our conservative politicians and citizens, to the end." And John Thompson said he wasn't "antiwar/ government as I volunteered for it." Rodney Wambold was equally positive in his takeaway: "I also developed a stronger feeling of gratitude for living in our country. It may not be perfect, but there is no other nation with so much opportunity, as well as the ability to express what you like or don't like, and have a voice in trying to improve things."

The Domino Theory of communism spread never came to fruition. Cambodia, Thailand, and Laos have their issues but communism never sprouted in those fertile fields. The pernicious effects of the communist victory are clear to me now after a two week vacation in South East Asia in March 2013. The south has been strangled by a corrupt bureaucracy and the hand of communism is heavy.

Jim posing at the entrance to a tunnel used during the Vietnam War. March, 2013. Courtesy of Jim DeCamp.

Every intersection is patrolled by avaricious police waiting for an accident or infraction so they can extract bribes. Vietnamese citizens rush to exchange information and settle before the police arrive. Our guide in Ho Chi Minh City, which he referred to as Saigon,* told us it would cost him $20,000 in bribes to get a job at the airport that would go for free to somebody's nephew from the north. The one domino that did fall was South Vietnam when the U.S. finally pulled out in 1975.

Chuck Freese saw some justification for our efforts in Vietnam:

"We were correct to step in and stop the communist takeover of Southeast Asia. The countries in that region would have fallen one by one. Much different map today and a much bigger problem with China. Did our government operate the war correctly, or to our best ability, I'm not so sure, but the war was fought trying to contain growing dissent at home. During a war a country has to commit all or stay out."

A clear contrast was provided by Cliff VanDerveer:

"Most people don't know the government has, knowingly, misinformed (LIED) about the slow poisoning of Agent Orange. We are dying at a higher rate than any other group! Our government (and our young) ignore history and continue to repeat it! A mandatory, 100%, three-year draft should be instituted - men & women. No exceptions! Lawmakers would hesitate sending their kids to their deaths! This government has to take care of the vets above all! We served, possibly gave our all - Got carried away! Sorry!"

Terry Alger agreed about a draft:

"I am very strongly in favor of national service. The current Army is the best in the world, but it allows the general public to become disassociated with war efforts. It is too easy 'to get them' when one has no 'skin' in the game. In a democracy the people have to be involved in all aspects of the governmental decisions and actions."

John Carney said he lost trust in government:

"War needs to be fought right. You fight to win, nothing else is acceptable. We need to take care of business at home. None of my sons or grandsons will be militarily involved."

*Under the name Saigon, it was the capital of the French colony of Cochinchina and later of the Republic of South Vietnam from 1955–75. The name was then changed by the communist government to Ho Chi Minh City and is the largest city in Vietnam.

Agent Orange figured prominently in the disillusionment many of us felt. Roger Johnson, whose son Wesley's life was cut tragically short by the after-effects of Monsanto and Dow's* contribution said,

"My attitude toward my government changed when I found out that Agent Orange, which afflicted my child's health, was ordered by the military and approved by the government.

As time went by my feelings about the war and politics became bitter as I now feel that the government dictating the war from Washington, yet having us fighting a half a world away, never allowed those in Vietnam to fight to win." - Roger Johnson

AWARD OF THE ARMY COMMENDATION MEDAL --Roger C. Johnson, ████████, Specialist Four, Company B, 5th Battalion, 46th Infantry, 198th Infantry Brigade APO 96219 was awarded the medal for service Jan. 1970 in the Republic of Vietnam by direction of the Secretary of the Army under the provisions of AR 672-5-1, for heroism in connection with military operations against a hostile force in the Republic of Vietnam. Specialist Four Johnson distinguished himself by valorous actions on Jan. 21, while serving as Rifleman with Company B, 5th Battalion, 46th Infantry. On that date, the company was conducting a tactical sweep near An Thinh when it was suddenly assaulted by heavy concentrations of small arms fire from a well entrenched enemy force. With total disregard for his personal safety, Specialist Johnson provided a solid base of protective fire for the advance of his fellow soldiers while repeatedly exposing himself to the hostile rounds. After the company succeeded in overcoming the enemy's resistance, the difficult task of searching the village and its insurgent fortifications began. Despite the extreme hazard inherent in the mission, Specialist Johnson unhesitatingly volunteered to enter and search the enemy bunkers and tunnel complexes. His search yielded many important documents and weapons, providing valuable intelligence information for his unit. Through his timely actions, he was instrumental in eliminating the enemy threat and in minimizing friendly casualties. Specialist Four Johnson's personal heroism and devotion to duty are in keeping with the highest traditions of the military service, and reflect great credit upon himself, the Americal Division, and the United States Army. Signed: John L. Insani, Colonel, GS, Chief of Staff. (Roger is the son of Mr. and Mrs. Charles H. Johnson

Livingston County Leader, 7/15/1970.

The fact that our government would spy on us, lie to us, and otherwise abuse us is not the news today that it was back then. Our bombers knew we were in Cambodia way before the official incursion of May, 1970. The unit I joined in July of '71, the 2nd/27th Wolfhounds, had often crossed the border into Cambodia in hot pursuit. How did they know it was the border? Because the demarcation was the Mekong River, as wide as the Mississippi.

The very open-ended query, "Do you have any other comments you'd like to make?" received equally open-ended responses. The shortest, "Why are you doing this?" from Don Peraino will be answered, I hope, by our completed project. Our responding vets gave reflective and personal answers. Dennis Staley said, "I am very glad the American people are behind all veterans. Do not hate the military. They did not declare war. They are the ones trying to win with what we have."

*The US Dept. of Defense contracted with Monsanto Corp. and Dow Chemical to manufacture the chemical defoliant known as Agent Orange.

Chuck McLaughlin had similar thoughts about the military and included a presidential endorsement:

"I think Colin Powell was absolutely correct when he said 'when are we going to learn to keep our troops home!' With more troops at war, we still have not learned. Colin, will you please run for president!"

Rod Bowles wondered why we jump into war without considering the overall cost to society:

"What would happen if we put as much effort into living peacefully together - would the differences between people be less? Would our happiness be greater?"

John Thompson thought the Vietnam-era veterans "didn't get the support and recognition that they deserve." Jim Creagan appreciated the recent attention paid to local veterans but found it shallow. "Livingston County has certainly made a nice gesture by soliciting local businesses to offer a variety of economic benefits to veterans. However, the judicial system offer nothing. No senior discount either."

SP 4 Charles McLaughlin arrived home Thursday to attend the wedding of his sister, Karen to Charles Tanis, at which he gave the bride away. After his tour of duty in Vietnam he spent a month's leave visiting his mother, Mrs. "Toots" McLaughlin of Geneseo. Charles will be stationed at Fort Knox, Ky.

Livingston County Leader.
11/8/1967.

Some responses were more personal. Pete Williams offered good advice:

"One of my biggest regrets was not staying in college. I was going to Geneseo State. I quit college and a couple of months later I was drafted and 5 months later I was in Vietnam. I had a great career with the U.S. Postal Service. I often wonder how much better my career would have been which, in turn, would have made my retirement all the much better if I had stayed in college. Go to college, get the best education you can. Education is the key to a better, more successful life!"

My personal response to the politics of the Vietnam War is from another point of view. I assess all men my age by how they navigated those treacherous draft waters. As an unsuccessful draft dodger myself, I respect all the choices made, except for "Chicken Hawks" like Dick Cheney who avoided war themselves and sent others into it. I used to sit in the all-male GCS faculty lounge as a substitute teacher before I was drafted and the Korean War-era guys would tell me to shut up about my anti-war views. When I came back from Vietnam they listened raptly to the same views. When I asked, "why, now?" they said, "Now you know what you're talking about."

The returning Vietnam vet is a much maligned figure in movies and popular culture. "Shell shock" morphed into "battle fatigue" from World War I to II, and picked up two syllables. We're up to eight now with "post-traumatic stress disorder." We have our share of PTSD but most have found a way to cope. Bruce Booher said,

"After meeting my wife, Rose, I had a great family, kept a full-time job. Now I'm retired, doing some house painting. Got some help from the Army who determined I have PTSD. Life goes on. I never spoke of the war until I went and talked to a counselor at the Army. Too painful. I have always been a happy-go-lucky guy but a part of me has changed."

The after-effects of the war have been physically debilitating for some with symptoms manifesting in various ways. Chuck McLaughlin describes,

"I am unfortunately dealing with ringing in my ears, skin cancer, and maybe Agent Orange disability."

Cliff VanDerveer, like many others, has to deal with his health and the VA:

"Dealing with Agent Orange health-related issues. VA continues to try to use 'lifestyle' as an issue to deny me my percentage of disability...If you wait long enough we will die and stop reminding them of their neglect."

Surprisingly though, when we asked our guys about how they are doing today, we received mostly positive responses. It appears the stereotypical Vietnam vet is not found among us. No Jon Voigt chaining himself to a fence, no *Deer Hunter* from Pennsylvania haunted by Russian roulette. As a rule we came home, married (mostly happily) and set about raising families of which we are rightly proud. Several of us carry the physical scars, all of us some psychological baggage, but for the most part we seem to resemble the succinct reply from Don Piraino, "Good! Great family."

My answer to how I'm doing is much milder – I'm great, very happy and satisfied. I would claim to be totally unscathed except I'm very claustrophobic, and didn't used to be: have to sit with my back to a wall in a restaurant and always plan an escape route. Recently in a recovery room from kidney surgery I was thrashing around and talking about Vietnam, according to the nurse. Most of the rest of the responses echo Dennis Staley's, "I am doing very well, very active, [with] submarine veterans, VFW, American Legion."

Right: Dennis Staley led the Pledge of Allegiance at the Livingston County Board of Supervisor's meeting, March 2012.
Courtesy of the Livingston County Veterans' Services Office.

Roger Johnson is upbeat as well, "Considering everything I feel myself very lucky. I have seen and experienced so many things, some bad, but most very good. I feel more knowledgeable; try to be more aware of people, government, what is most important to those around me. And I really know how special life is." John Thompson says he is "healthy, happy, and retired." And Rod Bowles is also retired and says he is has come full circle,

Image below courtesy of R. Bowles.

"Adjusting slowly, trying to figure out how I wish to live my life today. Luckily I have the love of my wife & children and am beginning to love myself again.

War crushed our youthful dreams, by the grace of God time heals and dreams return." — Rod Bowles

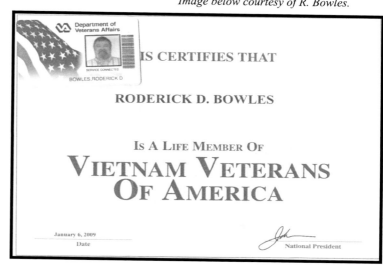

Jim Barber is "just fine," and Lenny Peri is "doing pretty well today," though he had prostate cancer due to exposure to Agent Orange. Carroll Teitsworth is well also – "Four kids who are all involved in aviation with me, each in his own way – oldest grandson is starting flight training."

Above: The Teitsworths have long been a familiar sight in the skies over the Genesee Valley. (Left) Carroll Teitsworth sitting on the side of his hot air balloon basket and (right) with his large family. Carroll formed Liberty Balloon Company, based in Groveland, in 1976 and from the beginning, it has been a family-friendly business. After serving in the Navy as a multi-engine airplane pilot, a fixed base operator, and flight instructor, Carroll became a full time professional balloonist logging over 3,400 hours of hot-air ballooning. He is also an FAA-designated balloon pilot examiner, and an FAA safety counselor. Photos used with permission.

Terry Johnston is philosophical:

"What I went through has made each day a little better and at the end of my life I can look back and say it was a part of my life. I wish no one to go and fight a war, but if it was for this country, I would be the 1st in line, but not somebody else's country."

Jim Creagan has no complaints:

"I am in moderately good health and can accomplish those chores I choose to take on. I retired four years ago so I'm not on demand to get things done. My marriage is happy and secure. I have two sons graduating with four-year degrees this spring, one of whom has recently been elected to Phi Beta Kappa. A third son will graduate from Syracuse with a Masters in Forestry also this spring. No complaint here."

Pete Williams says he's doing fine, "retired though working part time to stay out of trouble. Happily married to a beautiful woman, two wonderful kids, two super grandkids and enjoying life to its fullest."

Tony Gurak is doing well also:

"I retired in 2010 and am really enjoying myself. I try not to dwell on past mistakes. I just try to do the right things and live my life the best I can. I joined the Geneseo VFW post and it's an active post. We do a lot of things to help vets and the community. It gives life a good purpose. I enjoy it very much."

Life is good for Terry Alger too:

"My wife and I live in Victor during the warm months and go to our home in Florida during the winter. My children (two boys) are both doing well. I have no complaints and consider the generation born in the 40s to have been the most fortunate. Jobs were plentiful (for the most part) and most of us prospered. The war in Vietnam did hurt a large number of young Americans and I am appreciative of what the nation is now doing to help them."

Al Dietrich also describes a good life:

"I have been very fortunate with a wonderful family and friends. I have also had a good career with meaningful work and the opportunity to work with good people. My war service gave me a very deep appreciation of every single day and especially the little things in life that taken together mean so much. Hopefully, in retirement I can give back to others as I have been so fortunate."

Jerry Vickers enjoyed the organization and discipline of the Air Force, but suffered a life-altering experience in 1969 when he was seriously injured in an accident while off-loading a large shipment of helicopter rotor blades. After leaving the Air Force he continued to serve in the military in both the Army National Guard and the Army Reserve, retiring in 2001. In 2005, he went to work at Highland Hospital in Rochester and recently retired.

"Today, I am fine. I'm on my second marriage (and my last) to a wonderful woman I met fourteen years ago. We have been under the same roof for twelve years and as of September, 2013, married for ten years. And lest I forget: I am a very recent cancer survivor and have been pronounced cancer-free!"

Right: Geneseo Memorial Day, 2007.
Photo courtesy of Jerry Vickers.

Malcolm Stewart is doing great as well:

"After returning to California from England, and working for a couple of years, I attended law school and became an attorney, with a trial and litigation practice in Central California. I closed my Fresno office last year, and now serve as legal counsel for a private foundation, with my office located a mile from my home in the Sierra National Forest (between Yosemite and Kings Canyon National Parks). Although some-what age limited, I remain as physically active as possible."

India Company reunion 2007 in Texas. Malcolm Stewart was a platoon leader (not in photo). This is the same company that Bobby Henderson belonged to when he was killed on January 4, 1968. The photo was provided by Robert Harriman (2nd row kneeling under the 'a' in India) who was present when Bobby was killed.

Bucky O'Neil is doing fine too,

"Bumps along the way have been made easier by having a wonderful wife of 35 years, four daughters and four grandchildren. I am currently contemplating retirement and doing some long distance hiking, bird-watching, and golfing."

Left: Bucky O'Neil, his wife Ann and four daughters. Courtesy of Ann Dwyer O'Neil.

Wayne Tuttle says the good life started the day he arrived home after being discharged.

"I met my future wife. Four years on Conesus Lake, 33 in Springwater and now in Clarkson. My daughter is a Med Tech at Unity Hospital and has my two grandkids. My son is a geo-engineer in Denver. I enjoy golf all summer and an occasional golf trip to Pinehurst in the winter. I retired in 2004 at age 55 with 39 years of state service. Retirement and my pension are great. Social Security makes it even better. My wife and I have both won individual battles with cancer and I would do it all again."

Jim Adamson put it succinctly, "I'm fine, and after all this time I wouldn't change a thing."

Jim Adamson was employed at the Johnson Space Center from 1981-1992 and was selected by NASA during the Space Shuttle Program to be an astronaut. He worked in numerous capacities before becoming a veteran of two space flight missions. First aboard the Space Shuttle Columbia in 1989 and then the Atlantis in 1991. In total, Jim logged over 334 hours in space. Above: (left) Official NASA photo 1983; (top center) photographing the Earth from space onboard the STS-28 Columbia flight 1989; (lower center) On orbit STS-43, Atlantis flight 1991; Right: Jim and family, 2009. All photos courtesy of Jim Adamson.

For Chuck Freese, "Life is good, retired after 32 years with Niagara Mohawk, family is doing good, enjoy two grandkids, spending winters in Florida is great, helps keep me active and able to get outside with warm weather."

And Rodney Wambold sums it up for us on a positive note as well:

"Today I am doing well. I have had highs and great lows in my life but I have two great sons and two wonderful grandchildren. I am retired and spend winters in Fla. with a wife whom I love. Can't ask for more."

❀ ❀ ❀ ❀ ❀ ❀ ❀ ❀ ❀ ❀ ❀

From Don Peraino's "Good!" to Rodney Wambold's "Can't ask for more," the GCS vets are all right.

Geneseo VFW members (and <u>Blue Devils in Vietnam</u> authors) selling Christmas trees. From left to right: Dennis Staley, Roger Johnson, Jim DeCamp, and Tony Gurak. Photo courtesy of VFW Post 5005.

Conclusion

by Jim DeCamp

"We served in a hard war, far away; gave it what we had, or all there was to give in Butch, Bobby, and Charlie's cases; and came home, many back to the Valley that had sent us 'Blue Devils' away to fight in Vietnam."

- Jim DeCamp

The GCS Blue Devils served from the Delta to the DMZ in all the branches of the services. From early advisors like Hal Witter and Terry Alger in 1963-4 to "turn out the lights when you leave" guys like me in July, 1971 and Gunnery Sgt. Percy Richardson whose second tour ended on January 30, 1973 - three days after the Peace Accord Cease-fire was signed in Paris ending the bombing of North Vietnam.

We flew on BUFFs, EC-121 Warning Star Super Constellations, P-3 Orions, C-141 Lockheed Starlifters and Huey, Cobra, and Loach helicopters. Off-shore we were on river patrol repair boats, the USS Oriskany (nicknamed the Mighty O), and "under the seas" in WWII diesel submarines. On the ground we were combat engineers, artillery men, radio operators, mechanics, drivers, and grunts; the rifle and mortar men who went into the "boonies" every night on APS in the dark, alternating sleep and guard duty in two-hour shifts waiting for some unlucky VC or late-night lover to stumble our way.

Above photo: Courtesy of Ron Hilfiker

We did our 365-day, or longer, tours while some "re-upped and bought a brand new car," as the 1970s marching refrain said. On our sleeves we wore patches of the Big Red One insignia *("If you're going to be one, be a Big Red One");* Black Horses of the 1st and 11th Armored Cavalry; Electric Strawberries of the 25th Infantry Division; Screaming Eagles of the 101st Airborne; Shamrocks of the 4th Infantry Division; Stars of the Americal; and Flaming Bayonets of the 198th Light Infantry Bridgade. And on my own shoulder - a Snarling Wolf in profile of the 2nd/27th with the Latin boast: *"Nec Aspera Terrant"* translated *"No Fear on Earth."* An untrue claim for me as I was afraid every day I was with those boys.

On our shoulders we carried the burdens of an un-won war, one America decided not to win, and chips of various sizes. In general, we did not join any veterans' groups, save for a few against the war, and didn't march in any parades, which was convenient as there weren't any that welcomed us for some time.

We gladly, if not always smoothly, slipped back into the lives we had left behind. Most of us went from important roles in the military with life and death consequences, to much less vital and exciting civilian ones. Other wars have come and gone or are on-going. Now we have joined the ranks of the grey-haired old guys from World War II and Korea. We don't look much different from these comrades but we're bound by a special bond that all conflicts produce. We served in a hard war, far away; gave it what we had, or all there was to give in Butch, Bobby, and Charlie's cases, and came home, many back to the Valley that had sent us "Blue Devils" away to fight in Vietnam. Now more than forty years have sanded down the sharp edges of our memories and our fears.

Why did we write this book? Not just to tell our personal stories but to set the record straight, get the truth off our chests, and to bring some peace to the warriors and their families that fought that unfortunate war.

❀ ❀ ❀ ❀ ❀ ❀ ❀ ❀ ❀

The battlefield looking East toward Mike's Hill taken approximately January 27, 1968, an hour before the Marines of India Company 2nd and 3rd platoons charged across the valley. Courtesy of Robert Harriman.

In Memoriam

❀❀❀❀❀❀❀❀❀❀❀

U. S. Army Major Charles D. Wilkie
June 6, 1934 – December 8, 1967

U.S.M.C. L CPL Francis P. "Butch" Rosebrugh
December 6, 1946 – October 22, 1966

U.S.M.C. Pvt. Robert C. "Bobby" Henderson
May 17, 1947 – January 4, 1968

U. S. Army Major Charles D. Wilkie

❀❀❀❀❀❀❀❀❀❀❀❀❀❀❀❀❀❀❀❀

June 6, 1934 – December 8, 1967

"Charlie loved Geneseo…when we had the dreaded conversation about what if something happened; he said he wanted to be buried in Geneseo, not Arlington." – Marge Wilkie

Major Charles D. Wilkie was killed December 8, 1967 while attempting to reach a fallen comrade. He was 33 years old and is buried in Temple Hill Cemetery. He was survived by his wife, Margery, and two young daughters, Jennifer and Susan. For his heroic actions on the day of his death, Major Wilkie received a posthumous Bronze Star Medal dated 30 January 1968:

> For heroism in connection with military operations against a hostile force: Major Wilkie distinguished himself by heroic action on 8 December 1967 while serving as District Advisor, Don Duong District, Republic of Vietnam. On that date, a Popular Forces outpost at Tahine was overrun by a numerically superior Viet Cong force. A Vietnamese relief force was quickly organized and dispatched to the scene. Major Wilkie, accompanying this force, moved with the unit to the area of fiercest fighting. At that time, a fellow advisor who was attempting to neutralize enemy fire from a flank position was critically wounded. Though in the face of continuous and overwhelming volume of enemy fire, so intense that the rescue unit had begun to withdraw, Major Wilkie attempted to reach the fallen advisor. In doing so he was mortally wounded. Major Wilkie demonstrated an inspirational and valiant fighting spirit and his heroic actions were in keeping with the highest traditions of the United States Army and reflected great credit upon himself and the military service.
>
> For the Commander:
>
> Walter T. Kerwin, Jr.
> Major General, USA
> Chief of Staff

Margery Wilkie has remained in Geneseo to the present day and her daughters attended elementary school here and graduated from Geneseo Central School before moving on to college, careers, and families of their own. All three have generously contributed their memories and emotions to this project, bringing a broader perspective as to how vital family, friends, the Presbyterian Church, and the community at large were in the healing process. Marge came from a family with strong military ties and recalls the sad times, along with happy times, with her own special style of wit and humor.

Left: Top photo: Korean War veteran, Richard Platt, in front of the Geneseo War Memorial. Memorial Day ceremonies in the Village Park, 2003. Lower: VFW Post 5005 gun salute, Veterans Day, 2002. Both photos courtesy of Michael Johnson, Livingston County News, Geneseo, NY.

Marge writes,

"Although your head knows the orders will come, your heart does not. I remember General Yancey coming over and saying 'Wilkie, I hear you got a short tour.' I blurted out 'SHORT TOUR?' Two weeks later on May 16, 1966 our second daughter was born. Two weeks after that Charlie left for 6 weeks of summer camp. Now the Short Tour had begun. We moved to Geneseo on August 1st. Charlie had a month of leave here and then went off to Fort Bragg Special Warfare School for six weeks. After that he had a week of leave and then off to the Presidio of Monterey [California] Language School for two months.

I was able to spend Christmas week with Charlie at the Presidio. He had day classes and at night would practice his Vietnamese. It was hard not to laugh hearing my 6'2" husband speaking in a falsetto voice. He was asked to stay two months more for an advanced class. It would not hurt his career if he declined. He opted not to extend as he had been away from his family four months and was ready to begin his tour. I do wonder if he had stayed if he would have had a different assignment.

Charlie had a week of leave before he left Rochester on Friday, January 13, 1967. Jennifer was two and Susan eight months when they last saw their father. While Charlie was at Fort Bragg and the Presidio we wrote letters and spoke on the phone. That all changed when he got to Vietnam. Letters became our lifeline. We numbered our letters and I kept his. I still reread them. I told Charlie in letter 102 that Susan had started to walk and in letter 189 that Jennifer insists Daddy will take her to Burger Park, her favorite drive-thru restaurant. Charlie's letters did not tell me bad things. They were thrilled to get a movie, and a food delivery. He would have to travel into Saigon and was glad to get back to Don Duong. The one time we spoke on the phone was the day before I met him in Hawaii. He let me know he had arrived in Nha Trang. It was phone and radio. When we were ending our part of the conversation we were to use the magic word, 'Over.' The operator said, 'Don't forget the magic word,' and I said, 'Please.' Charlie explained we had little kids.

The week we had in Hawaii was marvelous and something I will never forget. Charlie promised we would come back again. I have been back six times and the girls were able to see where we stayed. Charlie left Hawaii on Friday, October 13. There were other promises he was unable to keep. Birthday cards to the girls promised he would be there for their next birthdays after missing their birthdays that year. There was a much more light-hearted promise he made to me.

If I did not have a speeding ticket by our 10th anniversary he would give me a Mercedes 120SL. It was 8 months later we were heading to the shore when I was stopped for speeding. Jennifer informed the Trooper, 'I told her not to speed.' I knew Charlie was feeding her that line!"

Marge awoke crying the night of December 7, 1967. She didn't know why and went back to sleep. Thousands of miles and 13 hours ahead at that same time her husband was losing his life in Vietnam. The Army team tasked with notifying Marge was downtown in Geneseo a few days later. It was early Sunday morning and an Army Major and a Sergeant waited at the Normal Café on Main Street over coffee until 8:00 A.M. Some people in town already knew that Major Wilkie was MIA and when the Sergeant asked for directions to Oak Street, they knew it was bad news. Marge continues her story:

"The day I never forget is Sunday, December 10th. We were at my parents' home. The doorbell rang and I saw an Army Major at the door. I could not answer it. I knew it was bad news. Charlie was missing. Four days later I was informed that his body had been recovered. On the 21st of December, Charlie, accompanied by his best friend, Tom, was finally home. I will always remember the flags and the truck driver who jumped out of his cab and put his hand over his heart.

Charlie loved Geneseo. It was very different than Long Island. In fact when we had the dreaded conversation about what if something happened. he said he wanted to be buried in Geneseo, not Arlington. The years went by quickly. Jennifer, a Sociology major at the College of Wooster, wrote her Senior Independent Study on the returning Vietnam veteran. The next year she was asked to speak at the Memorial Day Exercises in Geneseo. I know her father would have been proud. Susan went to Allegheny College, majoring in Communications. Her thesis was a documentary on the history of the Genesee Valley Hunt, a subject near to her heart, as she had ridden for many years. Both girls live in Ohio, but Geneseo will always be home.

Charlie grew up in a small Long Island community, Bellerose Village, Nassau County. His father was an oral surgeon in New York City. He went to Xavier Military Academy in New York City. That was his first experience with the military. After two years he was able to go to Sewanaka High School. They had a football team and did not have daily drill. He went to the University of Michigan his freshman year (his father's alma mater). He transferred to the University of Vermont. He was a member of the Army R.O.T.C., in our day the first two years of R.O.T.C. was required. He stayed for four years and was commissioned as a Second Lieutenant in September of 1957. He was stationed at Fort Knox and Fort Benning and then off to Germany. A three-year tour was extended as the Berlin Wall was erected while he was there. He was Company Commander of A Company of the 37th Armor. Schweinfurt was close to the East German border, thus they were on high alert. In July 1963, he was assigned to St. Peter's College, a Jesuit School in Jersey City, New Jersey. He taught military history, a passion of his.

Charlie never discussed the war and his feelings about it with me. He was a career officer so he followed orders. In 1986, his friend, Tom, a Major General, wrote a letter to Jennifer for her Independent Study. He told her that he and Charlie were resentful of outside interference that kept them from doing the job they had to do. He also added that he hoped the military would only be used in the future when there was a clearly stated objective defined by the national leadership and supported by the national will."

Jim DeCamp's connection to the Wilkie family was tangential but deeply affecting for him. In December, 1967, he was working part-time at the Geneseo Post Office for the Christmas crunch while still in graduate school in the 5th year of a 2S deferment. Jim's task one day was to "return to sender" the unopened Christmas presents the family had sent to Major Wilkie in Vietnam before he died. Jim tells the story of how he was supposed to ring the bell and respectfully return the presents to the family. Instead, he couldn't bring himself to ring the bell, so he much less respectfully left the gifts on the porch.

These days Marge is still very active in the community, plays golf with friends, spends time with her grandchildren, and works at the local veterinary hospital. She is upbeat and doesn't dwell on the "what ifs." Rather, she has spent the last 47 years since Charlie's death thoroughly enjoying the quality of small-town life that Geneseo offers in abundance. Looking back, Marge readily admits she never liked the anti-war protesters during the Vietnam era and her husband Charlie agreed, but qualified his view by saying, "I don't like it [the protests] either but I'm willing to die for the right to do it." Charlie Wilkie is indeed a Geneseo hero.

Right: Livingston County Leader, 12/20/1967.

Military Funeral Thursday For Major Wilkie, Killed In Viet Nam

Friends may call at Rector's Chapel from 2-4 and 7-9 on Wednesday. Services will be held from there Thursday at 2 P.M.

Major Wilkie was reported missing in action early last week. However the family has received no details about his final service to his country.

Before going to Vietnam, Major Wilkie taught in the ROTC program and was assigned in Germany for three years. A graduate of the University of Vermont in 1957, he also attended the University of Michigan.

He is survived by his widow, Margery Ann of 48 Oak St., who is the daughter of Mr. and Mrs. LaVerne Spring of Geneseo; two daughters, Jennifer and Susan; his parents, Dr. and Mrs. Charles Wilkie of Bellrose, L.I.; and a sister, Mrs. Donaldson Kingsley of Hastings, Nebraska.

Full military honors will be accorded this week to the late Major Charles D. Wilkie, 33, in services to be held at Rector's Chapel, Geneseo. Major Wilkie was killed Dec. 8 at Don Doung, Vietnam, while serving as a sub-sector advisor to the civilian population. He had been in Vietnam since January 14. Burial will be in Temple Hill Cemetery, Geneseo.

Charlie's daughters, Jennifer and Susan, now both mothers, proudly and movingly describe how their father's death affected them growing up and how his legacy lives on.

Jennifer Wilkie Reynolds, Charlie's oldest daughter writes,

"My father left for Vietnam when I was two years old. I sometimes think I have memories of him, but more than likely they are just glimpses of my life with him from the few photos I have of us together.

I was blessed. Living in Geneseo, we were surrounded by family and friends. As a child I felt love not only from my family, but from the whole community. I grew up in a time when most children came from two-parent families, so that was difficult. I always felt the need to tell people why I only had a mother. Daddy/Daughter events were especially hard, but my grandfather, LaVerne Spring or family friend, Don Hamilton, always made sure we were included. I had a very happy childhood. I knew my dad was a hero and he died protecting others.

As I grew there were occasions I missed him terribly; my high school and college graduations, my wedding, and the birth of my children. However, I never dwelt on the loss but rather took comfort in knowing that my father would be very proud of the person I had become.

Growing up, I did not think about the war too much. I was so very young. I really just knew that I lost my dad to the war. Once in college, I began to have an interest in finding out what I could about the Vietnam War, how it changed our country, its citizens and even the country of Vietnam. I took a course in college on the Vietnam War. That course and my father's role in the war were the catalysts that led me to write my Senior Independent Study Thesis on the war. As a Sociology major, my thesis focused mainly on the role society played in welcoming back our Vietnam veterans.

As a mother myself, I marvel at my own mother's strength. My mother is the strongest person I know. I know there were sad, dark days, but she never let us see them. She picked herself up and made sure that my sister and I were always her first priority. I like to think that I am a strong person too. I believe my strength comes from both my parents. My mom for raising two daughters alone, and my dad for the courage, bravery and conviction he showed in serving his country.

I have had many people through the years say to me, 'Your dad was a real hero' and I agree, but I always add, 'My mother is one too!' "

Susan Wilkie Moses, Charlie's youngest daughter writes,

"It is my great honor to be the daughter of Major Charles David Wilkie. I am always proud to share our family story as it comes up in conversation with those unfamiliar with my background. Gratitude for my father's service and sacrifice is almost always a part of their response, and I accept it gratefully. But as much as I love talking about my father, there is a moment in the conversation I dread. And it always comes. **'So, you never really knew your father.'**

Sometimes it comes in the form of a question. Sometimes it's presented as a declaration. It is neither rude nor insensitive for the fact is my father was killed when I was only 18 months old. He'd already been in Vietnam for nearly a year. And before his deployment, he spent months away from us training for his assignment. So how could I know my father? I don't know how many times my father held me, fed me a bottle or laid me down to sleep. Did my tiny hand grasp his finger? Did I make eye contact with the brown eyes that mirror mine? I don't have the answers and cannot close my eyes and recall a moment in time with him. **But there is no doubt in my heart and mind that I have always known my father.**

My father was not a physical presence in my life. But through the love and foresight of my mother, grandparents and relatives who knew him, my father was always present and his name spoken on the most loving, joyful occasions. My sister and I can recite stories of his experiences in Germany, where he met my mother. Their first date was in an armored tank. We know stories of his boyhood growing up on Long Island. How he attended a Catholic military school and loved the Brooklyn Dodgers. So despondent was he when Wendell Willkie lost to FDR in the 1940 presidential election, my father stayed home from school. He was only 6 at the time.

We know he worried greatly about leaving us to go to Vietnam. But as a man of great honor, he made sure we were in a place where my mother would have support and my sister and I would be surrounded by love and family. He brought us to Geneseo. But the presence of my father in my life is deeper than the words spoken about him. I know my father through me. Our connection goes beyond the brown hair, brown eyes and the height we share. Quieter than my mother and sister. Introspective. A bit more serious. A heartfelt smile that can't quite surrender to the occasion. I am my father's daughter.

(continued next page)

My father taught me the right choices in life rarely are the easy ones. They require sacrifice. And sometimes they will make you unpopular. Your responsibility goes beyond the people in your life. It stretches to those who cannot fend for themselves, and those whose footsteps will follow in yours.

Today, I am the mother of two beautiful boys. My younger son is still a toddler. But my older son, who is 12, shares his grandfather's love of history and our nation's battles. He is thoughtful, reflective and a bit serious for a boy his age. He has that all too familiar smile. In him, I can see my father. It is a most cherished gift.

So how do you respond to, 'So you didn't know your father?' By smiling with his smile and saying 'Yes. Yes I do.' "

Top: Charlie and his daughters. Lower: Images from Charlie's Vietnam scrapbook. Courtesy of the Wilkie family.

U.S.M.C. L CPL Francis P. "Butch" Rosebrugh
✿✿✿✿✿✿✿✿✿✿✿✿✿✿✿✿✿✿✿✿✿✿✿
December 6, 1946 – October 22, 1966

Francis P. "Butch" Rosebrugh was killed October 22, 1966 in Vietnam while carrying the body of his platoon commander back to the command post amid heavy fire. He was 19 years old and a graduate of Geneseo Central School, Class of 1965. He is buried in Lakeview Cemetery, in the town of Groveland, New York.

Butch was attached to G Co, 2Bn, 3rd Marine Div, III MAF. His company commander at the time, Lt. John Kopka, is a retired Lt. Col. with a Silver Star Medal and he offered us his memories of that day:

"As the Commanding Officer, Company G, Second Battalion 3rd Marines CO, Co G, 2nd Bn 3rd Mar, I was LCpl Rosebrugh's company commander. Operation Kern (Oct 21-Oct 26, 1966) was a search and destroy operation in a region southeast of An Hoa, Quang Tri Province, Republic of Vietnam. Company G was the point company for the 2nd Bn 3rd Mar. We were to move to the north from a helicopter drop zone to an area called Helicopter Valley. The point platoon for Co G was 1st Platoon (1st Lt Robert Bates). A fierce firefight erupted as we approached the valley and 1st platoon was pinned down by heavy enemy small arms fire. LCpl Rosebrugh was in 1st Platoon. Our artillery forward observer requested/received artillery support and our section of 81mm mortars provided supporting fire. Heavy rain prevented any gunship support.

On October 22, 1966, 1st Lt Thomas Holden, Executive Officer, Company G; 1st Lt Robert Bates, Platoon Commander 1st Platoon; SSgt Louis Reed, Platoon Sergeant, 1st Platoon; LCpl Charles Riley, 1st Squad; LCpl Francis Rosebrugh, 1st Squad; PFC Alonzo Teague, 2nd Squad; Sgt Ivan Smith, 3rd Platoon and Cpl James Hightower, 3rd Platoon were all killed in action.

When the 2nd Bn returned to its home base a memorial service was held for all the Marines killed during Operation Kern. The service was conducted by the Bn Chaplain with the CO, 2d Bn 3rd Mar (Lt Col Victor Oranesian) and Sgt Maj, 2nd Bn 3rd Mar (Sgt Maj Wayne Hayes) providing remarks. Lt Col Oranesian and Sgt Maj Hayes were killed in action during February, 1967.

Wish I could provide more information, however, many years have passed and many Marine faces are in my memory bank. We hope our small contribution will help with your writing."

The Command Chronology for the period 1 to 31 October, 1966 has been de-classified and its 154 pages are available online (see insert this page). The Marine patrols of that period found 47 graves containing 93 NVA bodies contributing to the extant theory that body counts would turn the tide for us. We failed to realize that there was an endless supply of bodies willing to die for their own independence.

Operation Kern was a mess and even the cold, clipped prose of the summary can't conceal the horrors of that day. Cut off from retreat by a monsoon-swollen stream turned to a river, rained and fogged in from any medical evacuation or helicopter support or re-supply, the Marines had to hunker down amid their own dead and dying throughout the night. The report dated 22 October, 1966 stated,

"At 1310, enemy contact was made when Company G received sporadic sniper fire from Objectives D & F. Company G continued to move forward towards Objective D utilizing reconnaissance by fire. Sniper fire continued and one squad from the 1st Platoon of Company G, after crossing a waist deep stream and 200 meters of open rice paddies moved to Objective D at 1345 hours... Casualties in the Command Billets of Company G became critical as the XO [executive officer] was killed, as were the platoon commander and platoon sergeant of the 1st platoon. The platoon commander of the 3rd platoon was critically wounded and evacuated. In addition 6 squad leaders [Butch included] were either killed or wounded within one hour.

The stream that had been easily crossed earlier became un-fordable as the rains continued to fall...fog and rain precluded re-supply and medical evac. Of the casualties: Friendly casualties were 8 KIA and 18 WIA from Company G. Enemy losses were 18 KIA confirmed at Objective D."

* *From the Marine Corps Command Chronolgy, National Archives www.archives.gov.*

Geneseo Marine Killed in Viet Nam

LANCE CORPORAL FRANCIS ROSEBURGH

Mr. and Mrs. Paul Roseburgh of Geneseo were informed Sunday of the death of their son, Lance Corporal Francis Roseburgh, 19, in Danang, Viet Nam, by Marine Lieutenant Colonel Dale E. Shatzer, 3rd Comm. Co., Force Troops, U.S.M.C.R. A telegram of confirmation received Monday stated that Lance Cpl. Roseburgh was killed in a skirmish "in the vicinity of Danang, Viet Nam. He sustained a gunshot wound to the abdomen from hostile rifle fire while participating in an operation against hostile forces."

A June 1965 graduate of Geneseo Central School, Lance Cpl. Roseburgh had entered the service in March of 1965. He had been stationed in Viet Nam since July of 1966.

In his last letter home, he stated that he had just recently been promoted to the rank of Lance Corporal.

Lance Cpl. Roseburgh is survived by two sisters, Mrs. Mary Ann Orman, Geneseo, and Mrs. Betty Beach, Fort Lewis, Washington, and his parents.

It is expected that the body will arrive in about ten days, with funeral arrangements being completed by W. S. Rector and Sons. Burial will be in Lakeview Cemetery, Groveland.

Lance Cpl. Francis Roseburgh was the grandson of the late Ralph Roseburgh, who was Groveland's Highway Superintendent for many years. His mother is the former Ellen Munson of Geneseo.

Livingston County Leader, 10/26/1966.

Did Butch's death have a dramatic long term impact on his family? Butch's nephew, Jeff Orman insists, "Absolutely" as he began an interview. In fact, his first remembrance as a child was seeing his mother come home crying. He recalls that at what was supposed to be a time of family celebration, there was conflict and confusion going on as notification of Butch's death came just before Jeff's 4th birthday. Jeff said this scene in his mind still "feels like it was yesterday."

Yet, the details surrounding what happened afterward are fuzzy except that he remembers his grandmother (Butch's mother) didn't want the kids going to the funeral.

Jeff describes his grandmother and his mother as the "greatest women in his life, always there, always strong…My mother was as strong as a rock, if there was a situation no matter how bad it was, you would never know there was a problem." It was just the opposite for his grandfather who never recovered from losing his youngest child and only son. "My grandfather was an alcoholic. My whole life I knew him just as an old guy who sat in the corner and drank beer…I'm sure that was his way of dealing." Even though he barely remembers Butch himself, Jeff's whole life has been defined by his uncle's over-arching presence. His mother, Mary Ann, who passed away in 2008, never talked much about the death of her younger brother but told Jeff that he and Butch would have been great together. "Most of the talk wasn't about his military service but about his love of hunting," he says, and as a little boy, Jeff was fascinated by Butch's gun collection and eventually the gun cabinet came to him. He describes feeling a "special kinship through an object, more so than a kinship knowing Butch." Jeff has a small box of precious mementos: including Butch's diploma, his dog tags, graduation picture, and his Marine notebook - the only item with his handwriting.

The aftermath of the war, along with Butch's death, most likely influenced Jeff's parent's insistence that he go to college and not into military service. Jeff admits he has struggled with unsettled emotions and feelings throughout his life and always wondered if the Vietnam War had ended differently then there "would [have been] a whole different meaning and pathway that things took afterward." He is thankful his Uncle Butch and Vietnam vets in general are finally being given the level of recognition they deserve. Most of all Jeff is appreciative of the opportunity to let his story be told.

Jeff's older sister Brenda also shared her remembrances of her Uncle Butch.

"My earliest memories of my Uncle Butch were as a playmate. He was eleven years old when I was born, his oldest niece. I recall kickball and games of croquet on the front yard that he would play with us, his nieces and nephews. Letting us play with his wooden blocks, marbles and his toy soldiers, cowboys and Indians or reading to us from his latest comic book. His model airplanes and ships on the other hand were off-limits!

Butch towering over his nieces and nephews. Clockwise from front: Brenda (sitting) Jeff, Bob, Dianne, Mike, and his beloved dog, Zeus. Courtesy of Brenda Orman.

(continued next page)

(Brenda Orman continues) I know he frequented Long Point Park because there was a stack of unredeemed Skee Ball coupons that Grandma kept among his things in his bedroom...I have absolutely no memories of him ever being angry or saying a cross word. I especially remember him as a hero, when my toddler brother, Bobby, had wandered off and eventually seeing Uncle Butch walking into our yard carrying him home upon his shoulders. I am now in possession of the letters he sent home to his parents, Ellen and Paul, and his oldest sister, Mary Ann, my Mom. His letters were always upbeat and very regular. I can remember how my Mom would read his letters to us and feeling so special when he would mention us by name. How she and my grandparents would get together to share his letters. He kept his family informed about his training and how he was doing...In his letters he would ask about family happenings and how his dog, Zeus, was behaving. He wanted to know the latest news about his friends. He enjoyed reading western novels...He always talked about the future things he would do, like saving his money to purchase a new car or the traveling he intended to do when he got out of the service.

I believe it was in late August of 1966 that he purchased an Olympus camera. I have three photographs of him while he was in Vietnam. Two are of him standing alone in his fatigues. In one he is holding his M-14. The third is my most precious. Unfortunately the quality of this particular photo is pretty bad, but it shows him standing

with two small Vietnamese children. He is smiling. His left hand coming gently over the shoulder of the boy, who is holding one of his fingers. I feel a bit of jealousy towards these children as I think that it should be my hands and the hands of my brothers and sister that should be in his grasp. But then I remember that one of the reasons he signed up with the Marines was to protect the innocents of the world and I am grateful that these children had a moment of their lives captured by the lens of a camera showing me that my Uncle Butch cared for them. *(continued next page)*

Left: Butch with Vietnamese children, 1966. Courtesy of Brenda Orman.

(Brenda Orman continues)   I remember years after his death, my grandmother explaining why she did not want us children being present at the calling hours or funeral as that was not an image she wanted us to remember of our Uncle Butch. In hindsight I wish I had thought to write down the stories that she would tell us of him and his growing-up years, of being a Cub Scout and Boy Scout. His school days at GCS. Hunting and fishing with his buddies. Working for Bryce Adair and buying his car, the "Yellow Banana." Even though I yearned for more stories, I didn't ask many direct questions about him for fear of causing her sadness. That also goes for my mother, I remember as an eight-year-old, seeing her cry over Butch's death and feeling completely helpless.

I was at my grandparent's home when Lt. Col. Dale Shatzer of the Marine Corps presented the Purple Heart and the National Defense Service Medal. I remember the sense of awe to be in the presence of the Marines that came that day along with the sadness of what it represented. I know that the flag that draped his casket and had been presented to his mother along with his Purple Heart, Bronze Star with Combat "V", medals for National Defense, Conspicuous Service from New York State and the Republic of Vietnam. We have a scrap book containing his Marine Corps Certificate of Acceptance as well as the certificates appointing him Private First Class and the one appointing him Lance Corporal, which happened just 22 days before his death.

I am very proud of my uncle and how he felt the need to serve his country. To this day, I still watch Vietnam documentaries or look at photos of the war scanning the faces in hopes that maybe one of them is my Uncle Butch. I cannot hear Taps played without remembering Uncle Butch and shedding tears for ALL who gave the ultimate sacrifice."

Above: Images of Butch growing up. Left - In his mother's arms; Center - With his father and sisters, Betty and Mary Ann; Right - With the Marines in Vietnam. Courtesy of Brenda Orman.

Butch's surviving sister, Betty, gave us short but eloquent replies to our queries. Forty-seven years after Butch's death, Betty's husband told us, "Finally got Betty to answer…Hope these answers help…It's all I could get her to do. I think it is too painful to relive in much detail." In response to several questions Betty writes:

"He was a good kid and although he was 3 years behind me in school, and worked at Warner's [farm]…We were proud of him when he enlisted…I had one or two letters from him but he was only gone for 2-3 months….Mom was worried that he would be killed…Initially we felt pain…Mom and Dad never felt peace. I believe I did, but I was away. My husband was in the Army…I am sorry there was a war. There was no end to it."

For Butch's close friends there was "no end to it" either. Fellow classmate and Vietnam veteran, Tony Gurak, describes how devastating his friend's death was, not just to him but to the whole community:

"As many of Butch's classmates that could possibly be there, along with family, neighbors, and friends, attended his funeral. No one who was there will ever forget that day. However, I don't think anyone remembers everything about that day. It was just too traumatic. The mind just mercifully blacks some things out. Butch's funeral was the first time that I had heard taps played at a military funeral. Mr. Falconio, our high school music teacher, honored Butch by playing Taps for his final salute. He played beautifully, perfectly. It was just too much for everyone. I can see it all so clearly in my mind. At the first notes of Taps all who had tried so hard to hold back their emotions no longer could. The uncontrollable sobbing, wives collapsing into their husband's arms. Just awful. Everyone knew it was the final goodbye.

Every time I hear Taps played now it tears at my heart, and I'm right back at Butch's funeral. Butch's parents never recovered from their loss. Butch's father was never the same, his grief was too deep. A year later, when home on leave I ran into a young lady from our class who had attended Butch's funeral. The instant she saw me, she began crying and buried her face in my shoulder. All she could think of was Butch's funeral. All the pain from that day was still very much there for her. Another of our classmates confided in me that at times when he needs to get away for some quiet, personal time, he goes to the cemetery and just talks to Butch like he used to. Such a sincere act of friendship all these many years later."

Without a doubt no one besides Butch's immediate family was more devestated than his best friend Bobby Henderson, whose own compelling story and short life on this earth is defined by his strong will, charismatic personality, and undying devotion. Butch and Bobby's lives were interwoven and sadly Bobby's death in Vietnam just 14 months later once again rocked the small-town communities of Geneseo and Groveland. And as Tony Gurak explains:

"The emotional roller coaster began all over again. Those of us who knew Bobby best knew how hard he took Butch's death. Bobby had convinced Butch to join the Marines. He blamed himself for Butch's death. Bobby was home on medical leave recovering from malaria from his first Vietnam tour when Butch was killed in Vietnam. Bobby did not wear his Marine Corp uniform to Butch's funeral. That could only mean that he was not proud to be a Marine at that time. In the weeks following Butch's funeral, Bobby lashed out at the world. He started fights with college students, got thrown out of bars. It was a very hard time for Bobby."

Best friends Bobby Henderson (center) and Butch (right) on a fishing trip with Carmen Griffo, close family friend. Courtesy of Brenda Orman.

U.S.M.C. Pvt. Robert C. "Bobby" Henderson

❀❀❀❀❀❀❀❀❀❀❀❀❀❀❀❀❀❀❀❀❀❀❀❀

May 17, 1947 – January 4, 1968

"Bobby" Henderson, age 20, was killed January 4, 1968 while on a combat mission a few weeks before the Tet Offensive and is buried in Arlington National Cemetery. Bobby was in the Geneseo Central School class of '65 but had left school for the Marines prior to graduation. After being wounded and stricken by malaria in his first tour of duty he volunteered for a second tour determined to avenge the death of his best friend Butch Rosebrugh.

His younger brother Mike, GCS Class of '73, tells of his big brother's character and his "stand-up guy" mentality:

"I knew Bobby to be a tough, no-nonsense guy who would take on any physical challenge that presented itself any time, anywhere and whoever wanted that challenge. I laugh to myself occasionally when I reminisce as a child coming out of grade school noticing all the high school kids by the big tree off campus to settle one's differences...for some reason or another my brother seemed to be involved in the mix...daily!

Bobby was a street-smart kind of guy who wasn't interested in school and could not wait to get out. Bobby would talk to Butch eventually talking Butch into going in the Marines under the buddy plan. Also fondly recall when he came home and told us all he had joined the Marines wanting to serve his country, which he felt he needed to do as Vietnam was soon approaching. During our conversation over dinner I could tell my father was concerned but proud of the decision he made. I asked him later why...and he replied with a grin, 'Because, Mike, if I don't stand up to the bully next door no one else will. It's important to me to protect this country and the people I love from others who can't defend themselves, I owe this country that much.' I never really gave it much thought until many years later as I prepared for the military myself, fully understanding the great responsibility of protecting our country.

Finally...the greatest memory of the man he had grown to be....was a time, I won't name the family of boys who lived up the road from us, but they had been working me over pretty hard on the bus, which was a daily activity. Each time I disembarked off the bus I ran home a hundred yards ahead of this group of brothers so I would not have to endure another beat down. I remember as I turned into the yard through the trees seeing my brother waiting for me, thus forgetting

Pvt. Robt. C. Henderson

*Livingston Republican,
January 11, 1968.*

Local Marine Killed In Action In Vietnam

Six months and six days before his tour of duty ended in Vietnam Pvt. Robert C. Henderson, 21, of Groveland was killed while serving his second tour of duty with the U. S. Marines.

Pvt. Henderson, who joined the Marines July 10, 1964, was killed on Jan. 4 and the family received notification on Sunday. During his first tour of duty in Viet Nam he was twice wounded and twice had malaria. During the second attack of Malaria in Sept., 1966, he was sent home two weeks early for treatment at Bethesda Naval Hospital in Md. During this time he was able to visit at his home here

He was later assigned to Henderson Hall in Washington for a few weeks and went from there to Key West, Fla. Then he again volunteered for duty in Viet Nam and was sent to Camp Pendleton, Calif., in Sept. and left for overseas in October, 1967.

His tour of duty would have been up on July 10, 1968.

He was born in Warsaw on May 17, 1947, the son of Major and Mrs. Robert L. Henderson of Groveland. He attended Geneseo Central School.

His father, who retired in 1962 from the U. S. Air Force where he served more than 20 years of active federal military service, is now a patient at Northside Hospital in Rochester.

Other survivors include his mother, a sister, Mrs. James McDowell of Lewistown, Ill., a

Continued on Back Page

(Cont. From Front Page)

brother, Michael, and another sister, Barbara Ann, both at home; his paternal grandfather, Robert W. Henderson of Groveland who is a patient at Dansville Hospital, and his maternal grandparents, Mr. and Mrs. Keith Kickman of Lewistown, Ill.

Arrangements are being made for his body to be sent directly to Arlington Cemetery for burial.

Those desiring may contribute to a Memorial Fund being handled by Mrs. Herman Adamson of Hunts Corners.

In a recent issue of Geneseo Central School's Valley Echoes there was a letter from Bob Henderson.

He wrote in part, "I'm presently stationed at C-2 an artillery outpost, which is approx. 2 miles from Con Tein, and the DMZ....

"Our living conditions are a lot better than the first time I was over here. We live completely underground in bunkers and we have trench lines that run every where. We don't have to walk on ground level at all, if it is so desired. (All of this is due to enemy artillery.)

"As for being here, it's really hard to say, what with all the protests, but as far a I'm concerned we are in too deep to get out now and too close to victory.

"Thanks to the people back home, my squad had a great Thanksgiving. We combine all our packages in to one big al among the squad."

(cont. from page 205) what had occurred to me earlier and him giving me a hug, asking him why he was home with him replying, 'I'm home on furlough.' Bobby then noticed something was wrong as I had tears in my eyes…and not having a very good poker face, only telling him I was so proud of him for being my brother, but he was smart, seeing right through that bullshit and subsequently getting the real reason why I was crying.

As I explained the situation of the ganged up beatings I was taking daily he proceeded to walk out into the middle of the road standing like John Wayne in a gunfight confronting the band of brothers. With them all stopped and spread out on the road frightened and rightfully so, I watched from the driveway as he stated to each and every one of them in no uncertain terms that if he ever heard of anyone touching me again he would personally take care of business and they would not forget. Needless to say from that time forward I never was bothered again. As he walked to the house after he made his statement he never said a word to me, but I knew this was his credo: to stand and face adversity in the eye and deal with it how he knew best."

We now know much more about Bobby's death than the bland announcements the military provides. Coincidentally, his platoon leader was Lt. Malcolm Stewart, GCS class of '61. Through Malcolm we have gathered an eyewitness account from his fellow Marine squad mate, Paul Harris of Carlsbad, California, who shared some of his memories, which he admits were difficult to write down. Paul was right behind Bobby as he stepped on the anti-tank land mine left over from the disastrous French war with Vietnam 15 years earlier. Paul writes eloquently about Bobby as he recalls the events of that day:

"Hardly has a day gone by in the last 45 years that I have not taken a few minutes to think of him. He was simply a great guy, a good combat Marine, and his death was so sudden and terrible…My memories of January 4, 1968 are incomplete and fragmented. Others have mentioned that day in terms of our activities but I'm not able to recall it so clearly. I believe that is a result of trying to reconstruct events after more than 45 years and is also attributable to the fact that I suffered a severe concussion and other wounds that day as a result of being so close to the mine blast. But as I recall it was a cloudy day, not wet, but gloomy. I think the explosion occurred in mid-afternoon… I do remember Bob Henderson well. Arriving at C2 on or about December 14, 1967, fresh from the states, I was immediately assigned to his fire team. This was his second tour in Vietnam…

From a leadership standpoint, I had a lot of respect for him. He clearly understood how to work in the bush: setting a perimeter or an ambush, how to walk a trail, use flankers, set trip flares, read a compass and a map; he had an excellent knowledge of all of it. He taught me a lot in the few weeks I knew him, and I intentionally pushed him to learn as much as I could.

He was hot-tempered, abrupt and to the point, yet he possessed a mischievous sense of humor, and was liked by all of us. He was also from New York, as I was, so we shared a certain kinship as a result. I knew that for that short time that I knew him that he liked and re-spected me as I did him. We were fast building a solid friendship that I'm sure would have endured a lifetime. Everything that was promised about what Vietnam would be like that I heard throughout boot camp and advance infantry training were realized after only a few short weeks of being in-country, including firefights, witnessing my first KIA and wounded (both enemy and friendly), enduring incoming sniper fire, losing a very good friend and being wounded myself only 2.5 weeks into my 12-month and 20-day tour of duty.

Bob's death was particularly shocking to me since he was such a well-rounded, experienced and proven field fighting Marine. From his death I took stock of the fact it mattered not how good you were or how well-prepared or how handsome and fit you were; if you were in the wrong place at the wrong time you could be taken in a millisecond, as quickly as the sound that comes from snapping your fingers. After January 4th, 1968, with over 11 months remaining in-country, I took absolutely nothing and no one for granted. I seriously doubted I would survive it all, but somehow, miraculously, I did.

It has often occurred to me throughout my life that I could easily have been the one who stepped on the mine instead of Bob; as I was behind him he simply got to it before I did. Bill Waldrop was ahead of him but took the right step, and Bob found it first. A few days later, when in the rear for medical treatment of my wounds, I was taken to Graves Registration at Dong Ha combat base to identify him, and after doing so I personally signed his death certificate. Had it been the other way around he would probably have been the one who would have put his signature on mine.

Not a religious man, but I know, have always believed, that God was with me that day, and he spared me for a reason. Bob's death was swift, he felt no pain. On identifying him, I will never forget the look on his face. His face was not damaged by the blast, but he wore a slight grimace, a slight tightening of the eyes, suggesting that for a moment, however slight, he knew what took him. *(continued next page)*

Sometime in 1987, I sought out Bob's parents. I called information for Geneseo, New York, and asked for a local Henderson phone number. It took three or four inquiries, but in a short time I found them. I spoke with his father for several minutes. He was eager for information on how Bob died. I explained it all while closely guarding details that I felt would be too difficult for him. He told me Bob was buried in Arlington. The entire family was devastated by his death, and based on what Bob's father shared with me, his mother was never the same again. He thanked me profusely for calling. We both cried a little. He too died a short time after that and I think he is buried in Arlington as well as he was retired military.

I can't but wonder what Bob would be like were he alive today. Like the rest of us, he would occasionally look back in time on certain indelible anniversary dates, or as we all do he would daily engage in a light reflection of the long-gone past and return to the field for a few short moments, opening short windows of memory for minutes at a time remembering who we were, what we did, and the many good friends, now long dead, many forgotten, who gave all they had."

Bobby's high school sweetheart, Janice (McDonald) McFollins agreed to share "their story" as well. Her personal perspective clearly reveals what kind of guy he really was deep inside and the tremendous impact the loss of his best friend Butch Rosebrugh and the war itself had on him. Through the gentle (and persistent) encouragement of Butch and Bobby's friend and fellow Vietnam veteran, Tony Gurak, Janice agreed to do an interview, speaking into a recorder alone in her living room. And despite her initial reluctance, she did a remarkable job, describing in vivid detail a painful, but enlightening, story that has been frozen in time for more than 46 years. In the process, Janice unleashed pent-up emotions that she has kept buried, driven solely by her desire to set the record straight and to give thanks to all involved in this publication. We are grateful for her contribution that has helped us better understand the sacrifices Bobby Henderson made.

Note: Janice McFollins was given a list of questions for this interview that was tape-recorded in February 2014 over the course of a few days and subsequently transcribed by Holly C. Watson, Deputy Livingston County Historian. Only minor edits have been made such as removing words and phrases inadvertently repeated, and a few explanatory words were inserted in brackets. Otherwise the interview is presented in its entirety.

"This is Janice McFollins, formerly Janice McDonald. I graduated in 1965 from Geneseo Central School, therefore I was in the same class as Bob Henderson. First and foremost, I'd like to thank the guys who are writing this book as I know the difficult time I'm having with this… I cannot imagine what you guys are going through, but if it helps you to do this, I'm very glad. I have found out about myself from this, and I've put it off as long as I can, and now I'm just going to sit, and do it, and whatever comes out, I'm going on live because I've found out that I really have never dealt with this. To me, Bob is not deceased. I don't know – I just can't handle that part. To me, he is still alive and roaming around somewhere. So I'd like to thank you guys, and it means a lot to me, and I certainly want a copy of this book. So thank you, and here we go.

"I believe it was our sophomore year when Bob came to our school from Niagara-Winfield, I believe. And shortly after that, we became – well, we started going steady, let's put it that way, that's what it was called in those days. And through him is how I became friends with Butch. And the three of us used to do a lot of getting together, and laughing, and, you know, having a good time. The one – one thing that I remember about Butch is that I believe it was Warner's, where he used to work as a farm hand, and Bob and I were down there one day, and Butch came out of the barn, and just threw around the F-bomb, once. Well, Miss Prim-And-Proper got so indignant about it that I just wanted to get out of there. I just wanted to leave, I didn't want to know anything about him, and Bob took me off to the side and tried to tell me, you know, this is just farm-talk, that's how farmers talk. Well, I didn't care how they talked, I didn't want to hear it. Well, Butch was so, oh, so upset, and this went on for some time, that he was so uncomfortable around me, and he vowed to me that day he would never, ever use that word in my presence again. And he kept his word. He was a guy of his word. And also he was very loyal; he and Bob were extremely, extremely, tight. I mean, they both knew what was going on with the other all the time. And we used to go around in Butch's – I think it was a '52 Chevy… we palled around, the three of us, a lot.

"…Bob got this brainy idea that since he and Butch enjoyed hunting so much, that I should learn to use a – I don't know what it's called – a 30F – 6 – Central – a shotgun, anyway, so we met halfway, Bob lived in Hunt's Corners, I lived up on Groveland Hill. And we used to do this often, we met halfway between our houses and we would just go walking. So we met at Butch's house, and Butch at this time lived on the Groveland - Mt. Morris Road, and as we were walking up the driveway

(continued next page)

(Janice McFollins continued) Bob and I were laughing, and I looked, and I see Butch trying to scramble something off to his side, but I could still see his bloody hands, and it's like, what the heck?

"Well, on his lap was a squirrel that he was skinning for as he told me later, after Bob had to pick me up off the ground 'cause my legs went out from under me – it was just gory and disgusting – that his mom was going to make them for dinner. Well, I'm telling you, if I had eaten anything that day, I'm sure I would up-chuck, because the thought of squirrel, and seeing that tiny little thing on his lap with no skin was just... So, here he goes again, he's getting all nervous, and finally after I came up after having my head between my legs because I was so dizzy over it, they got to laughing, and I got to laughing, and I said, 'No, that's quite all right.' "

"…Bob and I [would] go up through the woods, up and down … they used to call them Seven Gullies and all that. And we get to this spot, which I look at every single time I go back to my mother's house. She's deceased now, but my niece lives there. And it's up at the top of Chestnut Hill, just as you get over the top. And there's this field. Well, we ended up there, and he had me steady myself on the fence and he taught me right, he told me, you know, 'Hold it [the shotgun] tight, you have to hold it very tight to your chest.' Well, I weighed maybe 95 pounds soaking wet at that time, and I didn't have any problem with it because my brother had a rifle and he was always shooting. So, you know, I didn't think anything of it. Well, when it decided it was gonna kick, there was this tiny little ditch there that I ended up in, with my legs up in the air, my head up in the air, and my fanny caught in this little, kinda, whatever it was, just a small ditch. And he had to pick the gun up and put it away properly and then try to get me out of the ditch. And I can remember him saying, 'she's holding on to me' because I was just stunned. 'Well, I guess we can forget about that,' and forget about that we did. So, those are two stories that come to my mind when I think of Butch and Bob.

"I think of many things; he has never left my mind. I think your first love is a very important love, and it just stays with you – I think of him often...

"What did I think of the war before Bob went into the Marines? Well, it scared me. I had really never been through a time when we were in a war. I used to watch it faithfully with my parents, we always watched the news together at night, and it was scary. And yes, I believed the government when they said that we were winning the war, you know, and that we belonged there. *(continued next page)*

"At that time, I mean, the government…the politicians, the people who were making all the rules, were next to God to me. What did I know? I mean, I'm 17 years old, 18 years old, but…no, it just scared me. To watch it was a horrible thing, and I used to pray for all the guys that were over there at night. And the protesters, I just thought … I thought they were rather gutless…and for them to run away, and their parents to help them…I don't know…it's been such a long time…

"After Bob died, it's a different story. I can remember that my main thing about the protesters and the people who didn't believe in the war and thought the government was wrong, was Jane Fonda. I could not stand her, I swear to God, if she was standing in front of me at that time I would have spit in her face. But that was after he died. My thoughts changed incredibly about the war. As far as were we right to be there, to tell you the God's honest truth, I don't even remember why we were there… to tell you the truth, all I felt was rage. Just this rage would come over me, and then it changed. I never watched when Vietnam came on. And after going through all this, and thinking about this…I realize now that whenever, you know, like it'll come on TV, I walk out of the room, or I grab something and start reading it, and I tune it out. I don't want to know anything about it. I don't want to see about it, hear about it…it just is a bad time. And I never had any conversations with Butch about being in Vietnam, because after Bob went into the service, I don't even know if I even saw Butch about it or not…it's kind of a blur because I can't remember…

"I know I rode to the airport with him [Bob] and his family when he first went into the service and I think it was when he found out he was going to Vietnam that he decided – well, we had become engaged December 25th, 1964 – but he had decided because he was going to Vietnam that it wasn't a good idea for us to be engaged. That, you know, that I should go out, I should have fun, I should do this, I should do that. And I was crushed over it… But even though I didn't have a ring on my finger, you know, that ring doesn't really mean all that much, your feelings do not change. And, so we went our separate ways. Although I still wrote to him, and in our letters he was absolutely insistent that we not talk about Vietnam…he would not tell me what was going on over there, he might tell me what the weather was, or…a story one of the guys had told…he always talked about the future. That was it. Always talked about the future…well, actually, the main thing I think was to just protect me so I didn't really know, so I didn't have to worry. Although…of course I worried, he's in a war. But he always made everything sound like it was OK… *(continued next page)*

(Janice McFollins cont.) "I know it's probably hard to believe, but I mean, I think when he wrote to me, it took him out of that zone, and he could feel more comfortable because, like I said, we kinda went our opposite ways, and the very last time I saw him…he was home on leave and we got together, this was when he was gonna go back for the second time, and again, he didn't want to talk about it, but we met up somewhere… when he was ready to take me home – and we were in my driveway, he stopped the car and I noticed, as we got closer to home, that he seemed to be trembling…[He] pushed the seat back and he just started trembling terribly, and he was sweating profusely, and at that time, is when I learned that he had malaria, because I mean, I didn't know what the heck was going on. He told me…he had malaria, but he'd gotten over it, but every once in a while he'd have a small bout with it…looking back on it, this was not a 'small bout' because it scared the hell out of me, to tell you the truth…

"I don't know if he was hallucinating, because I don't know, he was just really out of it, and I was just holding him. And he became very angry, and this is when, in broken words, he was talking about Butch, and he had a break-down…He said that he was going back to Vietnam to kill all those gooks, every single one he saw, whether it was a woman, child, man, animal – he was going to kill every single one of them over there, because Butch didn't deserve to die, and it was his fault…that Butch was dead, because he's the one who convinced him that the Marines was a good thing for him to get into. That he [Butch] was the type of guy that would enjoy it, would be good for it, and make the country proud. I mean, that was a big thing to him, to make the country proud. So yes, he went over there to avenge Butch's death, and yes, he blamed himself for Butch's death. No doubt about it… when he finally got to the point – because I wanted to go in the house and get my father, and God knows, you know, he wasn't about to let that happen - but when he finally gathered himself and got his emotions together and got himself together…

"To read this [Tony Gurak's questions and notes] that many people knew it and I didn't see… I didn't know a lot of stuff, apparently. But I will say that when he got home that time before he went in [the military and to Vietnam] the second time, yes, he was different. He was not the same happy-go-lucky person that he always was before, laughing and joking. And there was a bitterness about him. And I can understand why… It's almost like he had a mean streak in him…He wasn't the soft-speaking guy…with me, I'm saying. He tried to be.. and I knew, when he found out about Butch…　*(continued next page)*

I think that's how we got together again, is because, you know, we both felt bad, and we both kinda knew where the other one would be, and just got together. He didn't want to talk about, you know, Butch's death…we kinda just, as you would say today, hung out. And this is when I found out he had malaria, was when he had that attack…

"I was living in Rochester in January of 1968 and working at Schlegal's on Jefferson Road. But I always went home on the weekends. And that's when I walked in the house, I could tell something was different with my mother, and she called for my father to come out into the kitchen, and she got me a cup of coffee and told me to sit down, she had something to tell me, and of course whenever a person does anything like that…you know something is wrong.

"I need to back up a little bit. I started this on Sunday, and today is Thursday. Last night when I went to bed, which was Wednesday night, I had this totally on my mind, because I have wanted to just get this out of the way, get it done, so I could give it to Tony and be done with it. Well, laying in bed last night, thinking about it, and thinking about it, you know, because this is the most I have ever thought of it. And at first, I felt sadness, and I felt some tears, you know, welling up behind my eyes, and I can tell you now, I have never sobbed about this. NEVER. And I felt sadness. And then, as the minutes wore on, and I was thinking about it, I felt nothing but rage. Just sheer rage. And then, as the minutes wore on again, I just felt an emptiness, like there was a hole in the pit of my stomach. And that's how I finally went to sleep.

"So…I'll tell you now: my mother finally told me, as we were sitting there having a cup of coffee, that Bob had been killed, and to her knowledge, he had been killed by stepping on a land mine. And I didn't know what to say. Actually, I don't think I said anything…I don't remember the drive home. I do remember thinking about it, and trying to put it into perspective…he had been my life, and around me for, gosh, I don't know how long, even though we had broken up, we still were just – it was just a connection, OK, I don't want to get really…mushy or gooey here, but I mean, you know, that connection. And I get back to Rochester to my apartment and I just sat there because I was alone. I lived with three other girls, but I was alone.

"And still, trying to think of it, and understand it, and realize that it was real. And guess what – it wasn't real. It just wasn't real. I thought…if there's a funeral, then I'll have to believe this. But I just didn't believe that it could be true. Well, they had a memorial – and stupidly again, they'd have to have a memorial – I remember going to it alone, it was at Rector-Hicks. *(continued next page)*

(Janice McFollins cont.) I walked in the front door, and then I walked in the door to where the casket is, and I signed my name. And this is all that I remember: I just slowly walked, I saw his picture on a casket, I walked out the other door, turned around, walked out the front door, got in my car, and…that's all I remember of it…like there was a fog in that room, and to tell you now, I am extremely embarrassed because I never went through a line, I don't remember Mr. and Mrs. Henderson being there, Bob [probably means Bob's brother Mike] or Barbara - nothing…I have never, ever – if this is the way you want to put it, come to terms with it, in the natural way – the normal way, I guess – because for me, I have to see something.

"I don't want to be really terrible here, but I mean, Butch was laying in the casket and I saw him. And I grieved. And I cried over him. But see, I didn't have that with Bob. So in my mind, this person that I really, really loved, and meant everything to me, really wasn't gone… I know I'm talking goofy, but this is the most I have ever thought of it, I ever talked about it – I've never talked about it to anybody else, but this stupid machine I'm holding in my hand. So, anyway, that's that…to this day, now that I think about it, I don't watch anything that has to do with Vietnam. I won't talk about Vietnam…that whole part…just cut it out of my life and I'll be thoroughly…comforted, that way. Just take it out of my life. But it's not, and I still feel his presence. That's the most I can say.

"How has it affected my life? Well, I can tell you now, I hate war. I watch the Olympics now, and I watch how the different countries, the competitors, that are competing against one another. When somebody wins or does a good job, it doesn't matter if they're from Russia, Canada, or whatever. Watch them on TV. They all run up to one another, and hug, and embrace one another…So I think to myself, and I've said to my husband, why in the hell can't the politicians, the leaders of these countries, see that? Here they are, competing against one another. It means the world to them because they've trained so hard. They get along, they hug, they kiss, they say wonderful things about one another. Why can't the leaders do that? And this whole world would be a lovely place in which to live. Well, I don't feel that way because they aren't that way. I hate our government, I can honestly say that. I think they're all out for themselves. The money, you know, war – war means money – that's how it's affected my life. When I think war, I feel bitterness, and I've never realized it before, but when we talk war – any war! – the war that's going on now – it really goes back to Vietnam.

(continued next page)

"...No, I didn't think we belonged in Vietnam. I don't think we belong over in Iraq and all of those places, I think it's about time we took care of business at home. Take care of our guys and gals that have fought the war, treat them decently. They're very brave, they're very courageous, and I'm very proud of them...I've never liked war, who likes war?...how has it affected my life, and my future? What would my future have been like? Well...I think it would be a lot different than what it is now, because I think I would have been Mrs. Robert Henderson.

"There is one more thing I'd like to add. My son and I in 1989 went to Washington, D.C. He had joined the Army, and he wanted to see the tomb of the Unknown Soldier. I wanted to visit Arlington. I did; to make a long story short. That place is humongous. I found the gentleman who told me the lot number where Bob was buried. And I found it; my son is looking at me weird, like, you know, why is this so important to you? And when I told him, he... couldn't see his mother being engaged to anybody else, and it was unknown to him... my son's a very good guy, and he just let it go and walked with me. And I said, you don't have to come with me if you don't want. But I must have been acting...a little bit strange. He came with me. I found it, and I stood in front of that gravestone with Robert C. Henderson written on it and just stared at it.

"It was like I was trying to...believe. Because in my heart of hearts I knew that he was deceased...but I'm looking at that, I'm seeing everything, I'm seeing his date of birth, yep, that's correct. But to believe it...no. It was just like...I just didn't. And my son put his hand on my shoulder, and he says, 'are you all right?' And I just looked at him and I said, 'sure.' 'Well – because you've been standing here an awfully long time. Are you all right?' So, you know what, I guess I'm not – well, obviously, I'm not all right when it comes to this, but you know what, this is the way I have handled it for 45 years, and this is the way I will leave it.

"One other little funny thing I'd like to tell you is, I asked Bob one time, I said, what is your middle name? ...it was, after we'd gone together for a while... I can't remember, but we had to write out our names, and I think it was in Mr. ____'s class, and I saw the C. So we were at his house, and I said, 'what does the C stand for?' 'Ah, nothing, it doesn't matter.' And I kept on, as I do, because I'm relentless. When I want to know something I don't stop. And finally he said to me, I'm not going to tell you. If you can guess it, I'll admit it, but you'll never guess it in a million years!   *(continued next page)*

(Janice McFollins cont.) Well, guess what. It was so ironic – he had to read <u>Catcher in the Rye,</u> and I can't remember the guy's whole name, but part of his name was Caulfield, C-A-U-L-F-I-E-L-D.

"So, we're back at his house, this one time, because I knew not to say anything around anybody else because obviously he hated it. And I looked at him, and I said, 'Robert Caulfield Henderson.' Oh my God, he – I mean, he sprung out of his chair. 'Where did you find that name? You can not tell anybody what it is.' ...I couldn't stop laughing! He said, 'It's humiliating, it's a horrible name. So, anyway, that's his entire name: Robert Caulfield Henderson. I think it's pretty darn neat, but he didn't like it.

"... I just want people to know... a lot of people saw him as... oh, what do I want to say...a rebellious person. Well, he had some issues with his dad...However, he loved his father very much and his father loved him. But, I kinda think maybe they were too much alike and he did things sometimes to just get his father's goat. But with me, I'm telling you, there couldn't have been anybody more protective, more loving, more gentle, more kind, thoughtful, fun. Just fun... when I'd get on my little snits, he'd explain things to me, he had just a way of calming me down.

"So...this is my story... in closing, I just want to say that the world lost two really, really good people when Butch and Bob were killed. I think the Vietnam War never should have been. But it was. I'd like to just cut that part out of my life. And once again, I would like to thank you guys that are writing this book. This has caused me nothing but a headache, my stomach turning, I feel vile this week, and really agitated. I don't know. That's how it's left me. I guess, apparently I haven't dealt – well, I've dealt with it in my own way...

"I cannot imagine the turmoil that your minds are going through each time you work on this...Because right now, I'd just like to be a bear and hibernate for about a month because my brain is totally twisted over this...thank you for giving me the opportunity to contribute...and God bless you guys, I really think the world of you for writing this book. Take care. And all of you, have a good life. Bye-bye."

Above: Images of the GCS Junior prom May, 1964. Janice McDonald (center) is crowned queen with escort Bob Henderson. Courtesy of Janice McFollins.
Left photo: Bob and Janice dancing; Right photo: shows Bobby's good friend Terry Magee who went on to have a distinguished career in the Navy. Courtesy of Tony Gurak.

Left: Platoon mates. (pictured left to right) Rich Kovalsky, Bobby Henderson and Paul Harris. Christmas Eve, 1967 in the sandbagged bunkers at Marine Firebase C2, India Company, 3rd Battalion / 4th Marines, 3rd Marine Division. This photo was taken about ten days before Bobby was killed. Courtesy of Eugene Ogozalek and Paul Harris.

Lower: Mementos of Bobby Henderson's military service. Courtesy of his brother, Mike Henderson.

Memorial Day, May 25, 1987

❀❀❀❀❀❀❀❀❀❀❀❀❀❀❀❀❀❀❀❀❀❀❀❀

The day finally came when Butch, Charlie, and Bobby's names were etched in stone on the War Memorial and their ultimate sacrifice was commemorated by the entire community.

An exceptionally large number of Vietnam veterans marched in the Memorial Day parade in honor of Charlie, Butch, and Bobby. Livingston County Leader, May 27, 1987.

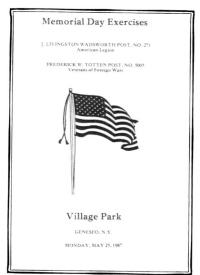

Exercises at the Village Park

MAYOR RICHARD HATHEWAY PRESIDING

Invocation and Lord's Prayer............Rev. C. Frederick Yoos
National Anthem................Geneseo Central School Band
General Logan's Memorial Day Orders......Douglas C. Mills
Reading Gettysburg Address.....................Leslie Riedel
Address....................................Jennifer Wilkie
Dedication.........Paul Hepler, Mayor Richard B. Hatheway
Salute.............................V.F.W. Firing Squad
Taps....................Scott Wilcox, Thomas Gilbert
Benediction.......................Rev. C. Frederick Yoos

Until May 25, 1987, none of the men who were killed in action in Vietnam with ties to the Geneseo community had been added to the Geneseo War Memorial for various reasons. Some of the VFW members argued that Vietnam was officially a conflict and not a war, others believed that because Butch Rosebrugh and Bobby Henderson had lived in Groveland, that disqualified them. And because Charlie Wilkie had never officially resided in Geneseo, that excluded him as well. However, Butch and Bobby both attended Geneseo Central School, which stands just to the west of the memorial, and Charlie Wilkie's wife lived in Geneseo when her husband was killed and chose to stay and raise their daughters in this community.

More than two decades passed and no public acknowledgement of the three men who lost their lives in Vietnam had been achieved. But they were not forgotten. Finally the day came through the undying determination and persistence of fellow Vietnam veterans Roger Least, Jim DeCamp, Roger Johnson, and Korean War veteran Frank Hicks. Now the names of Francis P. Rosebrugh, Charles D. Wilkie, and Robert C. Henderson are carved in stone and listed among all those from Geneseo and Groveland who died in the defense of this country.

The outpouring of community support on that sunny Memorial Day for the families was readily apparent in the enormous crowd and in Vietnam veterans themselves, as many proudly marched in the Memorial Day parade, most for the very first time. The ceremony in the Village Park was in the tradition of past Memorial Day events in Geneseo, and the highlight that day was the speech by Jennifer Wilkie, a tribute to all those who served and a genuine hometown "welcome home."

A Memorial Tribute

I remember standing in this park many Memorial Days listening to the speeches honoring those who gave their lives for their country. I would always ask my mother "When will Dad's name be on the monument?" Her reply to me was always, "Maybe Someday" - Finally Someday has arrived!

Vietnam was the scene of America's longest war. Begun in the early 1960's the last American Combat soldier left in 1973. 27 million men came of age during these years. 9 million served in the armed forces - equally out to be 1 in 3. The War, as well as changing the lives of those in service and the 18 million who didn't serve, affected the lives of parents, wives, children, and friends. No one went untouched. In a sense we all were the victims and the veterans of those difficult days.

For years this nation waged a war with one hand while denying it with the other. Our national indecision affected the conduct of the war and this nation's treatment of our returning veterans. When the war finally ended, we tried to forget it. No ticker tape parades down Broadway as we welcomed home our heros after World War II. But the Vietnam veterans found themselves going from rice paddy to civilian life in less than a day - upon their return they were greeted by taunts and jeers - not cheers.

Now almost 15 years later, all across the nation - the Vietnam veteran is being honored. The change in attitude seemed to have begun with the building of the Vietnam memorial in Washington, D.C. which in itself was a cause for controversy. To see each and every name of

those who died in Vietnam is a moving experience.

Movies such as "Platoon", "Garden of Stone," television drama, and books are bringing back sometimes painful memories. At my alma mater, The College of Wooster, a student inspired memorial "to all who suffered due to the Vietnam War" was dedicated this spring. The deep wounds that have caused so much pain for this country are beginning the slow healing process and parades of homecoming across the nation are visual signs of this healing.

This monument with the 3 names is not just to honor Francis Rosebrugh, Robert Henderson and my father, Charles Wilkie, but to remember and to honor all of you who served - it's Geneseo's way of saying - Welcome Home!!

Jennifer A. Wilkie
May 25, 1987

Left: Livingston County Leader, 5/27/1987.
Above: Jennifer A. Wilkie reads her essay at the Memorial Day ceremony in the Village Park.

HONOR ROLL

Left:
Butch Rosebrugh's extended family (including his two older sisters Mary Ann and Betty in the white jackets) in front of the Geneseo Memorial, May 25, 1987.

Courtesy of Brenda Orman.

Above left: Charles Wilkie's wife Margery, his sister Pat Kingsley, daughter Susan Wilkie Moses, and nieces.
Above right: (standing) Mary Ann Orman and Betty Beach; (seated) Bobby Henderson's sister Barbara Blizzard and his mother, Marguerite E. Henderson. Livingston Co. Leader, May 27, 1987.

Right: Jennifer Wilkie Reynolds and Pat Kingsley. Courtesy of Wilkie family.

ETNAM CONFLICT
FRANCIS P. ROSEBRUGH
CHARLES D. WILKIE
ROBERT C. HENDERSON

Vietnam – A History of Conflict   *By Tony Gurak*

Vietnam has a long history of constant struggle against foreign rule, revolt, and war. In the first millennium B.C. the Chinese referred to their southern neighbors, a distinct race of people, as "Nam Viet" (Southern People). In 111 B.C., the Chinese invaded, burned the capital, and conquered the country. Nam Viet remained under Chinese rule for the next 1,000 years. Although they learned much from the Chinese about their political organization and culture, the Nam Viet maintained a passion for independence and their own identity. In 939 A.D., The Nam Viet rose up against the Chinese. They defeated the Chinese armies and gained their independence. For the next 900 years the Nam Viet slowly and steadily pushed south to the Mekong Delta. In 1407 the Chinese re-conquered the country. They held on until 1427 when the Nam Viet once again defeated the Chinese occupiers. In 1527 a near three century long conflict between the North and South began. The Chinese continued to extend their influence throughout the country.

An insurrection in Annan state in 1774 drove Emperor Gia Long into exile in Cochin, China. In order to regain power, Gia Long signed a treaty with France in 1787. In trade for military aid, the French gained several bases in Annan. However, the French Revolution delayed military aid until 1802. With the help of French troops, Gia Long was able to retake the throne and reunite the country. Several French officers remained in service to the Emperor, further extending their influence. Gia Long's successors turned against the French Missionaries and those who converted to Catholicism. The French fought back and in 1857 seized Danang. In 1861 a large French expeditionary force began a successful military campaign. By 1867, Cochin, China was completely under French control and became a colony. In 1883, a treaty of protectorate gave the French complete control of Vietnam. In 1885 the French quelled an uprising in Tonkin, in the North. What followed was a decade of ruthless slaughter against all opposition by the French. By the 1890s the French had complete control of the entire area: Cambodia, Laos, and all of Vietnam.

In 1919, the Versailles Peace Conference following WWI saw a young, highly educated, and fiercely patriotic nationalist named Nguyen Ai Quoc, come to the forefront of Vietnamese independence. Quoc, who would later become known as Ho Chi Minh, presented an eight-point program for Vietnamese independence to President Woodrow Wilson. He had hoped to appeal to American ideals of freedom and independence. His proposal was completely ignored. This was the first time Quoc would be disappointed with the U.S., but not the last. In 1910 Quoc left Vietnam to spend the next 30 years living and studying in France, Russia, and the U.S. In all that time he continued to work tirelessly for the independence and reunification of Vietnam. In 1930, he formed the Indochinese Communist Party. He then began to study revolutionary theory and tactics with Mao Zedong (also translated as Mao Tse-tung) in China.

In 1930, the French quickly put down another revolt. However, the Annamese nationalist movement continued to strengthen throughout the 1930s. In 1932, the French installed a puppet government under a powerless emperor, Bao Dai. This further antagonized the nationalists. Following France's defeat by Germany in WWII, the German-controlled Vichy French government allowed Japan to use Indochina as a base of military operation. Japan eventually took over complete control and removed all Vichy French from authority in Vietnam. In 1941, Ho Chi Minh returned to Vietnam to fight the Japanese. He led the League for Independence of Vietnam, called the Viet Minh. The goal of the Viet Minh was to rid Vietnam of the Japanese and the French. They received aid from the Chinese communists and the U.S., through the Office of Strategic Services (O.S.S.) Their guerrilla tactics successfully kept the Japanese off-balance. The commander of Ho Chi Minh's forces, General Vo Nguyen Giap, would go on to command Vietnamese communist forces in two more wars. Ho Chi Minh, hopeful of U.S. aid following the war, petitioned President Harry Truman for support. However, the U.S., torn between French colonialism and the spread of communism, did not reply to Ho Chi Minh.

Following the Japanese defeat in 1945, British and Chinese troops briefly occupied Indochina in an effort to counter the Annamese independence movement. On September 12, 1945, Ho Chi Minh with American officers of the O.S.S. at his side, declared the independent democratic Republic of Vietnam.

Ho Chi Minh, the communist, began his declaration address with a quote from our own Declaration of Independence, "All men are created equal, and are endowed by their creator with certain unalienable rights, and among these are life, liberty, and the pursuit of happiness." Ho Chi Minh was still hopeful of American support even after being snubbed by two U.S. presidents. One week later French troops under General Leclerc landed in Saigon to "reclaim their inheritance," thus igniting a war that would last nearly another decade.

In 1949, Mao Zedong's communist forces took over China. Thereafter China and the Soviet Union began to send aid and support to Vietnam. Now the U.S. had a decision to make: support French colonialism or watch the spread of communism. The U.S. sided with France and in 1950 began supplying arms to the French. The U.S. also sent 35 men, the first American Military Assistance Advisory Group (MAAG), to Vietnam to train the French on the new weapons. By the end of 1952, the U.S. was financing half the cost of their war. France was nearly financially depleted after WWII and the French people were quickly tiring of the war. Causalities were mounting, along with the financial burden. Ho Chi Minh was well aware of this and knew he could wait the French out. In 1953, France sent to Vietnam one of their best generals, Henri Navarre, to take command. Navarre decided to bait the Viet Minh forces into one big battle and wipe them out, but he grossly underestimated the Viet Minh's resolve, manpower, and arms.

Navarre made a very poor choice in locating his forces at Dien Bien Phu, in a valley surrounded by high hills. By now the Viet Minh had modern Chinese artillery as well as Soviet anti-aircraft weapons. The Viet Minh by pure brute force dragged their artillery and anti-aircraft guns to the top of the hills. The French were surrounded; the Viet Minh had mobilized 64,000 troops, the French had 11,000. On March 13, 1954, the Viet Minh began heavy shelling of French fortifications with devastating effect. General Giap then threw human wave assaults at two French positions. The Viet Minh lost thousands of fighters, but overran both positions in one day. After a successful French counter attack in April further depleted the French forces, General Giap switched tactics. The Viet Minh began digging trenches and surrounded the French troops. The trenches came so close to the French positions that they could not call in the artillery or air strikes for fear of hitting their own positions. The final assault came on May 6th. Again, screaming human waves poured out of the trenches and over ran the French who were defeated in 56 days.

During the battle, the Viet Minh were being resupplied by bicycle caravans from the North over jungle paths that would later become known as the "Ho Chi Minh Trail." The French suffered 2,200 causalities and 6,000 wounded. 6,000 were taken prisoner with over half not surviving captivity. There had been 4,000 foreign legion paratrooper reinforcements to no avail. The Viet Minh had over 10,000 causalities and 20,000 wounded. They were willing to sacrifice any number to win. The Geneva Accords officially ended the Indochina War. Vietnam was to be temporarily divided at the 17th parallel. The French withdrew from the North and the communists took control. The non-communists took control of the South. Cambodia and Laos were granted independence. There were supposed to be nation- wide elections in 1956 to determine the future of Vietnam but the elections never happened.

By the end of 1954, the U.S. had 342 men serving in the MAAG and allocated $100 million in aid to support France in the war in Vietnam. The U.S. took charge of training the South Vietnamese army and was already secretly gearing up for a war against the communists. The figurehead leader of the South, Bao Dai, selected a Catholic nationalist named Ngo Dinh Diem to be the new Prime Minister. This encouraged one million Catholic refugees from the North to pour into the South where they found favorable treatment over the Buddhist majority. In 1955, bolstered by the support of the Catholic refugees, Diem proclaimed the South the Republic of Vietnam. He named himself as President and began a "land reform" that took land from the peasants and gave it to his rich supporters. Anger and discontent was quickly rising. By refusing to hold the Geneva Accord mandated elections in 1956, Diem set open unrest in motion. Diem knew that if he allowed the elections to take place, the communists would win. He became even more repressive and by the end of 1957, the Viet Minh communists were fully engaged in guerrilla warfare, sabotage, and murder of South Vietnamese officials. On October 22, 1957, 13 Americans were wounded in three separate bombings of MAAG and U.S. information services locations. The end of 1957 also saw 37 Hanoi-organized armed companies operating in the

continued

Mekong Delta. On July 8, 1959, two American MAAG soldiers were killed in a guerrilla attack on their compound. They were the first Americans to lose their lives in Vietnam. At the end of 1959, Hanoi ordered the next stage of the conflict: open insurgency.

The year 1960 saw increased movement of men and supplies down the Ho Chi Minh Trail. Assassinations of South Vietnamese officials increased, as did ambush attacks on South Vietnamese troops. Diem attempted to respond by cracking down even harder on any opposition. At the same time he neglected the increasingly desperate social and economic situation of the people. This resulted in an even more violent dissent from the peasants. Hanoi formed the National Front for the Liberation of the South, a Hanoi-controlled coalition of South Vietnamese political and religious groups. They became known as the Viet Cong. The end of 1960 saw approximately 685 American troops in Vietnam. Still, very few Americans had ever heard of the country.

In 1961, Senior White House advisor, Walt Rostow, proposed to President Kennedy that the time had come to step up operations in Vietnam. Following an unsuccessful summit meeting with Nikita Khrushchev, Kennedy agreed and the build-up was done piece-meal. In May, 400 Special Forces troops and 100 other military advisors were sent in. In October another advisor, General Maxwell Taylor, pressed President Kennedy for a massive joint effort to help the South Vietnamese. Kennedy was hesitant, but did order in more troops, military aircraft, and two army helicopter companies. There would be 16,000 American troops in Vietnam within two years. By the end of 1961, one of the most controversial operations of the war was authorized. Operation Farm Gate, a massive airborne defoliation operation (the long range effects of Agent Orange are still being felt today by civilian and military personnel.) The first North Vietnamese army regulars moved south in 1961. MAAG troops numbered 3,200 and $200 million was spent in U.S. aid with 14 Americans killed or wounded in combat.

The year 1962 saw many changes in U.S. involvement in Vietnam as there was a significant build-up of troops and aircraft. In January the Fleet Marine Force Radio Company arrived. The first Air Force C-123s arrived to begin Operation Ranch Hand. On January 20th, MAAG personnel were authorized to accompany South Vietnamese troops (ARVN) into the field for the first time and aircraft and aircrew losses increased. On February 14th, MAAG forces were officially authorized to return fire. Until this point they were advisors only. The first regular U.S. Army unit, the 39$_{th}$ Signal Battalion arrived on March 23rd. On October 6th, the first Marine deaths occurred. Five Marine and two Navy medics died in an accidental helicopter crash. By the end of December 1962, U.S. troops strength was 11,326: 31 Americans were killed, 78 were wounded.

In January 1963, 2,500 ARVN troops with their MAAG advisors, supported by armor and air units, were soundly defeated in a battle by 400 Viet Cong fighters. The deficiencies of the ARVN forces became glaringly clear. In early 1963, an attack was ordered by Diem official on the participants of a Buddhist celebration. This attack resulted in nine deaths and 20 wounded. Violent political unrest followed. Hatred of Diem and his pro-Catholic policies grew. In June 1963, the first immolation by a Buddhist monk occurred. Many more followed. In August, Diem secretly ordered an attack on Buddhist temples and sanctuaries that resulted in the death of hundreds. The Diem government was in shambles and there were violent demonstrations throughout South Vietnam. In August 1963, newly arrived ambassador Henry Cabot Lodge found the South Vietnamese in chaos. CIA operative Lucien Conein informed Lodge of a planned coup by General Tran Van Dong and General Duong Van Minh. Lodge and Conein began urging the Kennedy Administration to support the coup. Kennedy knew that the U.S. had supported the wrong man, but stopped short of giving the coup full support. For the next few months Kennedy's uncertainty continued, at times supporting the coup, and at times not.

Finally, on November 1st, Lodge, knowing full-well that the coup was to take place later that day, paid a call on Diem, supposedly to assure him of the U.S. continued support. About noon, Conein reported that the coup was starting. On November 2nd Diem and his much-hated brother Ngo Dinh Nhu, after being assured safe passage into exile, were both shot to death. General Duong Van Minh took control of South Vietnam. While not fully supporting the coup, the U.S. did nothing to stop it. The end of December 1963 saw over 16,000 troops in Vietnam. There were 78 deaths and 411 wounded.

In January 1964, General Nguyen Khanh, commander of the ARVN corps, overthrew the ineffective General Minh. Khanh himself proved to be ineffective and corrupt and once again, the U.S. found itself propping up an unworkable and corrupt regime. By 1964 South Vietnam was in an absolute mess with coup after coup, violent protests, death, destruction, and rampant corruption. There was no real leadership in South Vietnam. On February 16, 1964, the Viet Cong exploded a bomb in a Saigon theater killing three U.S. soldiers and wounding 50. On August 2, 1964 the U.S. Navy destroyer *Maddox* was attacked by three North Vietnamese patrol boats in the Gulf of Tonkin. The *Maddox* was targeted by torpedoes but all torpedoes missed and the Maddox opened fire on the patrol boats. With assistance from Navy jets, one boat was sunk, and the others crippled. On August 4th, the destroyers *Maddox* and *Turner Joy* came under a supposed attack by North Vietnamese torpedoes. The destroyers returned fire, although no enemy vessels had been spotted, and there were no torpedo strikes.

It was later determined that their sonar screens had been affected by a weather anomaly. This incident was the opportunity President Johnson had looked for and he ordered reprisal air strikes on North Vietnam. The President made a television address to explain his actions and assured the world, "we still seek no wider war." On August 7th the Tonkin Gulf Resolution passed the House and Senate with only two dissenting votes in Congress and the President was given broad powers to take all measures necessary to repel any armed attack against U.S. or ally forces.

The year 1964 also saw the Ho Chi Minh trail vastly improved to allow the use of trucks to move troops and supplies south. Eventually, the time required to move troops south was reduced from six months on foot to just days in trucks. U.S. Navy and Air Force jet fighters increased bombing attacks on North Vietnam and the Ho Chi Minh trail. Despite the tons of bombs, napalm, and defoliant expended, traffic on the Ho Chi Minh trail increased. Late in 1964 and early 1965, North Vietnamese regular troops, along with approximately 34,000 Viet Cong were quickly moving into the South and joined the 80,000 sympathizers already there. December 1964 ended with 23,310 American troops in Vietnam. There were 147 killed in action and 1,039 wounded. This year was the last year American troops would be called "advisors."

1965 saw great escalation of the war. In March, the 9th Marine expeditionary force arrived in Da Nang. The ARVN troops were still proving to be inadequate while the Viet Cong were proven to be very capable of simultaneous coordinated attacks, bombings, and sabotage. They proved to Americans that they could strike anywhere, inflict casualties and damage, and then simply disappear into the population or jungle. U.S. troops found themselves in a new kind of war where the combatants were indistinguishable from ordinary civilians. America was beginning to learn what the French, Japanese, and Chinese had already learned. President Johnson became convinced that air bombardment would achieve the U.S. goals and in March 1965, Operation Rolling Thunder began. Air Force, Navy, and Marine jet fighters began a campaign of intense attacks on ammo dumps, fuel supplies, truck convoys, and military personnel in North Vietnam. Rolling Thunder would continue for three years. All areas of North Vietnam except Hanoi were targeted. President Johnson and his advisors personally selected each target. In June 1965 Operation Arc Light began and Air Force B-52 bombers stationed at Anderson Air Force base in Guam began around the clock bombing in South Vietnam. Eventually they would also be stationed at Kadena, Okinawa, and U-Tapao, Thailand. Six bombers flew in formation, each raining down tons of bombs from high altitude, absolutely terrifying the Viet Cong and the NVA regulars on the ground. The B-52s became a very effective weapon throughout the war.

General Westmoreland, commander of U.S. forces in Vietnam, requested a buildup to 17 combat battalions by the summer of 1965 and in April the Johnson Administration agreed to double the existing commitment of troops to 82,000. In May, the first Army combat units arrived including the first American artillery unit. In June, the 173rd Airborne Brigade attempted its first mission and the American ground war was officially started. President Johnson announced that troop strength would be increased to 125,000, so in order to meet this demand, draft numbers increased from 17,000 to 35,000 per month. Most young men at the time accepted the call to serve their country as their duty. However, at college campuses across the country students began to question U.S. involvement in a jungle war in a country halfway around the world that few people had, until recently, even heard of. Sit-ins, marches, and protests increased around the U.S. and the world. This did not go unnoticed by Ho Chi Minh. Again, as he had done with the French, he would use this to his advantage. *continued*

In May 1965, U.S. Navy ships began shelling Viet Cong targets in South Vietnam. The 7th fleet with 125 ships and 64,000 men was stationed in the waters off Vietnam. The fleet included aircraft carriers, destroyers, cruisers, and river "swift" boats. They would remain an integral force for the remainder of the war. One of the Navy's primary duties was to enforce a blockade of Vietnam to stem the resupplying of North Vietnam. Chu Lai Airfield near Da Nang was the scene of the first all-American battle. The 3rd Marine tank division was delivered by helicopter, a new tactic developed for Vietnam, supported by fighter bombers and Navy guns. The year 1965 also saw the deployment of the 1st Air Cavalry with their Chinook and UH-1 "Huey" helicopters. The Huey became one of the most familiar and lasting images of the Vietnam War.

By 1966 the war was bogging down and becoming a war of attrition. Replacement soldiers arrived on a continuous basis with neither side gaining an advantage. The year 1967 saw growing disenchantment with the war. Americans following the war on television nightly news broadcasts were becoming weary of the daily body counts and kill ratios. Scenes of bloodied soldiers being loaded on to helicopters were alarming. The forced relocation of villagers was gaining the U.S. more enemies. Their villages were burned and the jungle defoliated or bull-dozed, all to drive the Viet Cong from an area. As soon as the troops left an area, the Viet Cong moved back in and resumed operations as before. The villagers lost all for nothing. 1967 also saw a "new" tactic by General Diap: massive attacks on U.S. fire bases. Nightly artillery and mortar attacks were followed by human wave assaults, sometimes resulting in hand-to-hand combat. His goal was to spread the American forces thin and demoralize the troops with constant fighting. Even without Secretary of Defense McNamara's policy of inflating enemy body count, the Viet Cong and NVA regulars lost thousands of men and the U.S. lost hundreds of men. Ho Chi Minh had told the French in the 1950s, "You can kill ten of my men for every one I kill of yours. But even at those odds, you will lose and I will win." The same men who directed that war were directing this war.

An October 1967 poll reported that only 44% of those polled believed our involvement was not a mistake. McNamara stepped up the public relations campaign to convince America that the war was going better than it actually was and that we were winning. At the same time, McNamara had his own doubts and was considering a job offer from the World Bank. On November 3, 1967 a 19-day battle at Dak To Military Base began and the fighting was furious and continuous. The NVA and Viet Cong threw massive numbers of troops at the U.S. position but after U.S. reinforcements arrived with incredible air attacks and artillery, the enemy withdrew. The enemy had lost a reported 1,455 men, the U.S. had lost 285, and 985 wounded. General Diap wanted to create another Dien Bien Phu. Not so much to defeat the Americans and end the war, but to create widespread destruction, alarm, confusion, and destroy morale among the troops. Also to weaken the will of the American people to continue supporting the war, just as had the French people after Dien Bien Phu. Dak To was not that battle.

Dak To was just the beginning. The real battle would begin in January 1968. Diap had massed between 20,000 - 40,000 troops in the vicinity of the fire base at Khe Sanh. On January 20, 1968 the Tet (Lunar New Year) Offensive began. The artillery, mortar, rocket, and grenade attacks were relentless. Hand-to-hand fighting was required to drive back the attackers. The defenders were reinforced by a Marine and ARVN battalion, but could do little except hunker down in trenches and bunkers. On February 23rd alone, the NVA poured 1,300 shells into Khe Sanh. General Westmoreland ordered Operation Niagara II to commence. For the next nine weeks, B-52s and fighter bombers dropped 100,000 tons of bombs around Khe Sanh. Artillery fired 150,000 rounds onto enemy positions. The enemy died by the thousands, but the battle continued. On February 7th, the NVA brought Russian-made tanks into battle for the first time. On April 6th the battle ended. The communists had lost 10,000 men, mostly to B-52 strikes. The U.S. had lost 500 men.

Two months after the battle, Khe Sanh, the base Westmoreland had called the most critical of all, was razed and abandoned by the Marines. The communist forces simply walked in and claimed it. It was never fully determined if Khe Sanh was the true objective, or if it was just a costly diversion for Tet. In 1789 there had been a legendary Tet battle. The emperor of Vietnam had driven the Chinese from Hanoi. The Tet Offensive of 1968 marked a big change in the war, a new commitment by communist forces. On January 20, 1968 simultaneous attacks broke out in nine of South Vietnam's largest cities and 30 provincial capitals. For several weeks, Viet Cong guerrilla fighters had infiltrated Saigon.

On January 31st the Viet Cong blew a hole in the wall surrounding the American embassy and for six hours the 19 invaders attacked the embassy with anti-tank rockets and automatic weapons. American troops arrived and killed or captured all 19. Seven Marines had been killed. That night millions of shocked viewers saw the filmed attack on television. An hour earlier the Viet Cong breached the gate of the presidential palace but were quickly driven back. The Viet Cong spread out through Saigon and had to be rooted out in street-to-street, house- to-house fighting. That day TV viewers saw national police chief General Loan execute a captured Viet Cong guerrilla with a pistol shot to the head. The grizzly horror of the Vietnam War was viewed in full color in living rooms around the world.

The ancient imperial capital city of Hue saw the worst fighting of the Tet Offensive. Over 25 days of the most intense fighting of the war, more than half the city was severely damaged or destroyed. Three-quarters of the population was left homeless and 5,800 civilians had been killed. South Vietnamese officials and foreigners were targeted for the most cruel, inhumane, and barbaric assassinations. Some were even buried alive in mass graves. Some were never found. The out-manned U.S. forces were forced to fight 20-hour stretches at a time. Most thought they would not survive the battle. U.S. losses were placed at 216, with 1,364 wounded. ARVN losses were 384 with 1,830 wounded. Communist losses were reported as 5,000 dead and 89 captured. Once again, the communists proved they were willing to sacrifice any number to achieve their goal.

The Tet Offensive was the turning point of the war. The communists did not achieve their military goal, but did achieve their main goal, changing the hearts and minds of the American people sickened by the daily coverage of the carnage. No amount of public relations stories could undo the damage. The disillusionment and rage the American people felt towards the war spread to the press, Congress, and to Johnson's own staff. McNamara was out as Secretary of Defense and Clark Clifford was in and began his own review of the war. He discovered much to his dismay, that the only U.S. military goal was attrition, to out-kill the communists. Clifford began a low-key movement to disengage from the war. General Westmoreland was relieved of his command and his replacement, General Abrams, began moving away from Westmoreland's strategies.

In March 1968, Senators Eugene McCarthy and Robert Kennedy announced their candidacy for the Democratic nomination for President. Both were opposed to the war. On March 31st, President Johnson announced on television that he would not seek a second term. He had been beaten by his own war. In 1968 there had been 221 major anti-war demonstrations against the war. The Democratic National Convention in Chicago saw one of the largest and most violent demonstrations to date; 10,000 anti-war demonstrators battled the Chicago police. Again, America saw all the brutality on their TV screens, this time it was Americans against Americans. Ho Chi Minh was accomplishing in America what he had accomplished in France, turning the civilian population against the war. Democratic Presidential candidate, Vice President Hubert Humphrey failed to distance himself from Johnson's policies until too late in his campaign and lost the election to Republican Richard Nixon. Nixon promised an "honorable" end to the war telling the American people what they wanted to hear. However, the war would drag on for another seven years.

By 1968, the American troops were becoming frustrated by the war, and showing increasing rage. The almost constant fighting, the land mines, snipers, booby traps, and an enemy that could just disappear into the jungle or mix into the civilian population after an ambush. It was becoming evident that there was no clear plan for victory in Vietnam. To meet the heavy demands of the war, draft boards were becoming less selective. The quality and attitudes of the new replacements was in decline. All of this took a heavy toll on morale. On March 16, 1968 all of the rage and frustration came together in what has become known as one of the saddest and most shameful acts of the Vietnam War. A platoon from Charlie Company of the 20th Infantry Brigade was ordered to attack a Viet Cong battalion in a village called My Lai, known to be heavily infiltrated by the Viet Cong and was always a very dangerous area. However, the platoon found no enemy combatants and no shots were fired at them. In total frustration, Company Captain Medina gave orders that "implied" it was time to get even and kill everyone. Unspeakable savagery followed; men, women, and children were shot, beaten to death, and bayoneted. Two young girls were raped before they were killed. Lieutenant William Calley ordered 150 villagers to be forced into a drainage ditch and machine gunned them to death. In all, 400 villagers were murdered that day. The same day in the nearby village of My Khe, 90 villagers were killed in similar fashion. The only American casualty that day was a soldier who shot himself in the foot. *continued*

The Army tried to cover up My Lai, but it could not. Lieutenant Calley and his platoon became so kill-crazy that they forgot they were in the company of news photographers. The whole horror was recorded and over a year later the pictures began to appear in American magazines. For Americans it was just too terrible to believe. They had seen pictures of atrocities like this before, by Nazis or communists, not by American troops. The Army demoted a couple of generals but Lieutenant Calley was the only person convicted of a crime and spent just a few years in jail before his sentence was reduced, and he was released. Captain Medina, for his part in the massacre received a special commendation. My Lai was truly the beginning of the end of the Vietnam War. By mid-1968 there were 500,000 troops in Vietnam, with another 25,000 slated to arrive.

In February 1967, President Johnson had sent a secret letter to Ho Chi Minh with proposals to bring an end to the war, but Ho Chi Minh refused to negotiate until the complete withdrawal of U.S. troops. Ho Chi Minh further stated that the Vietnamese people would never submit to force, so the effort went no further. In the spring of 1968, President Johnson became persuaded that the only way out was through negotiations. After his announcement that he would not seek a second term and a partial halt to the North Vietnam bombing, the North Vietnamese agreed to meet in Paris. The Paris Peace Talks began on May 13, 1968 with only the North Vietnamese and Americans excluding the South Vietnamese and Viet Cong. Hanoi's representative began with a war of words against the U.S. and a total impasse was immediate. In December, the South Vietnamese and Viet Cong joined the talks but before long the talks deadlocked again. The only thing finally agreed upon was the shape of the table. For months there was no progress, then President Nixon directed his National Secretary Advisor Henry Kissinger to begin secret talks with Hanoi in Paris. These talks would eventually (much later) lead to a breakthrough.

In order to keep up pressure on the South Vietnamese and Americans, the North started a new offensive. On May 5, 1968, "Tet II" began with a shelling of 119 cities. Communist gunners shelled the heart of Saigon and followed up with heavy ground attacks. Intense fighting drove the communist troops from Saigon and Tan Son Nhut Airport. Once again, communist forces attacked areas around Saigon and were again driven back by ground troops and air attacks. By May 13th, the communists had lost a reported 5,270 troops, the U.S. had lost another 154 troops. On May 25th, the communists struck the same areas again but in greater numbers this time. Days of heavy fighting finally drove them out. For five weeks following, they sent numbers of rockets into Saigon. Hundreds of civilians were killed, thousands were wounded, and thousands were left homeless. During this same time period, the communists struck 19 American and allied positions around South Vietnam. At one location, American troops had to fight house to house for days to drive the communists out. A month later, the communists returned to the same location in even greater force. The same grueling battles had to be fought over and over again. The North Vietnamese proved that they could and would keep the war grinding on and on indefinitely until the U.S. could take no more and pull out. In 1968, 14,492 Americans died in Vietnam.

By 1969 the new American strategy was to pull American forces back to defend Saigon. Airborne assaults would replace fixed positions. This would require the South Vietnamese Army to take more responsibility for the fighting. "Vietnamization" had begun. In mid-May 1969, American and ARVN troops were sent back to the Ashu Valley, for the third time, to drive the communist troops out. It was discovered that an NVA regiment was dug in on the top of Hill 937. Army historians would later remark that the hill had no tactical or significant value other than the fact that the NVA were there. "Hamburger Hill," as it would become known, turned into one of the most grueling and controversial battles of the war. For days the Americans and ARVN troops fought their way up the hill, into heavy gunfire and each time they were driven back. On the ninth day they secured the hill. Hamburger Hill had cost the lives of 56 Americans and a reported 630 communists. Incredibly, one week later, the hill was simply abandoned. When the news reached the U.S., members of Congress, as well as the American people, were shocked at this most senseless and irresponsible battle. Nothing had been accomplished.

In 1969, President Nixon and Henry Kissinger believed that increased bombing was the key to ending the war. Nixon ordered secret B-52 bombing of communist sanctuaries in Cambodia and a 60% increase in bombing of the Ho Chi Minh trail over 1968. In an effort to show the American people that some progress was being made, Vietnamization was increased and delivery of weapons, artillery, aircraft, and helicopters was sped up. Training of ARVN officers and troops was increased all with few positive results. For the most part the ARVN troops lacked the heart and will of their North Vietnamese counterparts. Nonetheless, on July 1, 1969 the first U.S. battalion exited Vietnam. By the end of the year, an additional 60,000 troops would be withdrawn.

In November 1969, the largest anti-war demonstration took place in Washington D.C. Among the 250,000 demonstrators were very notable leaders of education, commerce, and labor. Forty members of Congress endorsed the Vietnam Moratorium, as it would be called and 20,000 "Wall Streeters" rallied their support. Even some soldiers in Vietnam wore black arm bands to show their support as the anti-war movement had reached Vietnam. President Nixon proclaimed that he would be unaffected by the protests. In 1969 Ho Chi Minh died, the ensuing power struggle led to the decline of General Giap, and that year 9,414 Americans lost their lives in Vietnam.

In May and June of 1970, Nixon ordered a force of 30,000 American and 48,000 ARVN troops, with air support, to strike at communist sanctuaries in Cambodia. The operation was considered a success, but the backlash of the widening of the war was far greater than expected. Protests at universities across the country grew increasingly violent and pervasive. In early May 1970, a demonstration at Kent State University turned tragic as a detachment of the Ohio National Guard opened fire on the student demonstrators. Four students were killed, two merely passer-bys, not involved in the demonstration, and ten were wounded. The rage that followed was tremendous. Two hundred colleges and universities were forced to close because of violent protests. The American people flooded Washington with an avalanche of mail protesting the escalating war into Cambodia and the shameful handling of Kent State. Many State Department employees, aides, and members of Congress had also joined together to condemn the actions.

Nixon became more defiant in the face of increased criticism and ordered the formation of a covert spy team to report on any dissenters in or out of government. The American military had killed unarmed Americans and now Americans were spying on Americans. Morale of the troops in Vietnam was down, drug use and addiction was up. American servicemen returning home were faced with hostility and often were spat upon. In January 1971, the decision was made to cut the Ho Chi Minh trail in half in Laos to forestall a large communist buildup. After the attacks into Cambodia the previous year, American troops were forbidden to Cambodia or Laos so the operation fell to ARVN troops. 30,000 troops were airlifted into Laos; their objective was a town 200 miles inside the border but they were slowed by stiff resistance from the NVA. The town had been leveled by B-52 bombers by the time the ARVN reached it. However, the NVA was still there and attacked in force. The ARVN panicked and ran in full retreat. Many ARVN troops dropped their weapons and clung desperately to the evacuation helicopters. The ARVN lost 3,800 dead, 5,200 wounded, and 775 missing. Vietnamization was far from a success.

The year 1971 saw an increase in American anti-war demonstrations. A radical group called the Weather Underground exploded a bomb in the Capital building, beginning a week of demonstrations in Washington D.C. A group of veterans calling themselves "Vietnam Veterans Against the War" threw their combat ribbons and their uniforms onto the steps of the Capital. That year, 1,386 soldiers lost their lives in Vietnam and troop levels had dropped to 159,000. The "secret" Paris Peace Talks, like the public talks, went nowhere. By 1972, the U.S. ground war was winding down but the air war was heating up. The Peace Talks had stalled and the B-52 bombers became the main U.S bargaining chip.

In April 1972, Nixon ordered Operation Linebacker and massive airstrikes were resumed against North Vietnam. On the 16th of April, B-52s and fighter bombers struck the cities of Haiphong and Hanoi and in May, Nixon ordered all major North Vietnamese ports to be mined. Throughout the second half of 1972, the bombing raids intensified. The bombing had a positive effect, the peace talks resumed and by October, it was announced that a cease-fire was near. Nixon ordered a halt to the bombing but again, negotiations failed as the talks stalled. Around Christmas time, Nixon ordered Linebacker II. What followed was the most intensive and concentrated air offensive of the war. 40,000 tons of bombs were dropped on Hanoi and Haiphong and 26 American planes, including 15 B-52 bombers, were shot down. By the end of the operation, the North Vietnamese were out of SAM (surface to air missiles) and heavy anti-aircraft shells. The bombers ranged at will. Nixon called off the bombings on December 30th after Hanoi agreed to resume talks. This time the secret talks made rapid progress. In 1972, 4,300 Americans lost their lives in Vietnam and troop strength was down to 24,000.   *continued*

On January 23, 1973 Nixon announced that the agreement to end the war had been reached. On January 27th, the agreement was signed in Paris by the U.S., North Vietnam, South Vietnam, and the Viet Cong but the air war in Laos and Cambodia continued for several months. By March 29, 1973, all but 209 American servicemen were out of Vietnam. On June 16, 1973, Captain Samuel B. Cornelius and Captain John J. Smallwood became the last Americans to lose their lives in combat when their F-4 fighter was shot down over Cambodia. On August 15, 1973, all U.S. aerial warfare ended. The last B-52 mission left Cambodian airspace at 11AM. America's part in the Vietnam War was over and Nixon had achieved "peace with honor." In 1973, 34 Americans lost their lives in Vietnam.

By 1974, Congress began cutting off aid to South Vietnam and by 1975 funding was down to $300 million. The loss of American military support and funding began to rapidly weaken the performance of the ARVN and North Vietnam was massing troops and supplies in South Vietnam. It was not to be a peaceful reunification as stipulated in the Peace Accords. When the inevitable fighting began, the ARVN made a miserably poor showing. The NVA seized city after city with relative ease; the rout was on.

By 1975, the defending ARVN troops had pulled back to Saigon as the communists surrounded the city. Saigon was in chaos with thousands of South Vietnamese frantically searching for any way out. In the previous weeks, 50,000 American civilians and South Vietnamese left the country. In early April, a fleet of 70 U.S. helicopters began shuttling people to awaiting aircraft carriers offshore. One thousand Americans and 6,000 South Vietnamese were evacuated.

The last evacuation scenes of the long war were unforgettable. Thousands South Vietnamese were waiting on the roof of the U.S. embassy for helicopters to lift them to safety. Thousands more desperate people surrounded the compound. On the evening of April 29th, Marine guards held off terrified South Vietnamese begging for help with guns and bayonets as they pushed people off the overloaded helicopter. As the last helicopter lifted off the embassy roof, thousands of North Vietnamese troops poured into the city with little opposition, screaming as they had 21 years before at Dien Bien Phu, pouring out of their trenches into the French lines.

On May 7, 1975, President Ford proclaimed the end of the Vietnam War. The Vietnam War lasted 12 years, 4 months, and 15 days at a cost of $139 billion. 8,744,000 Americans served, 58,282 Americans lost their lives, and hundreds of thousands were wounded. Thousands more had lifelong wounds that did not show. Some never came completely back from Vietnam. Most, at the time, were left to deal with the pain on their own. The war left a generation and a nation forever changed. It was the end of innocence.

Bibliography
Books:
Barnes, Jeremy. *The Pictorial History of the Vietnam War*. New York: Gallery Books, 1988.
Kamps, Charles T. *The History of the Vietnam War*. New York: Military Press, 1988.
Welsh, Douglas. *The History of the Vietnam War*. New York: Exeter Books, 1984.
VFW Magazine:
Kolb, Richard K. and Van Cline, Kelly. "America's Advisory War in Vietnam 1962-64." Aug. 2011.
Kolb, Richard K. "Last days of the Infantry in Vietnam, 1972." Aug. 2012, p. 36.
Hemingway, Al. "Into the Teeth of the Tiger." Nov/Dec. 2012, p. 32.
Kolb, Richard K. "GI's leave behind the Vietnam War in 1973." Aug. 2013.
Kolb, Richard K. "1973: U. S. Military Actions and hostile deaths in Indochina" Aug. 2013.
Fournier, Richard. "Last days some of the best ones die." Aug. 2013.
The New Funk and Wagnalls Encyclopedia, 1950.

Glossary of abbreviations and terms

3.2 Beer – named for the alcohol content of beer in Vietnam

Agent Orange – a toxic chemical defoliant used to kill vegetation

AIT – Advanced Infantry Training

AO – Area of Operations

APC – Armored Personnel Carrier

APS – Ambush patrols

ARCOM – Army commendation medal awarded for acts of heroism, extraordinary achievement or service

Armored Unit – mechanized unit comprised of APCs and tanks

Article 15 – non-judicial punishment for minor disciplinary offenses

ARVN – Army of the Republic of Vietnam, a.k.a. South Vietnamese Army

B-52 – Boeing B-52 Stratofortess, US Air Force high-altitude bomber plane, see BUFF

Billet – civilian's home or other nonmilitary facility where soldiers are temporarily lodged

Black Pajamas – term associated with enemy Viet Cong clothing

Booby Trap - a concealed explosive device

Buck Sergeant – SGT E-5 or 3-Stripe; a nickname to distinguish senior grades of sergeants

BUFF – "Big Ugly Fat Fucker" nickname for B-52

Bunker Guard or Perimeter Guard – a manned line guarding a specific area

C-141 – Air Force cargo aircraft, specifically the Lockheed C 141 Starlifter

C-4 – a plastic explosive

CA or CAs – Combat assault(s) by helicopter

CAP Team – Civil Action Program (Marines) providing various means of support to a combat area

Charlie - slang for Viet Cong; short for phonetic spelling "VC" which is "Victor Charlie"

CHI-COM – Chinese Communist grenade

Chieu Hoi - see Kit Carson Scout

Chopper – nickname for Huey helicopter

Chu Lai – brigade headquarters for the American Division I Corps

CIB – Combat Infantry Badge

Claymore Mine – American above-ground anti-personnel mine

Commo Wire – U.S. communication wire

CP – Command Post

C-Rations – canned combat rations

Deuce and a Half – 2.5 ton transfer vehicle

DEROS – date estimated rotation overseas or date of expected return from overseas

D.I. – drill instructor, a.k.a. drill sergeant

Dike - mounded soil dividers in rice paddies to retain water

Dink – derogatory term for Vietnamese enemy soldiers

DMZ – Vietnamese Demilitarized Zone, dividing line between North and South Vietnam during the Vietnam War, a.k.a. "the 17th parallel"

Door Gunners – soldiers armed with a machine gun and positioned on both sides of helicopter

Donut Dollies - single, young females used primarily as morale boosters for U.S. troops in Vietnam as part of a Red Cross program

Draw Down – decrease of troops and bases in combat zone

Dust-Off – medical evacuation by helicopter

E-5 – see Buck Sergeant

E-5 Board – group responsible for determining promotion to E-5

EM Club – club open to non-officers

Firebase – also called artillery base, and supporting artillery, cannons, howitzers, and crews

Firefight – brief and intense exchange of small arms fire with enemy

FNG - "Fucking New Guy"; term for new soldiers in a unit or in-country

Free Fire Zone – an area with no friendly inhabitants, all considered enemy

Freedom Bird – airplane taking U.S. soldiers from Vietnam back to the U.S.A. or to the "world"

Friendly Fire – accidental firing on or bombing of American or ally troops

G.I. – Government Issued; an American soldier

Grunt – infantry soldier

Gunship – heavily-armed helicopters, specifically the UH 1 H Huey or Cobra

Gyrene – member of the U.S. Marine Corps

H & I – Harassment and Interdiction, firing on enemy positions to disrupt movements and possible attacks

Hootch (sometimes spelled hooch)– hut or simple dwelling used by the Vietnamese

Hot LZ – landing zone of helicopters or aircraft under enemy fire while transporting troops

Hot Spots – term used to describe areas of frequent enemy attacks or hostility

Howitzer – artillery piece, or cannon; described in part by size of barrel and caliber, (ex. 105mm, 155mm, 175mm, etc.)

HQ – headquarters

Huey – UH 1H helicopter; the primary vehicle used to transport infantry, supplies and medical evacuations

In-country – in Vietnam

I Corps – Northernmost military region in Vietnam

KIA – Killed in Action

Kit Carson Scout –enemy soldiers who surrendered or defected to the S. Vietnamese Army or US; a.k.a. Chieu Hoi

Klick or Klik – distance of 1,000 meters or 3,280.84 feet

KP – kitchen patrol duty

LOH or Loach – Light Observation Helicopter

Long Binh Jail or Stockade – prison for those who have broken military law

LZ – helicopter or fixed wing aircraft landing zone

MIA – missing in action

Mama San – an older Vietnamese woman

Medevac – medical evacuation from field by helicopter

M-16 – basic infantry rifle used in Vietnam

MP – military police

My Lai – small hamlets numbered 1 through 6 in Quang Nai province

NCO – Non-commissioned officer

NDP – Night Defensive Position

NVA – North Vietnamese Army soldiers

OCS –Officer Candidate School

Pack # or PAC Number – used to identify individual soldiers

Popped Smoke – use of smoke grenades of different colors to show location of a secured area

POW – Prisoner of War

Punji Stake or Punji Pit – sharpened bamboo stakes placed in shallow pits used as a booby trap

PRC 25 (Prick 25) – Portable Radio Communications, Model 25, a back-packed FM receiver-transmitter used for short-distance communications

Purple Heart – military award given for being wounded in action

PX – type of retail store found at U.S. military installations worldwide

R & R – rest and recreation out-of-field

Rear – the portion of concentration of military forces that is farthest from the enemy

Recon – short for reconnaissance, a military term for gathering information

REMF – Rear Echelon Mother Fucker; a soldier with no combat experience

Reventment Walls – concrete walls to protect and separate B-52s on base

Rice Paddy – a field flooded and divided by dikes for growing rice

Ringknocker – slang for military college or university graduates.

ROTC – Reserve Officers' Training Corps; college-based program to train commissioned officers for U.S. Army

Ruck or Rucksack – soldiers' backpack for carrying supplies

RVN – South Vietnam, officially the Republic of Vietnam until 1975

Sapper – enemy VC or NVA soldier carrying explosive weaponry to destroy U.S. troops and supplies

Satchel Charge – explosive carried in a satchel-style package and used by enemy to destroy artillery or bunkers

Sea-Tac – Seattle-Tacoma International Airport located in Washington State

Shit – slang for enemy contact or battle

Short-Timers – soldiers whose tour in Vietnam was nearly completed

Stand-Down – rest from the field in rear or base camp

SSGT – abbreviation for staff sergeant; E-6 Army or E-5 Air Force

Soda Girls – young girls who sold soda to infantry soldiers in the field

TDY – temporary duty assignment away from permanent duty station

Tet Offensive – launched January 30, 1968 by the Viet Cong and NVA against South Vietnam, U.S., allied forces.

Trip Flare – small flares ignited by tripwires to illuminate area, exposing enemy

Trip Wire – thin steel wire used to ignite flares and Claymore mines to expose and kill enemy troops

Tunnel Rat – soldier who enters underground holes and tunnels to search for enemy and supplies

VA – Veterans' Administration

VC or Viet Cong – Communist-led forces in South Vietnam

Ville – abbreviation of village

Warrant Officer - designation by warrant rather than by commission as for helicopter pilots

WO - Warrant Officer

WIA – Wounded in Action

World – referring to back home or the USA

Acknowledgements
❀ ❀ ❀ ❀ ❀ ❀ ❀ ❀ ❀ ❀ ❀ ❀ ❀ ❀ ❀

The book committee wishes to thank everyone who participated in this project. We are overwhelmed with gratitude for all who generously shared their proud and often painful memories. From the onset, we realized that the only way to paint a clear picture of how the Vietnam War impacted the our small community, was to have as many perspectives as possible. In our view, this goal was achieved.

Sincere thanks goes to the families and friends of our fallen comrades including: Margery Wilkie, Jennifer Wilkie Reynolds, Susan Wilkie Moses, Brenda Orman, Jeff Orman, Betty Rosebrugh Beach, John Kopka, Mike Henderson, Paul Harris, Robert Harriman, Eugene Ogozalek, and Janice McFollins.

In addition to the narrative support from all our fellow Blue Devil and area guys mentioned at the beginning of the book, we want to recognize Jim Adamson, Jim Creagan, and Malcolm Stewart for their generous financial support as well.

Also to Rodger Engler for his graphic art design work; Ben Beagle, Howard Appell, Michael Johnson, and all the staff at the Livingston County News for news stories and assisting with photographs; Michael Hager of Museum Photographics, for scanning old slides; Tim Hayes, GCS Superintendent, for allowing us to promote our project in a public forum; Doreen DeCamp and Holly Watson, Livingston County Deputy Historian, for their acute editing skills; and Carol and Todd Baker at Pioneer Print and Copy for making us feel more like old friends than just customers.

Most of all to our den mother/taskmaster, Amie Griffo Alden who listened patiently to our war stories then got us back on track to actually write the book she so capably edited. Without Amie, we would still be sitting around a table telling tales.

Blue Devils in Vietnam book committee in front of the Geneseo Memorial in the Village Park.

Left to right: Jim DeCamp, Amie Alden, Roger Johnson, and Tony Gurak.

Photo by Michael Johnson, reprinted from the Livingston County News, March 27, 2013, p.1

We also honor all GCS Blue Devils who served in Vietnam

✿✿✿✿✿✿✿✿✿✿✿✿✿✿✿✿

Here are just a few of the many brave men that have passed on.

Norman S. Culbertson, USAF Lt. Co. Retired

GROVELAND — Retired USAF Fighter Pilot Norman C. Culbertson, 86, died June 30, 2006 after a long battle with cancer. He was a former resident of Buffalo, Clark Mills and Phelps.

He was born May 9, 1920 in Dreyden the son of Percy and Ruth Culbertson settling in Groveland. He graduated in 1938 from Geneseo High and 1949 from Veteran's Agricultural School.

In 1939 he joined the Air Force. During World War II he flew 37 combat missions and was awarded the Silver Star, South Pacific Battle Ribbons and Distinguished Flying Cross. He separated from the service in 1946 and joined the 183th TAC Fighter Reserve Squadron known as 'The Boys From Syracuse' during the Cold War. He later transferred to the 136th TRS Reserves in Niagara Falls. During the Vietnam War he was awarded his second DFC, achieved 236 combat missions and 20 air medals and Vietnam ribbons. In 1980 he retired from the military with 28 years of service.

Livingston County News 7/6/2006

Above: "Hal" Witter with Vietnamese children. Photo provided by Sally Witter. Article: Liv. Rep. 12/19/1963.

Capt. Harold Witter, a member of the 7th Special Forces unit at Ft. Bragg, is visiting his parents, Mr. and Mrs. Kenneth Witter, Sr., and family prior to returning to his base from which he will leave soon for duty in Vietnam.

George J. 'Jimmy' Young, Lt. Col., U.S.A., Ret.

GENESEO/SAN ANTONIO, TEXAS — George J. 'Jimmy' Young, Lt. Col., U.S.A. Ret., 75, died May 9, 2003.

He was born July 28, 1927 the son of George and Hannah Bovill Young. He lived in Geneseo until enlisting in the Army in 1945, serving in Germany, Okinawa, Japan and Korea. He was commissioned in 1952. He was a veteran of the Vietnam War and a rated Army aviator. He retired in 1972 with over 27 years of service.

During his years of service he was awarded many distinguished medals including Distinguished Flying Cross, Air Medal with 20 oak leaf clusters, Legion of Merit with 10 oak leaf clusters, Vietnam Service Medal with five bronze service stars and Vietnamese Cross of Gallantry with palm.

Livingston Co. News, 6/12/2003.

Peri — John Peri of 5397 Lakeville Rd., Geneseo, died Aug. 26.

His was the 11th traffic death in Livingston County this year.

A graduate of Geneseo Central School, Mr. Peri had lived most of his life in Geneseo. He attended Alfred Agricultural and Technical College.

He recently worked on the assembly line at Stirling Homex Corp. and also did some farming. He was a member of St. Mary's Church.

He reached the rank of specialist fourth class during Army service in Vietnam.

Livingston Republican 8/31/1972

Leader — Apr. IL 26, 1967

L/CPT. STANLEY H. MILLER 2224042, Supply Bn. 1st FSR, Supply Co. Storage Sect. Plt., FPO San Francisco, Calif. 96602, received promotion of Lance Corp. on March 21, 1967 serving his 9th month in Red Beach, Viet Nam. He is the son of Mr. and Mrs. Harold Miller, 5051 Lima Rd., Geneseo. He will be home around the 11th of August. (Taken from colored photo.)

Sgt. Faulds In Vietnam

Lead Jan. 1968

Sergeant James J. Faulds, son of Mr. and Mrs. Alexander J. Faulds of 50 Second St., Geneseo, is on duty at Tuy Hoa AB, Vietnam.

Sergeant Faulds, a personnel specialist, is a member of the Pacific Air Forces. Before his arrival in Vietnam, he was assigned to Ent AFB, Colo.

The sergeant is a 1958 graduate of Geneseo Central. His wife, Marcia, is the daughter of Mrs. Marion G. Manning of 176 Rock St., Norwood, Mass.

Vietnam Veterans Memorial by Matthew T. Carroll/ Moment/Getty Images. Asset ID: #99641443. Licensee: Livingston County Histo
Images of rubbings added.